WAKING THE GIANT

WAKING THE GIANT

Inside the Rebirth of Aston Villa

GREGG EVANS AND MATT MAHER

HarperNorth
Windmill Green
24 Mount Street
Manchester M2 3NX

A division of
HarperCollins*Publishers*
1 London Bridge Street
London SE1 9GF

www.harpercollins.co.uk

HarperCollins*Publishers*
Macken House, 39/40 Mayor Street Upper
Dublin 1, D01 C9W8, Ireland

First published by HarperCollins*Publishers* 2025

3 5 7 9 10 8 6 4 2

A catalogue record of this book is
available from the British Library

[HB] ISBN 978-0-00-874100-6

Printed and bound in the UK using 100%
renewable electricity at CPI Group (UK) Ltd

This book contains FSC™ certified paper and other controlled
sources to ensure responsible forest management.

For more information visit: www.harpercollins.co.uk/green

CONTENTS

Foreword by Tyrone Mings 1

Introduction: A Night to Remember 3

1. Rock Bottom 9
2. Rescue 25
3. Restart 39
4. Goodbye Steve, Hello Dean 53
5. The First Miracle 69
6. Promotion 89
7. Balancing the Books 113
8. 'Doing a Fulham' 119
9. The Great Escape 137
10. Key Window 157
11. Selling Jack 173
12. Dean's Dream is Over 183
13. Gerard Experiment 197
14. Downfall 209
15. A Blank Piece of Paper 225

16. No Time Wasted 235
17. March to Europe 253
18. Control 271
19. The Giant is Awake 283

Acknowledgements 305

References 307

FOREWORD

BY TYRONE MINGS

A lot of people say to me I made a smart decision to join Aston Villa because of the great trajectory we have been on. The truth is I just wanted to play and Dean Smith and Christian Purslow gave me that opportunity.

I was looking to go somewhere where I was really appreciated and that was the feeling I got, unequivocally, from both Dean and John Terry. I was told that if I joined I would play the next Saturday and be a big part of what the club were doing.

There were big plans to push for promotion. That was it. That was my story. I got to Villa and they were true to their word. I started the next Saturday.

Now if you had offered me what we have had this season – Champions League football – when I first signed on loan more than six years ago, I'd have said: 'I don't know how we're going to do that, it seems like a mad ride, but one that I'm willing to go on!'

So much has had to happen to get us into this position. Even some of the negative things, for example, we just had to go through. You need the tough times to realise what you don't want. Periods of uncertainty make the better times even more powerful, and players and managers always come and go.

Unai Emery is very, very clear on the thing that doesn't come and go: the fans. We owe them a hell of a lot of respect every time we represent the club, on and off the pitch.

Players like myself and John McGinn, who have been here for a long time, know to put the fans first and make sure that we represent the club in the right way.

One part of the journey that is not spoken about enough is our survival season in 2019–20 so I'm hoping this book – written by Gregg and Matt, who I thank for giving me this opportunity to share my thoughts – will explain that story in full.

It has been an honour to represent Villa for this period where we have tried to do the best for the club. Every player – probably hundreds since I've been here – has contributed in either a small or big way. I'm just so happy the club is competing at the level the fans want it to be.

I honestly owe the fans so much. I've had some tough times here. But the love and support from those who follow the club is real. The connection we have built over the years is incredible.

I don't know what the future holds. As we've already figured out over the last six years, it's impossible to predict what is next because this has been a wild journey.

I do think the one thing that all fans, and us as players, are craving is a trophy. I hope we can deliver that in the next few years.

INTRODUCTION

A NIGHT TO REMEMBER

Wednesday 2 October 2024 was a night like few others at Villa Park.

Aston Villa 1 Bayern Munich 0 might not have delivered the European Cup, as the same scoreline had when the two clubs met 42 years previously. That previous match remains, without doubt, the greatest moment in the Birmingham club's 150-year history. But for the 40,000 home supporters packed into the famous old ground, a future king among them, and the many thousands more watching around the world, it was an occasion to cherish almost as much.

After more than four decades, often spent in the wilderness, this felt like the moment their club re-announced itself among European football's elite, beating a Bayern team who, not even a couple of years before, had appeared to be on a different stratosphere.

At the centre of it all stood Unai Emery, the manager who had engineered a stunning turnaround since taking charge less than two years previously, at a time when Villa appeared at real risk of being relegated from the Premier League.

In his first full season at the helm, the Spaniard had secured qualification for the Champions League, the competition which had replaced the European Cup as the pinnacle of club competition. It was Emery's image which dominated the huge banner draped over the Holte End when the teams emerged onto the pitch. Surrounding the Spaniard on the design were pictures of his players, including the mercurial Colombian striker, Jhon Durán, who would score the stunning goal which earned Villa their victory.

Yet while it is Emery who has taken Villa to heights long thought impossible, in what feels like the blink of an eye, the true story of one of European football's most remarkable revival acts actually began long before his November 2022 arrival.

With Villa back battling with the elite, now seems the perfect time to tell it.

Journalists crave a good story, and in that regard those of us who have covered Villa over the past decade have been spoiled.

Two takeovers, one humiliating relegation, a near financial implosion, an extraordinary eleventh-hour rescue followed by a club-record winning run to clinch promotion, an improbable escape from the drop, the first £100 million British transfer and an enthralling surge back into the European elite. Those are just a few of them.

Certainly, the period from 2018 to now ranks among the most dramatic in the club's illustrious history, perhaps only bettered by the 1970s and early 1980s when, in the space of little more than a decade, Villa rose from the third tier of English football to become European champions.

That remains the pinnacle of the club's achievements, the benchmark upon which all teams are judged. Unai Emery's current unit has come closer to matching it than most.

Founded in 1874, Villa hold an important place in football history. One of 12 founder members of the Football League, the latter was the brainchild of their director William McGregor and it was Villa who became the sport's first dominant force, winning five league titles and three FA Cups during the 1890s.

They remain among the English game's most decorated clubs, albeit most of their honours were won before the advent of television. Since 1920, Villa have claimed just a single league title and FA Cup, along with the aforementioned European Cup triumph. There have been five wins in the League Cup to keep filling the trophy cabinet, but the last of those was in 1996, and the current wait for major honours is comfortably the club's longest since the end of the Second World War.

Regardless of their fortunes on the pitch, in Birmingham and the wider West Midlands, the Villa have always been the biggest show in town, pulling in crowds larger than their rivals even during the periods when they played in a lower division. Big stories at Villa are always just that bit bigger than anywhere else.

It is on a national level they have struggled to punch their weight. As the millions and then billions of pounds began pouring into the English game, Villa were among those clubs left behind. Only now, with Emery at the helm, does it feel like they are catching up. Early in the 2023–24 season, banners appeared around Villa Park proclaiming: 'The Giant is Awake'. For much of the club's recent history, such a statement would have been laughed at. Now, it feels a fair assessment.

The rise has not been straightforward. For supporters, much of it has felt like a rollercoaster. It really wouldn't have needed much for the club's recent story to have been very different. Multiple times on the journey from Championship to Champions League, Villa stood at a crossroads and needed a good decision or, quite often, simply pure blind luck to send them down the right path.

Back in the summer of 2018 the club stood on the brink of disaster, out of cash and seemingly destined for administration as beleaguered owner Tony Xia and his executive team scrambled to find new investment. The story of the whirlwind rescue takeover by billionaire duo Nassef Sawiris and Wes Edens, sealed in the space of 10 days when the club stood on the very edge of the abyss and completed with just hours to spare, is told here in more detail than ever before.

It is Sawiris and Edens, ambitious and hugely wealthy, who have set the tone ever since they first walked through the doors of Villa's Bodymoor Heath training ground.

Qualifying for the Champions League was their dream, spelled out in their very first meeting with supporters, at a time when the very notion appeared pure fantasy. It is their determination, and most crucially their continued financial backing, which has made it possible – in the face of financial controls set against clubs making the kind of rapid rise Villa have experienced.

But like any sporting success story, it has also required a different kind of fortune; the fates conspiring when a big decision needed to be made. None more so than when former Arsenal and France striker Thierry Henry turned down the head coach's job, paving the way for the appointment of boyhood supporter Dean Smith, who would lead the club to promotion and consolidation back in the Premier League.

The latter achievement was undoubtedly aided by the onset of the first global pandemic in a century, which halted the season and bought Villa time just when they were looking odds-on to be relegated straight back to the Championship. Even then it required them to overhaul a deficit of seven points in the final four games to claim survival.

Those, of course, are some of the big twists. Yet, just as in life, it is the little moments which so often make the difference. You may not know, for instance, just how close Tyrone Mings came to joining Villa's local rivals instead, or how Jed Steer nearly left the club completely, eight months before he was the hero in a crucial penalty shoot-out win which helped alter the course of club history.

Neither will you know the inner workings of Villa's recruitment decisions and some of the key players they missed out on, or in other cases conveniently swerved.

So many stories are told here for the first time. We hear from Tony Xia in his first comments after six years of silence, some of which he reveals were spent in Chinese detention, in which he confirms his attempt to buy back the club in May 2019. Also included are Christian Purslow's accounting wizadry, Prince William's action-packed visits, Jack Grealish's reasons for leaving his boyhood club and joining Manchester City and how John McGinn was almost forced into a move away.

We will take you inside the club to understand precisely why Steven Gerrard's reign as head coach ran so badly aground after a promising start, and reveal the extraordinary tactic Sawiris used to convince Emery to return to the Premier League with Villa – comfortably the most significant turning point in the whole picture.

All the details, from the big to the small, the immediately important to the superficially insignificant, are documented here, told by those who witnessed events or, in many cases, made them happen.

And still the story goes on. Villa reached the quarter-finals of the Champions League in the 2024–25 season, a hugely impressive achievement for a club competing back on the biggest stage for the first time. The team were ultimately beaten by Champions Paris Saint Germain in April, on a night perhaps more extraordinary even than the fixture against Bayern. Champions League glory might have proved just beyond their grasp this time, but if anything the dream is more alive than ever. After all, if there is one lesson to take from Villa's journey from 2018 until now, it is that nothing can be ruled out.

1
ROCK BOTTOM

To fully appreciate the present, you have to know the past, though precisely where best to start this story isn't so easy to pinpoint.

An obvious place would be 20 July 2018, the day Nassef Sawiris and Wes Edens completed a whirlwind takeover to acquire a controlling stake in Aston Villa. They would save one of English football's most famous clubs from possible oblivion and set in motion a chain of events which, less than six years later, would see it back among Europe's elite.

But then you'd want to know exactly how Villa reached the point where such a rescue was required. To fully appreciate the climb, you first must understand the fall.

The story begins, arguably, more than nine years previously, in the final months of the 2008–09 football season, Martin O'Neill's third as manager. Helped by heavy investment from Randy Lerner, the American billionaire who had completed a £62.6 million takeover of the club in 2006, O'Neill had established Villa as the most likely challengers to the Premier League dominance of Manchester United, Chelsea, Liverpool and Arsenal.

In 2008, those four clubs had finished in the division's top four positions in four of the previous five seasons, thereby securing qualification for the Champions League, Europe's lucrative elite club competition. Riches earned from participating in that tournament each season helped the quartet sustain supremacy on the domestic front. It was estimated Premier League champions Manchester United received more than three times the TV revenue of the bottom club, West Bromwich Albion. Breaking up the Big Four's hegemony, by qualifying for the Champions League themselves, was Villa's main aim and, two-thirds of the way through the 2008–09 season, they looked in prime position to achieve it. In early February they sat third in the table, seven points clear of fifth-placed Arsenal. They had also qualified for the last 32 of the UEFA Cup.

Sensing the opportunity but concerned his squad didn't have the necessary depth to sustain their challenge in the Premier League while also going deep into European competition, O'Neill decided to sacrifice the latter by fielding a team largely consisting of youth players in the second leg of a UEFA Cup tie at CSKA Moscow. What seemed a calculated gamble at the time backfired almost immediately when a full-strength Villa XI, supposedly fresh having been spared the midweek trip to Russia, conceded twice late on to draw 2–2 at home to Stoke the following weekend, starting a run of eight matches without a win which put paid to their top four aspirations. Villa eventually finished sixth, an achievement they would repeat twelve months later, though by now the momentum and excitement of the early Lerner years was fully on the wane.

The American's 2006 takeover and the appointment of O'Neill, a manager who had been linked with the likes of Liverpool and Manchester United during his time managing Scottish giants Celtic, had injected fresh energy into a club which had struggled for direction during the final years of long-time chairman Doug Ellis's reign. His association with Villa dated back to 1968 and was almost unbroken, barring a spell between 1979 and 1982 during which the club won the First Division and European Cup. A self-made millionaire whose travel business had been based in Birmingham, he was part of a group of chairmen who were prominent drivers behind the Premier League's formation in 1992, the catalyst for money pouring into the sport.

There were question marks, however, as to whether Ellis truly understood just how transformational that moment would be. Villa finished runners-up behind Manchester United in the inaugural Premier League season and won two League Cups in the space of as many years. But as the 1990s turned into a new century, so the club began to fall further back, unable to maximise the commercial opportunities as well as United, Liverpool and Arsenal. By 2006, Ellis, now in his eighties, was very much in the minority as a locally-based custodian in an increasingly global Premier League. Lerner, with his considerably deeper pockets and American charm, represented the bright future.

The trouble for Villa was they weren't the only underachieving Premier League club on the market and the 2008 takeover of Manchester City by the Abu Dhabi Group completely changed the landscape. Lerner might have been a billionaire, yet his wealth paled in comparison to that of City's new owner Sheikh Mansour. Villa's march back into the Premier League's elite suddenly had a rather large roadblock in the way and an increasingly disillusioned Lerner, who had pumped in more than £200 million by 2010 with no Champions League football or trophy to show for it, could see no way around the problem.

Frustrated at the American's reluctance to invest further, O'Neill walked out just five days before the start of the 2010–11 season, taking most of the club's coaching staff with him. It was a moment from which Villa never fully recovered and from challenging for Champions League football they very quickly became regulars at the wrong end of the table through a series of poor decisions, bad luck and an ever-tightening playing budget. Villa finished 16th in the 2011–12 season and then 15th in the following two before the 2014–15 campaign brought their closest brush with relegation and a 17th-placed finish.

By then, Lerner had already announced his intention to sell up. 'I owe it to Villa to move on, and look for fresh, invigorated leadership, if in my heart I feel I can no longer do the job,' he said in May 2014. The trouble was finding someone willing to pay his £200 million asking price.

By January 2016, Lerner was still at the helm and a rudderless Villa, having exhausted all of their on-field fortune, were staring relegation in the face. That same month, Lerner announced he was stepping down as chairman. His replacement was Steve Hollis, a Birmingham-based businessman with no previous experience of working in football. A strange choice at first glance, Hollis's selection became more understandable the more it became clear his primary instruction was to help broker the sale of the club.

Relegation from the Premier League carries serious financial repercussions. In 2015–16, clubs in the top flight were guaranteed to receive £55 million from the division's broadcast deal. By contrast, clubs in English football's second tier, the Championship, received only a fraction of that amount. Dropping out of the Premier League meant Villa's value would plummet, and while on the one hand this was very bad news for Lerner, it did mean there was no shortage of interested parties eyeing the chance to acquire one of the country's most famous clubs for a knock-down fee.

Among the various groups to approach Hollis in the early weeks of 2016 was Socfin, a company registered in Gibraltar and operated by Swiss-based businessman, Chris Samuelson, an offshore finance specialist with two well-publicised previous involvements in football.

In 2004, Samuelson had been involved in a failed takeover of Everton by Russian businessman Boris Zingarevich.[1] Eight years later, he was more successful in brokering a deal to buy Reading, led by Anton Zingarevich, Boris's son. However, things quickly turned sour. Reading were relegated at the end of the 2012–13 season and Zingarevich sold up with the club deep in debt.[2] A decade later, the Royals were playing in League One, English football's third tier.

Those failures did not deter Samuelson who, having previously used his contacts in Russia, now turned his attention to China. In early 2016, the Chinese FA unveiled a plan to make the country a 'football superpower' by 2050, with the aim of eventually winning the World Cup.[3] The domestic league, previously largely ignored, became flooded with cash which allowed clubs to attract some of the biggest-named players from Europe. More than $450 million was spent by Chinese Super League clubs on transfers in 2016. At the same time, Chinese businesses were encouraged to make inroads into the established European market. Villa, with Samuelson's help, were about to become one of several clubs to be bought by a Chinese investor.

In early 2016, through their contacts in the Far East, Samuelson and business partner Jamie Banfill had been introduced to Xia Jiantong, a Beijing-based entrepreneur eager to get involved in English football. Xia tasked Socfin with finding him a club and several were discussed, including Villa's near neighbours West Bromwich Albion, who just a few months later would be bought by his compatriot, Guochuan Lai.[4] Yet Villa were always the preferred option for Xia. In March, former Aberdeen and Everton chief executive Keith Wyness accepted an invitation to join Xia's consortium, initially on a short-term contract to assist with the bid.

Almost nothing was known about Xia, who went by his English name Tony, in the UK. In truth, there wasn't a huge amount known about him in China. A former student of landscape design at Harvard University, he had relocated back to the city of Hangzhou after completing his studies, where he made his fortune through a planning company called Teamex, which provided services in the building of hundreds of 'smart cities'. The majority of his businesses operated under an organisation titled the Recon Group.

By early May 2016, this relative unknown was in pole position to buy Villa. Xia, Samuelson and their business associates attended Villa's final home match of the season, a 0–0 draw with Newcastle which ended an 11-match losing streak and saw the hosts pick up just their 17th point of a miserable season in which relegation had long been a certainty. On the evening of 18 May, days after the season had concluded, the proposed £76.2 million sale of the club to Recon Group was officially announced.[5]

Xia and his entourage had been instructed by Lerner to fly out to New York and then send an email when they landed. No other details, were disclosed, nor even a phone number, so Xia didn't know where he would end up. When he arrived, he followed the instructions and Lerner then sent a helicopter to transport him to Long Island where a deal was struck within 30 minutes.

The official club statement said Xia was a Villa fan, having attended a match during a brief period studying at Oxford.[6] It also outlined his objective to take the club back into the Premier League and into Europe. Recon, it said, employed more than 35,000 people in 75 countries worldwide.

The following day, Hollis held a press briefing with local and national reporters at Villa Park, providing some background on the sale process. Of six serious bids on the table, he said Xia's had been the most appealing. 'This is a gentleman who has a proven track record of delivering,' he told assembled reporters of the prospective new owner. 'This is the single biggest football investment outside of China. The Chinese do not have a habit of doing things and coming second.'

Xia was equally bullish in his first interviews with the English press. Asked by the *Mail on Sunday* if he was a dollar billionaire, he replied: 'I think it is rather more than that,' before going on to boast he would soon be completing a multi-billion-pound takeover of a US logistics firm.[7]

His plans for Villa, both on and off the field, were hugely ambitious. Though the club had just been relegated having won just three of their 38 Premier League matches, collecting their worst points haul for a season in history, Xia was confident of an immediate return. There was absolutely no attempt to downplay aspirations. 'The aim, not just the hope, is to get back in the European field within five years,' said Xia. 'I wish we can succeed to get another trophy like we have here in eight or ten years. That is not an exact number, but we want to win the European Cup.'

Such a statement was extraordinary considering the situation Villa were in, having been relegated from the Premier League after one of the worst seasons in their history. But Xia even talked of building a theme park close to the club's Villa Park stadium.[8] In light of such bold ambitions, it is understandable why Hollis claimed Xia's takeover would be 'transformational' both for Villa and the city of Birmingham as a whole.

Yet, right from the beginning, there were discrepancies.[9] Villa's press release announcing the deal at first said Recon possessed controlling interests in five companies listed on the Hong Kong stock exchange, but it had to be quickly amended. Within a couple of days, after some digging by journalists at the *Financial Times*, a spokesman for Recon revealed that the Group had a controlling interest in only one company in May 2016, and it wasn't in particularly great shape.[10] Lotus Health, a large-scale producer of the food additive MSG, had made a significant loss in the previous financial year. Despite this, Xia told the *Mail on Sunday* the company's fortunes were in the process of being turned around[11] and told us directly that several companies were not disclosed at the time as they were held 'under legal trust structures'.

It took nearly a month from the deal first being announced to being given the green light by the game's authorities, but Xia did eventually pass the Premier League and Football League's fit and proper person tests after submitting a comprehensive business plan and proof of funds through his advisors, he told us.

Samuelson's involvement was ultimately shortlived. Initially, his role in Xia's new-look regime was going to be significant. Indeed, he was heavily involved in negotiating Villa's first three signings of the summer window: the £3 million capture of defender Tommy Elphick from Bournemouth, a £3.75 million deal for young Italian goalkeeper Pierluigi Gollini from Hellas Verona and a £5 million agreement for Reading midfielder Aaron Tshibola. He also had a hand in the new four-year contract for the 21-year-old Jack Grealish, a product of the club's academy and a Villa supporter. Having passed the EFL's owners and directors' test, Samuelson was all set to assume the role of Villa's deputy chairman. But by the start of August, he and Socfin were out of the door due to a deterioration of his relationship with Xia, which reached its tipping point during a business trip to India.

Keith Wyness was tasked with leading the day-to-day running of the club as chief executive. He and the rest of Villa's executive team were responsible for budget planning and management, while Xia also had sign-off. They were quick to note how, for a billionaire, Xia did not exactly adhere to the stereotype. For one thing, he had virtually no entourage and during visits to the UK preferred to do his travelling in Ubers and black cabs rather than hire a driver. Club officials who visited Recon's offices that summer said the owner operated the same policy there. Xia told us that he was 'honoured' not to appear to be a 'typical' billionaire. While he had a team of drivers in China, 'I still prefer to jump a cab when abroad as I enjoy seeing the local life and culture of a city'. He had, he said, been influenced by 'Thoreau's *Warden* [sic.] on the simplicity of life'. Plans for Xia to establish a permanent home in the UK came to nothing.

'It did make you wonder,' admits Wyness. 'But then you thought, maybe he is just a humble billionaire? Every question you asked yourself, there was some kind of logical explanation.'

The fact money was flowing was initially enough to allay any nagging concerns. While Villa could no longer count on cash from the Premier League's broadcasting deal, as a relegated club they did receive around £40 million in the first of three annual 'parachute payments' provided to help clubs cope with the financial shock of dropping out of the top flight.

This also gave them a financial advantage over many other clubs in the Championship and, determined to capitalise on this and encouraged by Xia's promise of monthly cash injections to cover day-to-day operations, Villa spent like no other second-tier club had ever done before. More than £50 million was splashed on new signings in the summer 2016 window in a bid to revamp the playing squad which had surrendered top-flight status so meekly. The big deals included a £12 million outlay on striker Ross McCormack from Fulham, pushed heavily by Xia because of his goal-scoring tally in previous seasons. Another forward, Jonathan Kodjia, joined from Bristol City for a fee which could eventually have been worth a Championship-record £15 million, while defender James Chester made the short trip from West Brom for £9 million. One move they couldn't secure was for Hull City's £14 million-rated striker, Abel Hernandez, represented by the agent Mino Raiola at the time, as the cost of the total package became too high and other players were still needed.

The big spending, however, did not translate into results. Roberto Di Matteo, a Champions League winner while caretaker manager of Chelsea four years previously, had been selected by Xia to be Villa's new boss. The then owner told us advisors presented him with two stand out candidates and 'Roberto had our unanimous vote', in large part because of Di Matteo's experience in obtaining promotion from the Championship with West Brom in

2010. He also liked that the Italian, capped 34 times during his playing career, had a higher status in the game and a business degree (which he says he only found out about after the appointment was made). Yet for Villa, Di Matteo proved a disaster in the dugout and was sacked in early October having won just one of his eleven matches in charge. He was replaced by Steve Bruce, a proven operator in the Championship with four previous promotions on his CV.

'My first meeting with Tony Xia summed up how crazy things were at Aston Villa,' ex-captain Tommy Elphick recalled a few years later. He had been called into Xia's office at the training ground after seven games with the promise of a gift. Instead, Elphick says, the owner wanted advice on who to select when he ditched Di Matteo.[12] 'What would Eddie Howe [Elphick's former manager at Bournemouth] do?' the owner asked. Xia was bypassing the manager he had just hired to consult with his captain about what his former coach at Bournemouth would have done. It was an early sign of loose and inexperienced leadership, especially as Villa had already appointed a technical director in Steve Round just weeks before. Wyness had identified the 45-year-old as an experienced operator given his work with England, Manchester United, Manchester City, Everton, Newcastle United, Middlesbrough and Derby County.

The CEO also tried to bring in David Moyes as manager – both before and after Di Matteo – and pair him up with his former assistant, Round, but the Scot insisted he was not a Championship manager. Even the offer of a ten-year contract could not sway him.

The process to appoint Bruce was more diligent. Wyness and Round pulled together a 50-page report centred on finding the right man to get Villa out of the Championship. With Moyes not interested, the two other options alongside Bruce were Sean Dyche and David Wagner. All three were open to it, but it was Bruce who came out on top.

By the January transfer window, Bruce had got Villa to within striking distance of the top six and a possible place in the play-offs, the end-of-season head-to-heads which offer clubs who miss out on the first two automatic places a final chance at promotion. Still hopeful of getting back into the Premier League at the first attempt, Villa spent big again, signing seven new players, of whom Scott Hogan, who joined from Brentford for an initial £9 million, was the most expensive.

Xia had set up an account on the social media network Twitter to directly engage with supporters and was being lauded for his largesse. He ran a 'sitting with Xia' competition for home games to help find out more about the club and listen to supporters' suggestions around improvements. Yet only a few weeks after the Hogan deal was completed concerns about finances were first raised within the club. Villa's financial model depended entirely on owner funding, with Xia transferring payments of between £4 million and £6 million a month to ensure the club paid its bills. By March 2017, Xia told Wyness that new 'cost control' measures introduced by President Xi were making it harder to transfer money out of China, with personal capital outflows capped and subject to new regulations. Xia confirmed this to us, saying 'we, like other clubs, had to take financial measures to enable funds to flow through the new foreign currency system that China had put in place. This system was administratively bureaucratic and delayed transfers out.' However, he denied that the restrictions had caused problems, saying 'the club's payments and obligations were all met and at no time was the club ever endangered.'

In June 2017, we have been told the club came close to missing a payroll deadline when Xia failed to transfer a payment in time – something the former owner denies. Ulimately, the Premier League provided the next instalment of Villa's parachute payment earlier than expected, ensuring the club was able to pay staff on time.

For those on the ground at Villa Park it was a huge warning, but from there the situation only became worse. Sources told us that payments from Xia increasingly arrived late and even then for amounts far less than expected, promised or required. Xia denies this, contending that payments that were budgeted for were paid but 'non-budget items appeared', before later saying, China's ODI [Outbound Direct Investment] policy made it 'impossible to permit wire money for daily operational use.' To make up the shortfall and ease the burden on cashflow, Wyness and the club's executive team entered into a policy of 'factoring', essentially borrowing money in advance against guaranteed future earnings. Factored items included parachute payments, sponsorship deals and portions of fees still to be received from the sale of players including midfielder Carlos Sanchez and defender Jordan Amavi.

'Essentially, we were spinning plates,' explains Wyness. 'We were factoring in transfer fees we were owed, sponsorship deals, anything we could to keep the club going.'

Factoring is a common procedure and widely used by football clubs to assist cash flow.[13] It is used as a process to access capital quickly. But Wyness knew such a strategy could not be performed forever. Factoring future payments was only a temporary fix and meant even more money would be required from the club's ownership further down the line. Without additional funds, trouble could only be averted for so long. In February 2018, Wyness was informed that Xia was open to bringing in more investment by selling a minority stake in the club.

Amid increasing uncertainty behind the scenes, performances on the pitch were building hope Villa's short-term worries might be solved by promotion and a return to the riches of the Premier League. Having ended up a disappointing 13th in their first Championship season, Villa's second was going far better and by the spring of 2018 Bruce's team were fighting near the top of the table. The free-transfer signing of former Chelsea defender John

Terry the previous summer, on wages of around £60,000 a week, helped establish a winning mentality in the dressing room. Villa beat a host of clubs to his signature with Bruce playing a leading role after the pair played a round of golf together in Portugal. The opportunity to learn from the experienced manager was a big attraction for the ex-England captain, who had ambitions of becoming a coach himself in the future.

Jack Grealish, meanwhile, had recovered from an early season injury to establish himself as probably the best player outside the Premier League. Born in Solihull, just outside Birmingham, to a Villa-supporting family, Grealish had joined the club's academy at the age of six and had long been tipped as a future star. He had duly burst into the national consciousness in 2015, aged 19, with a superb performance in an FA Cup semi-final win over Liverpool at Wembley which instantly saw him become a fan favourite. Yet his progress since had been far from smooth as Villa struggled and he became talked about more in the national press for partying than playing football. Now, under Bruce's guidance, he was finally showing the consistent form those who had watched him over the years at Villa knew he was capable of.

Behind the scenes, Xia's apparently bizarre behaviour continued as he sent players like Grealish and Hourihane direct messages on Twitter to discuss results.[14] On one afternoon when Villa were trailing 2–1 at Sheffield Wednesday, two sources told us the owner sent a message from China demanding midfielder Glenn Whelan be substituted at half-time and replaced by a more attack-minded player, or he would sack Bruce after the game. When we put this to him, Xia told us 'I only communicated with my assistant with my opinions about the squad, the match, but I never intervened with the manager.'

Villa won seven straight matches in January and February and, while their form was not enough to secure automatic promotion as one of the division's top two teams they did earn a place in the play-offs contested by the four teams finishing between third and sixth.

On 15 May 2018, a packed-out home crowd at Villa Park watched their team draw 0–0 with Middlesbrough to secure a 1–0 aggregate win across the two-legged play-off semi-final, setting up a date with Fulham at Wembley later that month in the final: a match worth £170 million to the winning team.

By that time the importance of winning that game and securing promotion had become crystal clear to Wyness and the club's executive team. Payments from Xia had ceased completely in early February, we are told (though he says otherwise), and Villa had exhausted all factoring options. Just £300,000 was left in the bank. A PAYE bill of £4.2 million was due on 21 May and the club did not have the means to pay it.

In a series of increasingly desperate messages to Xia and fellow Recon officials, Wyness says he tried to make clear what was at stake. Yet despite the warnings and despite repeated assurances from Xia that money would be sent, none was forthcoming. Again, Xia says payments that were budgeted for were made but 'non budget items' appeared which were difficult to settle under Chinese ODI restrictions.

On 21 May, Villa missed the HMRC payment deadline. On 26 May, Tom Cairney scored the only goal as Fulham won the play-off final, condemning Villa to another season in the Championship and any chance of averting the impending crisis was gone. For the few members of staff who recognised the situation the club was in, the trip to Wembley was a sad and sobering experience.

The days following the defeat were fraught for those inside Villa Park as more people internally became aware of what was happening. Wyness and his executive team were informed HMRC were prepared to begin winding-up proceedings as early as 1 June if the PAYE payment was not received. As a director, the chief executive had a legal obligation to seek the advice of insolvency practitioners.

All the while, the outside world remained largely oblivious to just how much trouble the club was in.

On 30 May, four days after the Wembley defeat, Xia finally gave in to supporter demands and issued a public statement in which he warned of 'severe challenges' ahead though, strangely, he suggested the largest of those centred around complying with Financial Fair Play (FFP) rules, better known these days as Profit and Sustainability (PSR), the following season. While there was little doubt Villa would face problems on that issue, it paled in comparison to the immediate worries.

Indeed, there was widespread concern inside Villa Park as to whether Xia understood just how deep the crisis was. Based more than 5,000 miles away, in a different time zone, the club's owner rarely spoke on the phone, preferring to do his business through either WhatsApp, WeChat [the Chinese equivalent], or email. In perhaps the most surreal moment, meanwhile, former colleagues say that Xia once enquired as to whether Prince William, a lifelong Villa supporter, might be contacted and asked to speak to his grandmother, i.e. the Queen, about the club's predicament. When we put this to him, Xia denied it calling the suggestion 'ridiculous and malicious', before adding: 'the beloved late Queen was an Arsenal supporter why would she help Villa?'

With HMRC demanding details of how Villa planned to settle the debt and growing increasingly impatient, Wyness chaired a meeting of the executive team in which he laid bare the extent of the crisis. Xia attended by telephone but at some point those in the room noticed the line had gone dead.

Wyness went to bed that night wondering if the message had got through. Early the next morning he received an email informing him he had been suspended with immediate effect. Around 10 hours later, news of his suspension broke, as did the fact Villa were being threatened with a winding-up order over their missed payment.[15] Now, the whole world knew Villa were in crisis.

2

RESCUE

In the same way people of a certain age can recall precisely what they were doing when man first landed on the moon, so Villa supporters vividly remember the moment they learned their club was faced with financial ruin.

Like many fans when the bombshell dropped just after 4.30 p.m. on that Tuesday afternoon, Mo Razzaq was sat at work. 'I still remember seeing the news flash up on the BBC website,' says Razzaq, a supporter since the 1980s, who in 2018 sat on the board of the club's supporters' trust. 'I just went numb. You think no, this can't be real. You just never think it is going to happen to your club.'

It was Mark Kleinman, business reporter at Sky News, who first broke the story.[16] 'Exclusive: Aston Villa Football Club suspends CEO Keith Wyness less than a fortnight after Championship play-off final defeat and amid suggestions that HMRC has served a winding-up order against Villa, one of England's oldest professional football clubs, for missing tax payment,' he wrote on his Twitter account.

The reality of Villa's situation, before then known only to a select group of people, hit like a sledgehammer. 'The reaction was, oh my

God, what on earth is going on here?' recalls goalkeeper Jed Steer. 'For everyone it was shocking news. We kind of knew that if we lost the play-off final the club might be in a spot of bother but we thought it would mean having to sell a player or two. But winding-up orders? We had no idea things were that bad.'

James Chester had already sensed the troubles as he bumped into the captain, John Terry, days earlier in Mykonos, where Chester was celebrating his honeymoon. 'I think he was hoping to carry on for another season but he'd had conversations with Steve (Bruce) who told him some details about the situation the club was in.'

Within minutes of Kleinman's tweet, the mobile phones of football journalists across the Midlands were glowing red hot as they tried to find out precisely what was going on. That the news of the missed tax payment and Wyness's suspension broke at the same time caused some initial confusion. At least a couple of early reports made the mistake of putting two and two together and making five, suggesting the latter had been because of the former. While they were quickly amended, it was an error Wyness believes to this day damaged his reputation.

'The way the story got reported meant people thought I had been up to no good,' he says. 'Even then people only see the headlines: Club misses tax bill, chief executive suspended. They assume the one event is a result of the other.'

Instead, the stunned chief executive had been informed his suspension was for an alleged breach of his fiduciary duties. Wyness stood accused of acting without the authority of the board on certain matters, among them talking to an administrator.

From his perspective, this was baffling. As a director of the company, he had a legal obligation to take the advice of insolvency practitioners from the moment Villa missed the tax bill. Nor was Wyness going to deny he had been talking to investors about a possible part-sale of the club. He had been doing so, he insisted, with the permission and knowledge of Xia, ever since their conversation in February in which the owner stated the club needed a strategic partner to help with investment. A consultancy firm had been tasked with establishing a valuation of the club, in order to determine how much might be received for a minority share. Discussions had taken place with a number of interested parties, of which Wyness claimed Xia was kept informed.

On 8 June, the chief executive resigned his position, claiming he had been constructively dismissed. Soon he would begin legal action against the club, which would culminate nearly 18 months later in an out-of-court settlement. By that time Villa were under different ownership. A club statement announcing the settlement said the current directors 'accept[ed] Mr Wyness' assertion that during this period he was seeking to act in the best interests of the club. We wish him well for the future.'

'People can have their own judgements on me but I was not responsible for nearly bankrupting the club,' says Wyness now. 'I was a victim myself, a big victim because it has impacted my life big time since it happened.'

While the suspension of Wyness was a huge story, the bigger issue was the state of Villa's finances. Regardless of the reasons Xia had for suspending his chief executive, there was no hiding the fact he had a major crisis on his hands. Villa had to find the money to pay the tax bill or be hit with a winding-up order which would at best lead to administration and at worst liquidation. Either way, the owner stood to lose it all.

Immediately prior to Wyness's suspension, Villa had been attempting to agree a Time to Pay (TTP) arrangement with HMRC, which would allow them to settle their debt to the tax authorities over an agreed timescale. In addition to discussions with potential investors, talks had also taken place with a number of companies offering the club short-term loans, albeit most at a high rate of interest.

Calls had also been made to anyone Villa thought might help. This included former owner Doug Ellis, who had sold the club to Randy Lerner in 2006. Ellis, by now aged 94 and still president emeritus of a club of which he had first become chairman in 1968, had been contacted by Wyness and asked whether he would be able to provide emergency funding by way of a £2 million loan.[17]

Xia had also been making calls. Among those he contacted was Howard Hodgson. A lifelong Villa supporter, Hodgson was a successful businessman with a background in recruitment and luxury hire. A director of the supporters' trust, he had previously fronted a consortium which came close to buying the club from Randy Lerner in 2015. After Xia did complete a takeover the following year, the pair established a strong relationship.

'I decided to try and get close to him,' explains Hodgson. 'We formed quite a strong bond. For his part it was quite unprofessional. He would tell me everything. He was like an open book. He used to tell me how he would go into the dressing room at half-time during matches.' Xia, it should be said, denies this, saying 'running a real club is not like an episode of Ted Lasso.'

In the days after Villa were beaten at Wembley, Hodgson received a call from Xia's executive assistant, Rongtian He. 'He called me first and then I got a call from Tony himself. The crux of it was, we urgently need £2 million, can you help?' he says. 'I said I could but I would need to know exactly what was going on because, if the club was sinking, that would be my money gone in a couple of weeks. Eventually I told them I wanted no part in it.' Xia denies this, too, saying 'I never personally asked Howard Hodgson for any money', before adding 'in June 2018 the club did ask for "emergency funds"' and speculating that his former assistant might have 'tried to ask for help'. He continues, 'I successfully obtained foreign currency exchange permit and transferred the funds myself eventually.'

In the search for investment, it was clearly all-hands-on-deck. Further adding to the confusion was the fact that a couple of familiar faces were back on the scene. One of the people to make contact with Villa's executive team in the days leading up to Wyness's suspension was Jamie Banfill, business partner of Chris Samuelson and very briefly a Villa director during the summer of 2016 while their company, Socfin, brokered Xia's takeover. Socfin's involvement at Villa had ended when Xia and Samuelson had fallen out yet, less than two years later, with the club in turmoil and the owner either not trusting or unable to understand the information he was receiving from the UK, Xia had turned back to one of the few people he knew in football for help.

Banfill was among those offering to help the owner out with a loan in his hour of need and it is known this option was on the table just prior to Wyness's suspension. Despite having no official capacity at the club, there seemed little doubt that two years on from brokering a takeover which had now turned sour, Banfill and Samuelson were back on the scene, advising the beleaguered owner and assisting in the search for investment.

Though Xia had now assumed the responsibilities of chief executive after suspending Wyness, the day-to-day running of the club fell to the three remaining members of the executive team, which comprised chief commercial officer Luke Organ, chief financial officer Ian Hopson and the club's lawyer, Victoria Wilkes. Over the next seven weeks or so this trio, who held virtually no public profile and who even today almost every Villa supporter would walk past in the street without recognising, played a vital and unheralded role in saving the club.

Another key figure was Rongtian He, who effectively acted as Xia's eyes and ears at Villa Park. Popularly known as Ho, he had joined Villa four years earlier as a marketing advisor after graduating from Loughborough University. Born in China, he had acted as Xia's translator in the press conferences which had followed the takeover. The owner had subsequently taken him under his wing, even promoting him to the club's board. With Wyness gone, Ho was the only person in the UK listed as a director of the club at Companies House.

Though none of Organ, Hopson nor Wilkes were directors, they knew they had been placed in a vulnerable position by Wyness's exit. Every payment was carefully documented and detailed notes supplied on why certain bills took precedence over others. Among the most urgent was from the company resurfacing the Villa Park pitch which, at that point, had only been half re-laid.

Even that paled when compared to the headache of how to pay the tax bill. The solution came through a combination of smart thinking and some welcome good fortune. The latter element came in the fact that Villa's former midfielder Ashley Westwood, sold to Burnley 18 months earlier, had played enough games in the previous season to trigger a payment as part of the deal. By pure chance, the clause had been met on the final day of the campaign and while it did not have to be honoured until later in the year, Villa were able to negotiate an earlier payment from the Clarets by agreeing to lower the price.

Further funds came via the play-off final gate receipts, money the club also secured early despite the request raising some eyebrows at the EFL, who in March had received the standard annual indemnity from Xia confirming he would be able to fund the club until the summer of 2019. Why would a club who had confirmed their finances were in order just a few months earlier now be so desperately asking for funds to be released? While Villa, technically, were only due to receive their half of the cash from the play-off final ticket sales, they were grateful to a longstanding, little-known gentleman's agreement which traditionally sees the loser of the final receive all gate receipts. Typically small recompense for missing out on the far grander prize of promotion to the Premier League and guaranteed broadcast revenue of £170 million, but for Villa in this case it was vital.

Then came the clever bit, exclusively revealed at the time by one of the co-authors, who was working at the *Birmingham Mail*.[18] Through an existing connection with the high-profile businessman and sport fanatic, Sir John Beckwith, who was on the board at a company named Puma Leasing, Organ was able to arrange a loan secured against a large staff car park near Villa Park. This sum, while modest when combined with the funds received from the Westwood deal and the play-off final gate receipts, was sufficient for Villa to reach a TTP agreement with HMRC.

On 7 June, two days after news of the winding-up order threat had broken, the club released a statement confirming as such which finished by claiming: 'Plans were being put in place to move the club forward.' Though this sounded positive, the stark reality was Villa were living a hand-to-mouth existence, with any money received immediately going back out to pay the bills. The next slice of parachute payments from the Premier League, though a smaller amount than received ahead of the previous two seasons, provided more funds and ensured June's bills could be paid on time. It was also decided to pay off the Puma loan, as it was determined this would make the club more attractive to potential investors. That spared the need to sell the car park, something which would help the club considerably in the future as future plans on the site would include building a state of the art inner-city academy to help bring through the next generation of local footballers.

In 2018, it was becoming clear Villa's best way out of the crisis was a takeover but no deal was close to completion, despite plenty of interest. Prior to being suspended, it can be revealed Wyness had approached a Major League Soccer club about a potential partnership. Those talks ended the moment Wyness left the club. Another US group had already made a formal written offer of £30 million for a 30 per cent stake, which Xia had rejected.

On the evening of Friday 6 July the club's owner finally broke cover when, just over a month after suspending his chief executive and having ignored repeated calls from the supporters' trust to explain what was happening, Xia issued a public statement on the club's official website.[19]

In an 800-word open letter to fans, Xia denied having put Villa up for sale but said he would 'consider minority investment stakes that bring strategic value to the club to help us achieve our goals', adding 'but this will be considered extremely carefully.'

This was, by any standards, an optimistic outlook. Xia, who had made such big promises when buying the club two years earlier, was desperate not to lose both his investment and face in his homeland. The trouble was the whole world knew Villa were in the mire because of an inability to effectively fund the club. Finding an investor willing to come on board at this stage, who would both give Xia money and allow him to remain in control, was going to be extremely difficult, if not impossible. Any potential partner who looked at Villa's books would understand how deep the crisis was and know if they waited just a matter of weeks the whole club would soon be available for almost nothing.

Time was once more running out. Villa's next PAYE bill was due on 20 July and, just as in May, the club did not have enough funds to pay it. Having already agreed one TTP barely a month earlier, the tax authorities would not be nearly as patient should Villa fail to meet their liabilities for a second time. Unless a solution could be found in the next fortnight, a winding-up order would be almost unavoidable. That would lead, at best, to administration and a 12-point penalty at the start of the following season. Those inside Villa Park once again wondered whether Xia truly understood just how close he was to losing it all.

The idea Villa could stave off trouble for a little longer by selling a player was also now looking unlikely. While frequent newspaper reports claimed Jack Grealish, their most prized asset and valued at around £25 million, would be sold to ease the financial crisis, the reality was this would not offer an effective solution. Tottenham, the playmaker's biggest suitors, knew Villa were in trouble and were prepared to wait until much deeper into the transfer window to make their move in the hope of landing their target at a much cheaper price. Villa certainly knew they weren't going to receive an offer which would be of any help to their financial predicament in time.

Work in the club's football department, meanwhile, had been further complicated by Xia's surprise decision to sack technical director Steve Round in early July a decision he insists was recommended to him by the club's executive board. Getting rid of such an important figure in the middle of a transfer window would, in any normal summer, have been a huge story. In this particular summer, when the club's very future was at stake, it was a mere sidebar. What Villa needed was a financial saviour. From what felt like nowhere, they were about to get one.

In the weeks since Wyness had left, the executive team of Organ, Hopson and Wilkes had held countless meetings with groups interested in buying the club, yet none had followed up with a firm offer. With any prospective buyer likely needing to invest north of £60 million merely to fund the day-to-day running of the business, this was a seriously expensive deal.

Then, on Tuesday 10 July, Villa's executive team were visited by a representative of the London-based investment firm Rothschild & Co, acting on behalf of an interested investor. They were told the club's financial forecasts and given a tour of Villa Park and Bodymoor Heath before departing. Three days later, on Friday 13 July, they made contact again to say their potential investor was interested in making an offer and enquired about the possibility of Xia travelling to the UK that weekend to negotiate a deal. The potential investor was Nassef Sawiris.

Born in Aswan, Egypt, in 1961, Sawiris is the third and youngest son of Onsi Sawiris, founder of the Orascom Group, one of the world's largest engineering and construction companies. After graduating from the University of Chicago in the early 1980s, Nassef had joined the family business and later assumed control of the construction side of the firm from his father. His own NNS Group, meanwhile, held shares in several major companies including the sport manufacturer Adidas, of which Sawiris sat on the board. In 2018, he was estimated to be worth around £5 billion and was the richest Egyptian in the world.

On Saturday 14 July, Organ, Hopson and Wilkes travelled down to London to meet further with Sawiris' representatives. Xia arrived a day later and it was in a conference room at the Metropole Hotel, on Edgware Road, at around the same time France were beating Croatia 5–2 in the World Cup final, that negotiations began.

The truth was at this stage Xia did not have much of a bargaining position at all. If the deal didn't get done, he would almost certainly end up with nothing. Merely taking into account the funds which would be required for the club's day-to-day operations and the fact Xia would likely be contributing very little, prospective owners were looking at this as a deal where they should offer nothing beyond a guarantee of financial support in order to secure a majority stake.

Xia, we are told, was desperate to get something by way of a cash settlement, no matter how small, although he insists that he had four offers that were more attractive, financially speaking. Sawiris was not present at the meeting but instead instructed his representatives by telephone. Xia would listen to a proposal and then sit in silence for minutes before responding. It was unbearably tense. The good news from Villa's perspective was Sawiris had now set his heart on getting the deal done.

On the flip side, Xia seemed determined to keep his options open as long as possible. While the Sawiris offer was the only serious approach to come through Villa's executive team, other parties were in the mix through Samuelson and Banfill, while Hodgson had also been sourcing potential investors after receiving another call from the owner. After first meeting with Sawiris' representatives at the Metropole, Xia went to speak with Hodgson's group.

'I'd just arrived in France for a family holiday on the Saturday when I got a phone call asking if I would be able to meet Tony in London on the Sunday,' says Hodgson. 'I flew back to the UK that night and met him the next day along with the investors I had. He looked terrible, ill with the worry of it all.'

According to Hodgson, Xia was asking for £100 million, while still seeking to retain control. His group were prepared to offer £40 million for the whole club.

'He said he had meetings with other groups and would think about it,' Hodgson recalls.

Finally, on Monday, Xia reached a verbal agreement with Sawiris' representatives. The latter would pay £10 million to Xia for a 55 per cent controlling stake, with a further £20 million loan secured against the latter's remaining shareholding. Xia left the hotel to meet Sawiris for lunch, while a heads of terms letter was drawn up. The blueprint for the sale of a majority stake was in place.

On paper, the deal looked a bad one for Xia, at least compared to some of the other offers floating around. Yet at least with this agreement he retained a significant portion of the club and saved a little face. Xia told us he chose NSWE in the best interests of the club, saying 'they convinced me they were serious about entering the football business and had a vision for Villa.'

Arguably the biggest factor influencing his decision-making was time. Though an agreement was in place, there was still plenty of work to be done before the deal could be rubber-stamped. Due diligence when buying into a business the size of Villa would typically take weeks, yet just days remained before the next tax bill. It required someone with the colossal wealth of Sawiris to boil the process down into a matter of days. In what might be deemed his first big show of financial strength, the prospective majority shareholder hired Deloitte to go over every inch of the club's books and work began in earnest early on Tuesday morning. The exact number of lawyers involved is not known but is believed to have run into dozens.

Xia, meanwhile, returned to China as Organ, Hopson and Wilkes based themselves at the offices of the club's legal representatives Squire Patton Boggs in Birmingham city centre. For three days and three nights they would not leave, as information was passed on to Allen and Overy, the firm conducting legal checks on Sawiris' behalf and hundreds of questions, from financial to commercial and everything in between, were answered. It was stressful for those involved and rooms were hired at the Hyatt Hotel but mainly used for showers. Opportunities for sleep were rare. This truly was a race against time.

Only as the deal neared completion did it become apparent Sawiris would not be buying into Villa on his own. The name Wes Edens did not crop up in conversation until things were almost over the line.

Born just nine months after Sawiris, Edens had grown up on a ranch in Montana and in interviews has often claimed to have sport in his blood. Unlike his business partner, who was born into a wealthy family, Edens is from a typically middle-class background. The son of a psychologist father and schoolteacher mother, as a youngster he was a competitive skier and a keen rock climber before gaining a degree in finance and business administration from Oregon State University and starting a successful career in finance. After getting his first job working for a small bank in San Francisco, things really took off when he switched coasts to New York in the late 1980s. In 1998, he and a few colleagues founded Fortress Investments, the private equity fund through which he would make the bulk of his fortune. Fortress had been bought by Softbank, a Japanese investment firm, for $3.3 billion in 2017. By then Edens had also moved into construction through another company, New Fortress Energy, which focused on clean energy infrastructure projects.

Most significantly, at least where the takeover of Villa was concerned, he also had experience of owning a professional sports club, having become co-owner of the Milwaukee Bucks NBA team in 2014. Under Edens' ownership, the Bucks had begun to shed their reputation for being chronic underachievers, reaching the play-offs in three of the previous four seasons, led by the brilliance of two-time NBA MVP Giannis Antetokounmpo.

Like many Americans, Edens also had a growing interest in football and it was during a series of social gatherings for the rich that he met Sawiris. The pair, though from very different backgrounds, bonded over their shared passion and discussed the possibility of buying a club. Initially, their focus was on the US market and Edens had held exploratory talks with David Beckham about investing in the former Manchester United star's planned Major League Soccer franchise in Miami.[20] Gradually, however, they realised buying a club in Europe would come with far greater potential. Sawiris, with his European base, was the driving force and when he began to push for the Villa deal he contacted his friend and asked whether he wished to come on board. Edens was keen.

By Friday morning, the paperwork was nearly complete and the story then broke in the *Birmingham Mail*. Both Sawiris and Edens had passed the EFL's owners' and directors' test, a process which had been fast-tracked by the league, who had been kept fully briefed throughout of the club's situation by the executive team. Nearly everything was in place.

There remained nagging doubts, however, simply because of Xia's unpredictability. Now back in Beijing, no-one knew what Villa's owner was really thinking. An argument over what his title would be once the deal was completed led to concerns he might call the whole thing off. Then finally, early on Friday afternoon, the call came through to the Squire Patton Boggs offices.

'Well done,' one of the firm's leading lawyers told Organ, Hopson and Wilkes after putting the phone down. 'You've just sold the football club.'

Later that afternoon Sawiris and Edens transferred £30 million to help cover costs for the coming months. The crisis was over. Paying tax bills was no longer a problem. Villa had been rescued.

'People really don't understand just how close Aston Villa was to folding,' reflects Hodgson. 'OK, it would have been picked up. But it might have been picked up by the wrong people and would never, ever have become what it has. That summer was such a sliding doors moment. It was extraordinary.'

3

RESTART

It was in the car park at Walsall FC's Bescot Stadium where Nassef Sawiris and Wes Edens took their first public steps as the new custodians of Aston Villa. It's a tradition for the club to play a pre-season match at the ground of their lower league neighbours but their opponents on the evening of Wednesday 25 July were actually West Ham United, the fixture scheduled for a smaller venue while work continued on the Villa Park pitch.

Not that the opposition, or the game, really mattered all that much. Every Villa supporter in attendance was keen to get a glimpse of the men who had breathed new hope into the future when their takeover had been announced the previous Friday.

The official statement announcing an immediate injection of 'significant investment capital' by NSWE, the company set up by Sawiris and Edens to complete the buy-out, almost made it sound like Tony Xia had achieved his ambition while retaining some semblance of control. Xia, it stated, was 'energised and excited' by the prospect of working with his new 'strategic partners'. He even retained an important title, remaining on the board as co-chairman.

Yet no-one was under any illusions as to who was really now running the show. The day of the West Ham friendly had already been a significant one for the new majority shareholders. Earlier that afternoon, Sawiris and Edens had conducted their first interview since completing the buy-out, a carefully choreographed, three-minute affair with Villa's in-house media team in which only four easy, open-ended questions were posed.

In a sign of things to come for two owners who rarely speak in public, both Sawiris and Edens were careful not to back themselves into any corners or outline any specific goals. There was enough there, however, to whet supporters' appetites.

Edens spoke of 'restoring Aston Villa to the highest levels of English football' while Sawiris went just a little further. 'We are here to bring the club back to its original glory,' he said.

Prior to filming the interview, the new majority shareholders had also held an informal meeting with members of the club's fan consultation group. Quizzed as to why they had decided to buy a club in Europe, as opposed to their earlier interest in the MLS, Edens is understood to have given a two-word response: 'Champions League.' It was another sign of their big ambitions.

'It was their representatives who came in first,' recalls Mo Razzaq. 'They wanted to know who we were, what we did, how long we had followed the Villa. Then shortly after Sawiris and Edens came in. It was very brief, probably no more than 25 minutes to half an hour. But you could just tell by the way they carried themselves they were completely different to past ownership.'

The most significant meeting the pair held at Bodymoor Heath that day was with Steve Bruce. A short while afterward and before kick-off at Bescot, the club released a statement confirming the manager maintained the 'full support' of the new owners. This was, obviously, good news for Bruce but he was in no mood to discuss it further with the assembled media at the final whistle. The days between the takeover and the Walsall friendly had seen newspapers awash with reports former Arsenal and France international striker Thierry Henry, then an assistant coach to the Belgian national team, was being lined up by the new owners to take his job. Bruce felt the stories had been disrespectful and took a modicum of revenge by shunning any media duties after the game.

Not that anything he might have said would have changed the story much for those journalists present. After a few days of uncertainty, the new custodians had taken their first big decision by sticking with the man who had come so close to taking Villa back to the Premier League the previous year.

Sawiris and Edens believed Bruce had the capabilities of taking Villa back to the Premier League despite falling at the final hurdle just a few months before. They sought the advice of trusted contacts who highlighted Bruce's record of four previous promotions from the Championship and despite all their ambition they were willing listeners, understanding that taking over a football club with such a rich heritage and tradition was not as straightforward as other business deals they had worked on in the past.

It was clear early on that this was one of the smaller projects in their portfolio. The real estate value alone was enough to protect the money they had put in and the most uplifting news for supporters quickly followed when Bruce was told there was no longer any intention to sell Jack Grealish or James Chester, the two most valuable players.

That was bad news for the clubs who were interested in the pair but had dallied when Villa were at their weakest. Tottenham Hotspur wanted Grealish and Stoke were keen on Chester but Sawiris and Edens refused to sell. Had either of the clubs pushed harder before the takeover, they would have landed a cut-price deal. Instead, Tottenham's opening bid of around £3 million plus Josh Onomah, the midfielder who had spent the previous season on loan at Villa, was knocked back. Stoke's £5 million offer for

Chester was also rejected as Bruce personally delivered the news to each player in a private one-on-one meeting.

'Me and Jack went in one after another and Steve told us that he had told the owners how important we were to the football club,' Chester recalls. 'The first conversation I had with Steve was about an offer coming in from Stoke for around the same fee that Villa had paid for me. That amount of money would have kept the club functioning for another month. It was that conversation when I thought there might be a real possibility that I would leave. Thankfully for me and the whole club in general, a deal was struck.'

Even with such strong resistance, Grealish expected to complete his move to Tottenham before the transfer window closed. He had mentally drawn a line through his Villa career, initially because he was told he would be sold to cover the financial burden, but also because the longer he thought about the move, the more he was looking forward to it.

The Tottenham and England striker, Harry Kane, spoke passionately about Grealish to those who asked and the manager Mauricio Pochettino was hopeful of adding him into an attacking unit that also included Grealish's friend, Dele Alli.

Pochettino's plan was clear: that Grealish was going to be the long-term replacement for Christian Eriksen. A contract starting at £50k a week – around double what he was earning at Villa – had already been discussed. The trouble was the transfer fee Tottenham were offering, even to a club then in financial crisis, was so paltry it was almost deemed offensive.

When the season got underway and Villa won 3–1 at Hull City, three days before the transfer window was due to close, the away end sang to Grealish: '*We want you to stay.*' It was a plea supporters hoped might sway the player's emotions but by that stage events were already out of his hands. Blowing kisses to the supporters was Grealish's way of saying this could be a goodbye. The topic of his future dominated the press conference after the game and Bruce didn't have the answers.

'If they get to the magical figure, then we will see,' he said. 'What that magical figure is I don't know.'

That 'magical figure' is believed to have been £25 million but when Tottenham finally did decide to move, they did so too late. Sawiris, despite being advised Villa still faced future issues around PSR, which a sale would instantly ease, informed them Grealish was not for sale and the deal was dead.

Grealish later admitted that the move was 'really close'. He thought the game at Hull would be his last and that he would move to Tottenham, play in the Champions League, and get closer to the England squad, a huge ambition of his. Instead he was now tasked with leading another charge out of the Championship, this time under a new regime. Picking up where he thought he had left off for good was not as easy as it seemed. For weeks his head was in the clouds and performances suffered. 'I was crap,' he later told the BBC.

At the same time as keeping hold of their talisman, Villa embarked on a busy transfer spree. There were less than three weeks between the takeover and the closing of the transfer window in which permanent signings could be made. The club had been previously operating under a 'soft' transfer embargo which was only lifted once the EFL had approved the takeover.

The first signing of the Sawiris–Edens era was a huge surprise to everyone bar the new controlling shareholders. Neither Bruce nor goalkeeping coach, Gary Walsh, had discussed Andre Moreira as an option, let alone scouted him, yet the 22-year-old Spanish goalkeeper was signed on loan as part of Sawiris' links with the agent Jorge Mendes, a background presence in the early weeks of the new regime.

Another goalkeeper, Orjan Nyland, *was* a player on the radar. Bruce had his eye on the Norway international for some time and a £1 million deal was agreed with German side Ingolstadt for him to become Villa's new number one. Defender Axel Tuanzebe, who had spent the second half of the previous season on loan from Manchester United, also returned on another temporary deal, this time for the whole season.

But efforts to strengthen at left-back were scuppered at literally the last minute when a £6 million deadline day deal to sign Joe Bryan from Bristol City collapsed, sparking a series of bizarre – and almost entirely incorrect – rumours on social media. Bryan was returning from completing his medical to Villa's Bodymoor Heath training ground, ready to sign a contract, when his agent got a call from Fulham, offering him a move to the Premier League.

'We were probably 15 minutes too late,' lamented Bruce at a press conference the day after the window had closed. 'When that happens, obviously, the financial lure of the Premier League, it blew us out of the water in terms of salary.'

While frustrated, Bruce understood Bryan's reasons. Both were quick to rubbish the fantastical claim, made by one journalist on Twitter, that the manager had set off in pursuit of the player down the M42 motorway while attempting to get him to change his mind. Neither had Bryan, as was alleged elsewhere, walked out on Bruce in the middle of dinner following a game of golf. 'I don't play golf,' Bryan would later tell the Fulham programme.

One player Villa did manage to sign, following a protracted chase throughout the summer, was John McGinn. A chance meeting in Portugal between Bruce and the Hibernian manager Neil Lennon got things moving. Bruce spends many of the summer weeks abroad, usually playing golf in Portugal, and that's where he first decided McGinn would be an ideal fit for Villa.

Over lunch, Bruce and Lennon talked about the tough-tackling midfielder who was emerging as a star of the Hibs team. Even as a youngster, McGinn was so likeable that his personality scored as high as his talent but at the point of the initial conversations Villa were still in a financial mess so Celtic – the other serious suitors – had a clear head start.

McGinn's grandfather Jack was a former Celtic chairman and such were the emotional ties to the club he had supported since he was a boy, a deal was considered a foregone conclusion north of the border. The Hoops manager, Brendan Rodgers, had met with the midfielder and discussed personal terms and all that was left to sign was the contract.

But Hibs were playing hardball over the fee and when Villa, financial woes now eased, were suddenly in a position to not only match Celtic's bid of £2.5 million but add an extra £250,000 on top, the Edinburgh club were happy to sell as it weakened a rival.

McGinn was in the Scottish capital, walking around the Fringe Festival, when he received the news about Villa's bid. Bruce called Villa's head of communications, Tommy Jordan, to help with the sales pitch ahead of McGinn's visit to Bodymoor Heath and Jordan, a fellow Glaswegian, rounded up other Scottish members of staff at Bruce's request to help make the 23-year-old feel more at home. Colin Calderwood, the assistant manager, and Kevin MacDonald, the academy chief, both played their part alongside Jordan, who discussed what it was like moving down south and relocating from a similar area.

Villa signed McGinn shortly before the transfer deadline but were open to moving on members of the first team if suitable fees were received. Albert Adomah, the top goalscorer in the previous season with 15 goals, was told by Bruce that he should consider leaving as Leeds United showed an interest. 'I thought I would be going because I wasn't even wanted,' Adomah recalls. 'There were money problems. They wanted to offload players and there was me expecting a new deal. The Leeds situation was odd and I said no. I also turned down Middlesbrough after speaking to Tony Pulis because I backed myself at Villa.'

When the transfer window closed, Villa still had a few weeks left to piece together the remainder of the squad with loan signings. In came Anwar El Ghazi, another player signed through the recommendation of Mendes, then Yannick Bolasie from Everton. The most important of the lot, Tammy Abraham, followed on the final day of the window. Bruce had pushed and probed all summer for Abraham, who was unable to break into the Chelsea team after a below-par period at Swansea City in the Premier League a year earlier. But with top-flight clubs also interested in his signature, the 20-year-old needed some convincing to step down into the Championship.

In the end it was only hours before the loan deadline on 31 August that Bruce finally got his man. The head coach knew he had signed a player with great potential, especially with the quality of Villa's wide players, and was confident he could replicate the form from a loan spell at Bristol City where he scored 23 goals in 41 games during the 2016–17 season.

There's no doubting that Abraham's arrival was a game-changer. Almost every club in the Championship were interested but Villa, with the support of Edens and Sawiris, were able to flex their muscles. Abraham's signing coincided with the arrival of Christian Purslow as the club's new chief executive. Then aged 54, and with 20 years of experience in finance before a career in sport, Purslow had previously worked as the managing director of Liverpool, overseeing the sale of the Reds from George Gillett and Tom Hicks to the Fenway Sports Group in 2010. More recently, he was the managing director at Chelsea. Through his contacts at Stamford Bridge, Purslow helped put the finishing touches on Abraham's move on his first day as Villa's CEO.

Building a strong management team was essential to the new owners, who had no previous experience of working in football and Purslow had been suggested to Sawiris through a mutual contact at Adidas. 'An Adidas executive I worked with at Liverpool and Chelsea called me and asked if I would meet Mr Sawiris to give him some advice,' says Purslow, 'but there was no commitment, it was essentially just doing a favour.'

At a meeting in Sawiris' holiday home in Greece, Purslow listened to the plans from the ambitious Egyptian, who was already very clearly the more hands-on of the co-owners. 'When I went to the lunch, there wasn't even a 1 per cent chance of taking the job at Villa,' Purslow says. 'But when Nassef said "we want a partner" that became more interesting.'

Purslow was out of work and planning a series of trips to destinations such as New York and Paris with his wife but the meeting forced him into a rethink. 'It was an excellent meeting in many respects, in terms of their vision and that they were very patient, long-term investors and builders. I was extremely happy retired until then,' he says. Purslow became a minority investor alongside the owners, and agreed to become the CEO, essentially assuming day-to-day control of a club in need of serious help.

With the financial backing of two billionaires, the leadership of Purslow, and the knowhow of chief finance officer, Ian Hopson, who understood the history of Villa's accounts having worked through the crisis, it felt like there was light at the end of the tunnel.

Purslow got stuck in immediately, and highlighted the most important areas of weakness. 'I spent a week with virtually no sleep doing the initial audit of the business,' he says. 'After eight days I wrote a very long paper to Nassef and Wes summarising the financial position which was … I guess the accurate way to describe it was that we had very heavy operating losses,' he explains. 'Very few valuable playing assets and therefore the club was going to be requiring a lot of further cash investment to keep it going while the turnaround plan was written and executed.'

The turmoil under Xia had left the club in a state which Purslow was in a hurry to fix. He continues: 'It was obvious and clear based on just one week's work that we couldn't expect any further investment from Xia.' It is a matter of public record on Companies

House that he failed to match the capital injections via share issue of Sawiris and Edens. On 8 January 2019, he ceased to be a person of significant control as his shareholding had dropped below 25 per cent. Purslow adds, 'Despite very regular board communications and capital calls to finance the losses in the early days, there was radio silence (from Xia). It was all on Nassef and Wes.' Xia disputes this, claiming he kept in regular contact with Sawiris.

Purslow made simple changes to his office at Villa Park, painting all the walls white and adding in a new desk, sofa and coffee table. 'I bought it myself from IKEA,' he says, smiling. 'It's important that a CEO is not spending money like water.' For the amount of time he was going to be spending in his new surroundings, a bed might have been a useful addition, too.

Big changes needed to be made because the wage bill was out of control and it was the final year of the parachute payment from the Premier League. Revenue was dwindling because thousands of seats inside Villa Park were unoccupied due to the unrest among supporters.

'It was a toxic combination,' Purslow says. 'The regime prior to our regime had bet everything on getting promoted and betting everything in football terms means retaining a high wage bill when turnover has dropped dramatically. It was literally a formula that means if you lose the play-off final you will be filing for administration unless you are rescued. And that is the story of Villa in one sentence.

'Nassef and Wes's willingness to step in and fund the club through that period saved it because it would have been bankrupted, liquidated, finished. It was truly a rescue takeover.'

Among those welcomed into Purslow's office during his first week at the club were Grealish's parents and the player's representatives. After Sawiris and Edens had put a block on a transfer to Tottenham a few weeks earlier, it was time for Villa to renegotiate the young playmaker's contract and it was the new CEO who took the lead. 'I met Jack's family and began the discussions on my third day at the club and he signed it a few weeks later,' Purslow says.

Grealish's wages increased considerably, to the extent he was now earning more than he would have had he joined Tottenham. Further clauses were inserted which would see his pay go up even further if Villa were promoted. The most important work had been done before the transfer window closed and this new deal was seen as reward for the player's co-operation.

Chester, the other player who had been close to leaving, was not so fortunate. Despite believing a new contract would be offered now the takeover was complete and the club free of financial worries, none materialised. When a few months later he began suffering the knee problems which would ultimately bring his Villa career to an end, any deal was off the table completely. A player who was so consistent and always available had cause to feel he was treated a little unfairly.

'I was of the belief when a takeover happened I would get a new deal,' says Chester now. 'The day after the takeover went through, Steve (Bruce) called me in and told us as such and when Jack signed his new deal I believe they told him I was next.

'But then my knee started to have some issues and I think the timing of that went against me. All of a sudden people were telling me those conversations had never happened. Of my whole time at Villa, that is the biggest disappointment.'

With Purslow in place, and the backing of Sawiris and Edens, Villa were about to start taking control of their finances. New deals would not be offered to the ageing and soon-to-be out of contract players. The wage bill had to be reduced to keep in line with PSR and it was important to start increasing other revenue streams.

It quickly became apparent there were issues on the pitch that had to be managed first as the new-look team struggled to gel. Terry's exit had left a void in the heart of defence and though

Elphick started and scored in the opening night win at Hull, Bruce had decided he was not going to be the man to fill it. 'The bottom line is that Bruce just didn't rate me,' Elphick recalls.

Instead, Bruce opted to play Mile Jedinak, a midfielder for most of his career, alongside Chester in the heart of defence, and keeping clean sheets quickly became a problem.

A stoppage time winner from Birkir Bjarnason earned Villa a dramatic 3–2 win over Wigan in their first home match. It was the first time the club had won the opening two matches of the season since 1999, but performances suggested the run would not last.

Three draws followed before a 1–0 Carabao Cup defeat at League One Burton which saw a portion of the travelling supporters turn their anger toward both the dugout and – strangely – the press box at the Pirelli Stadium.

If that was bad, it was nothing compared to what followed at Sheffield United four days later where Villa were thumped 4–1, their heaviest defeat since relegation. Nyland, who had looked shaky since making an error on debut against Wigan, struggled again while the Blades ran rampant against the visiting defence. The scoreline flattered Villa.

Bruce accepted responsibility after the game and had little to say about the chants of '*you're getting sacked in the morning*' from away supporters who were starting to turn on him in increasing numbers. His counter-argument to claims that he 'didn't know what he was doing' or that he was a 'dinosaur' came in the form of one of his stock answers: 'We can talk about tactics all we like but at the end of the day we didn't put our boots on.' In fairness that was a polite way of putting it.

But these post-match press conferences were rapidly becoming a chore, both for those asking the questions and the man having to think of the right words to say in response. There's only so many times you can ask a manager 'what are you going to do to fix this?' before it becomes clear that there is no solution.

The one thing Bruce could point to at Bramall Lane was the unavailability of Abraham and Bolasie, his two newest signings. Yet it was clear the head coach needed results and quickly.

Conor Hourihane saved him with a last-minute equaliser at Blackburn Rovers a fortnight later and a 2–0 win against lowly Rotherham United looked like it would offer some brief respite, only for Bruce's post-match comments to leave the boss in a deeper hole. Referencing his record of four promotions from the Championship, Bruce claimed it had been forgotten by the 'mad few' and added 'I hope it [the win] shuts up a few but I doubt it.' Those who had seen the carnage of the summer understood his frustration but taking on the fans only raised the stakes further.

A defeat at home to Sheffield Wednesday, memorable for a stunning if ultimately meaningless goal from McGinn, followed that weekend, before a draw at Bristol City left the head coach on the brink. Barely two years earlier, Bruce had entered Bodymoor Heath with a spring in his step and his personality was just what was required to energise a club reeling from relegation. Without results, however, patience was running thin and among a significant portion of the fanbase Bruce was now about as popular as a barman at closing time. The manager who had pulled Villa out of the rubble and nearly steered the club back into the big time looked increasingly lost and public humiliation would soon follow.

4

GOODBYE STEVE, HELLO DEAN

Nothing symbolised the broken relationship between Bruce and Villa's supporters like the cabbage.

Hurled from the Trinity Road Stand as the head coach made his way to the dugout shortly before a crucial home match against Preston on 2 October, the vegetable found its way onto the back pages of almost every national newspaper on what became another embarrassing night for the club and a fateful one for the man in charge of the team.

Almost every supporter would later agree the throwing of the cabbage, brought into the ground by a fan who had visited the supermarket on his way to the match and decided on a whim to practise his shotput technique, was a disgraceful, disrespectful act. Bruce, who had worked so tirelessly to make a success of things in his near two years in the job, deserved far better than that. By the same token, there was no hiding the fact patience among the fanbase had run out. Grumblings which had begun on social media had grown and were now being voiced openly in the stands. At the end of one of the most chaotic matches Villa Park had witnessed in years, the fanbase would be in open revolt.

Speaking of stands, the first thing journalists attending the match noticed was just how empty they were. That just 27,331 supporters had turned up, leaving 15,000 empty seats, showed how hard times had become. The upper tier of the Trinity Road Stand had been closed since relegation to save costs and re-opened only for select matches. Any optimism following the summer takeover had faded with Villa on a run of just one win in nine. After two years in the Championship, supporters feared another season was going to slide away quickly. They were sick of the division, and increasingly sick of Bruce.

Suggestions outside the West Midlands that Villa fans never fully embraced Bruce as a manager because he had previously managed their rivals, Birmingham City, with whom he had been promoted twice, were wide of the mark. The real – and justified – criticism was the way his side were playing. Yes, Villa could score goals, and understandably so with the attacking talent available, but keeping them out at the other end was an issue.

Other than in the home win over Rotherham, Villa had conceded at least a goal in every other league game. Taking on Villa was seen as a big day out for opponents and the chance to beat one of the most illustrious sides in the division. 'Bruce used to say that teams were out to get us,' Adomah recalls. 'He was right because a draw was massive for them but a draw for us was like a defeat.'

It had reached the point where you felt something had to give. For Bruce to stand any chance of keeping his post, Villa needed a win and a big one against Preston, who arrived sat bottom of the table having lost seven of their first ten league matches.

Villa Park was in no mood to hold back, and as many managers have discussed the often long and lonely walk from the corner of the stadium where the teams emerge at kick-off to the dugout – 'It feels like a mile after a defeat,' Tim Sherwood once said – Bruce was about to experience it, too. This would be the last night he would ever make those steps as a Villa manager and as humiliating as the whole experience was for him it was fortunate he didn't suffer any physical pain before the game started.

When the cabbage landed next to him, a nearby photographer, Tim Easthope, from the *Birmingham Mail*, was out on the pitch preparing to take pictures of Bruce and his opponent in the dugout, Alex Neil, the manager of Preston. He said that when the cabbage landed on the playing surface, his first thought was that an even heavier item, such as a brick, had been hurled from the stands. The weight of the cabbage made a loud thud and shocked Bruce and his assistant Stephen Clemence who was walking alongside him. Both reacted with disgust as they stared at the man in the stands who then let out a foul-mouthed rant in the manager's direction.

The story of the night was set there but of greater significance was what then happened on the pitch. At half time Villa looked to be cruising to a victory which would keep Bruce in post until at least the weekend trip to Millwall. Kodjia and Abraham both netted to give the hosts a 2–0 lead. The main question asked in the press room was just how many more goals they would score in the second half.

Yet when the match restarted, all of the flaws which had hindered Villa in previous weeks came back with a vengeance. Chester, who had not missed a minute of action since signing in 2016, conceded a penalty 10 minutes into the half and was sent off. Villa academy product Daniel Johnson scored from the spot for the visitors and by the 86th minute the turnaround was complete as goals from Paul Gallagher and Louis Moult had Preston in front. What then took place in stoppage time was enough to fill a standard-sized match report in its own right. Bolasie scrambled an equaliser before, seven minutes into the added period, Villa were handed a chance to take all three points and likely earn Bruce a stay of execution when Johnson inexplicably went through Bjarnason in the box. The only question was: who would take the penalty? Kodjia, Abraham and Hourihane, Villa's three most likely takers, had all been substituted. Grealish and McGinn remained on the pitch, yet to the amazement of almost everyone in the stadium it was Glenn Whelan, scorer of just one goal in the previous seven years, who stepped up. Chris Maxwell saved his weak effort and the full-time whistle sounded to a chorus of boos.

Bruce cut a forlorn figure on the final whistle and in the post-match press conference. 'He sounds like a beaten man,' former Villa striker Garry Thompson, then working as a radio pundit, opined on BBC West Midlands Radio.

There was no doubt Villa's owners had a decision to make, though in truth the only debate around Bruce was whether he went immediately or after the Millwall game four days later, which preceded an international break. Of far greater concern was who would replace him. Purslow would be tasked with leading the search but by now he was not working alone.

Though the appointment had not yet been formally announced, Villa had identified Jesus Garcia Pitarch as the man to be their new sporting director. The Spaniard, better known as Suso, had for several weeks been privately working on reports around the club after Sawiris had leaned on his friend and close contact, Jorge Mendes, for more assistance.

Sawiris wanted a director of football to work alongside Purslow and called on super-agent Mendes for recommendations. Suso was a high-profile name in the industry having worked at Atletico Madrid and Valencia in his native Spain where, during his period with the latter, the club won La Liga and the UEFA Cup. Atletico also lifted the Europa League and the European Super Cup with Suso at the helm of recruitment and he was recognised as both experienced and well-connected across the globe, albeit his knowledge of English football's second tier was lacking.

During initial calls with Mendes in August 2018, Suso made it clear he was not willing to work with just any Championship club but immediately liked the ambition around the Villa project. A number of other candidates were considered as part of the recruitment process and Suso's inexperience of Villa's current level was heavily scrutinised. He had no option but to be up front about it. During a meeting at Sawiris' office in London, Suso told the co-owner: 'I don't know much about Aston Villa now or the Championship, but football is football, and I would like to work with you. For me, it's a pleasure to help this big club to be promoted and if you give me the opportunity for sure, I will accept.'

When Purslow asked him to explain how he planned to get around the gap in his knowledge, Suso asked to attend a game and draw up a report and so, in early September, he attended Villa's 1–1 draw at Blackburn alongside the CEO. 'My first thought was that the team were better than they were playing, so they were under-performing,' Suso says. 'I started to share my thoughts about the system and certain players. I respected everyone at the club at the time, but I said: "We have a big problem with the coach." I said that for me to be the football director, we must change the coach. If you don't change the coach, I will not work with you.'

Suso says Sawiris and Purslow agreed with the assessment around the playing squad but not immediately with the decision on Bruce. 'They said they were not absolutely convinced to sack him,' he explains. 'They said let's speak later. I know after this meeting that they checked other sporting directors, other possibilities, other profiles.

'But a few weeks later, Christian called and told me to come back to London to discuss terms. He told me that the club didn't have much money right now and that I could not be signed for big money.

'The conditions were low but I accepted the challenge and put one condition in: a bonus if we were promoted and then also if we stayed up in the Premier League. Christian said to me: "This is a project for two or three years, we need to be promoted in that time."'

* * *

After discussing the manager's position, the embarrassment of Cabbage-Gate, and the worrying run of results, it was Purslow who delivered the news to Bruce the day after the Preston match. The remainder of Bruce's contract was honoured but there was a sour taste left by the manner of his final game in charge, a game Grealish says will haunt him forever: 'I'll never forget the atmosphere in Villa Park that night,' he recalls.

Adomah's take was interesting as he says the players needed to share some of the responsibility. 'We were the ones running around, but ultimately when a team is not producing then it gets put on the manager and Bruce was sacked because we weren't winning,' he says.

Kevin MacDonald, a stalwart of Villa's academy who had twice previously taken caretaker charge, was installed as interim boss for a game against Millwall in which the team again displayed their defensive fragility, falling to a 2–1 defeat after Abraham had fired them into an early lead.

By then all the talk was around who would be getting the job on a permanent basis and some big names were in the frame. For Villa, the next few days would prove one of the biggest sliding doors moments in club history.

The early frontrunner for the job was Thierry Henry. Touted to replace Bruce in the summer, the Frenchman represented the 'big name' preferred by Sawiris. Purslow promptly met with Henry's agent, Darren Dein, and a deal was close to being struck. But Villa were not the only club in Europe searching for a new manager and a day later Henry was given the opportunity to talk to Monaco. Sensing Henry was not fully committed, Villa switched their attention elsewhere.

'He might well have become the Villa manager, he was one of the candidates we met,' Purslow says. 'By the time it became a live deal it was obvious Monaco had come along. Sliding doors for him, maybe, sliding doors for us, maybe, but often when you're interviewing candidates, you have a suspicion when you are not their first choice.'

Eventually, Villa turned their attention to Dean Smith, who had topped virtually every fan poll run by the local press asking for their preferred candidate. Then in charge of Villa's Championship rivals Brentford, Smith had grown up in Great Barr, a north Birmingham suburb a short bus ride away from Villa Park and his close ties to the club were long established. His father, Ron, had worked for years as a steward in the Trinity Road Stand. Smith and his brother Dave would clean the seats before games in exchange for a free pass into the Holte End, from where they had witnessed some of the most famous nights in Villa's history in the early 1980s. The pair had also been babysitters to Pat Heard, a near neighbour and member of Villa's European Cup winning squad. They even got to drink out of the famous trophy when Heard brought it to the local pub.

Smith had gone on to forge a successful career as a defender in the lower divisions with Walsall, Hereford, Leyton Orient, Sheffield Wednesday and finally Port Vale. Having started his coaching career as assistant to Martin Ling at Orient, he took a job as head of third-tier Walsall's academy. It was with the Saddlers he got his first break in senior management, albeit at first reluctantly, following the sacking of Chris Hutchings in January 2011.

'I knew I was going to be asked to do the job because I was the only coach left at the club,' he would later joke. Smith had no ambitions to be a manager at that stage but quickly found he was rather good at it. A Walsall team which had lost 14 of its first 22 league matches and sat eight points adrift of safety when he took charge stayed up on the last day of the League One season. Smith took the job full-time and despite working on a notoriously tight budget, gradually developed a team attractive on the eye. In 2015, he became the first manager to ever take the Saddlers to Wembley when they reached the final of the Football League Trophy.

Brentford came calling later that year and during three years in west London Smith had won plenty of admirers. Earlier in 2018, he had come close to returning to the West Midlands as manager of Villa's rivals, West Bromwich Albion, only for the Baggies owner Guochuan Lai to ignore the recommendation of his board and instead opt for Darren Moore. It is a decision which went some way to shaping the region's recent football history.

By the autumn, Smith had another new fan in the shape of Suso, who had quickly been attracted by the style of Brentford's play during the hours he spent watching Championship matches. 'I loved them,' he says. 'Ollie Watkins, Said Benrahma, Rico Henry and several others. I told Christian that they reminded me of a Spanish team, not a British team, and Christian said he liked Dean's profile and pointed out that his allegiance to Aston Villa – as a lifelong supporter – would also help.

'My opinion was that we needed a coach who knew the league straight away. We needed someone already in the Championship or with very recent history so he could adapt quickly.'

It was on the evening of Tuesday 9 October that Smith's agent, Warwick Horton, himself a lifelong Villa supporter, returned home from watching the club's reserves to see Purslow's number flashing on his mobile phone. A short time later, at around 10 p.m., he and Smith walked through the doors of the Hyatt Hotel on Broad Street to meet with Villa's chief executive and Suso.

'Massive credit that he [Smith] got there so quickly,' says Purslow. 'I liked that he was prepared to work at my pace and I was immediately impressed. I said to him in the interview that I thought his middle name was 'attractive football' because every time I Googled his name, that came up. After five hours it was absolutely crystal clear that he was the one.'

Smith ticked a lot of boxes, including, as Purslow recalls, the 'obvious connection' with Villa. 'He knew the importance of our football club and I wanted that very badly,' he says. 'It wasn't clear whether it would take one, two or three seasons to get out of the Championship but I wanted to make Villa Park a great place to come. I had to get the top tier of the Trinity Road Stand open and I thought that a manager with a connection to the fans, and playing a brand of football that was so exciting, would help.'

Yet the interview was not merely a case of Smith selling himself to Villa. Regardless of his close links to the club, he wanted to be sure the move would be the right one. As he later explained at his unveiling: 'This was not an emotional decision. It was an entirely rational one.

'I was interviewing them as much as they were interviewing me,' he says now. 'I was in a good job at Brentford. I had seen what I thought was going on at Villa. I didn't know a lot about the new owners, they had only been there a few weeks.

'So I was asking what the plans were for the future, the club philosophy. Is there one? Or is it just about getting promoted? They were the questions I was asking to find out about them. What are the expectations this season? What are the expectations over the length of the contract? What does the staff look like? I left the room in the early hours of the morning thinking it had gone well but I honestly didn't know what they [Villa] would do next.'

One of the questions Smith had been asked during the meeting was whether he would be prepared to have John Terry on his coaching staff. Terry, who had announced his retirement from playing just a few days earlier, had been on Villa's initial shortlist to be head coach and the club were keen to bring him back in some capacity. Though Smith was assured that agreeing to have Terry on his team was not a dealbreaker, he had an advantage neither Purslow or Suso were aware of, in that he already had an existing relationship with the former England captain. Smith had coached Terry's older brother Paul at Leyton Orient and the pair had got to know each other during the younger sibling's visits to east London. So having left the Hyatt in the early hours and got just a little sleep, Smith's first move on Wednesday morning was to call Terry to discuss the potential move.

'I told Villa I would call JT and interview him,' explains Smith. 'He was playing in a pro-am golf tournament that morning and I called him at about 7 a.m. I spoke to him for about an hour on the phone and liked what I heard.'

Smith also sounded out Richard O'Kelly, his long-time assistant at both Walsall and Brentford. Another message went to goal-keeping coach Neil Cutler, who had worked previously with the pair at Walsall and would join Villa a month later from West Bromwich Albion.

The most important call, meanwhile, had been made the night before, ahead of the meeting with Purslow and Suso. While becoming Villa boss would be a big deal for Smith, he knew it would have even larger ramifications for his family. 'It would change our lives,' he says. 'Our son Jamie was at university in America but our daughter, Katie, was still at school. When I first spoke to my cousin he said: "It's Villa, you've got to do it." But I said: "No, I don't have to do it." I didn't get emotionally involved.

'That is how I spoke with Nicola and the kids, I said: "Listen, for Katie it is going to change because every time we don't get a win or don't play well, she is going to hear it at school. Can we accept that? Can she accept that?" To be fair, the family were all behind it. They were like: "No, come on, we need to have a go at this." Once I had the blessing of the family, I knew if I got offered the job I could start negotiating.'

It was later on Wednesday morning, while driving down to take training at Brentford, Smith took the call from Horton saying Villa were going to make an offer. 'I actually had Katie and her friend in the car, as they were going to a K-Pop concert at the O2 Arena that night,' says Smith. 'I was sat there with my headset on negotiating the contract with Villa.'

Smith made a call to Brentford's director of football Phil Giles to inform him of Villa's approach and his intention to take up the offer if it was right. Things were moving quickly, with Villa keen to get the deal over the line that night. For Smith, it spelled a hectic evening of travel on London's transport system, first on the tube to North Greenwich to drop the girls at the Arena, then in a black cab back across town to the Bulgari Hotel in Knightsbridge to meet with Purslow and Nassef Sawiris.

'The cab driver was a Millwall fan and recognised me,' says Smith. 'At one point he said: "Hey, you've been linked with the Villa job, haven't you?" Little did he know I was on my way to sign the contract!'

That wouldn't be the evening's most surreal moment. With the contract agreed, Villa needed access to a fax machine but the business centre at the Bulgari was closed. A cleaning assistant opened the lock and then acted as witness as Smith signed a two-and-a-half year deal to become Villa boss. 'I've still got the note with her signature on it,' smiles Smith.

Before signing, he had the chance for his first chat with Sawiris. 'He just immediately gave the air of a very successful businessman,' says Smith. 'I remember he liked the fact I was wearing Adidas because he has shares in them. Christian was running in and out quite a bit. I asked Nassef what were the expectations. He said you have a two-and-a-half year contract, the expectation is you get us up in that time.'

Deal done, Smith set off back to the O2. His appointment was formally announced just after 10 p.m. when he was more than a hundred feet underground on the Jubilee Line. 'I came up the escalator at North Greenwich tube station and I've got about four hundred messages on my phone!' he says. 'I met Katie and she was going mad at me because her phone had been ringing non-stop during the concert!'

Smith returned to Brentford on the Saturday to pack up his office before he and O'Kelly visited Bodymoor Heath for the first time the following day and were given a brief tour of the facility by the head coach's new PA, Jo Davis. The coaching team's first official day of work was on Monday, a busy day of introductions and training which finished with a formal press unveiling at Villa Park. Smith, Purslow and Suso, whose appointment had been officially announced at the same time as Smith, sat at the top table before separate briefings were held with the radio and written press in the players' lounge. Terry was also in attendance but conducted only one interview, with BBC 5Live.

Players were happy to see the former captain back as he set high standards, though not so much to talk about him publicly. Among regular press attendees there was a gentleman's agreement to refrain from asking the longer-serving members of the squad questions about Terry, largely because so much had been discussed the previous season. One player, who shall remain anonymous, almost cut short a pre-game chat with a group of reporters because the opening two or three questions were about Terry.

Even with no-one talking about Terry, he inevitably took some of the headlines. Having one of the Premier League's most recognised players in the building put a certain spotlight on the club. Every journalist in the country wanted to interview him, even though the majority didn't cover Villa because of their Championship status. Every set of away supporters wanted to take a pop, too. He was subjected to some awful abuse about his family but also the occasional non-personal chant that was quite amusing would draw a smile from him on the sidelines.

'I knew John well and he's incredibly competitive,' Purslow says. 'His big thing was always raising standards. Often he would come to me and say: "CP, the hotel is crap, can we have a better one?" If the food wasn't good enough or the soap in the showers, John would let me know. He was definitely the self-appointed king of high standards.'

Settling into life as a coach rather than a player did take some time. Terry turned up eager and ready on day one at 7.30 a.m. with a pen and notepad and – much to the amusement of his colleagues – a brand new pencil case. His other big mistake was wearing a pair of white boots. Some of the players ripped into him about it so he soon matched up with Smith and O'Kelly – coaching veterans in comparison – who were well-versed in black footwear.

Smith would soon split the defenders with Terry, and attackers with O'Kelly, but oversee everything himself. Training sessions were shorter but more intense than they had been under Bruce. 'The players perhaps weren't used to that and we probably picked up a couple of injuries because of it,' says Smith. 'But that's what I wanted in terms of the sessions and I think the players enjoyed it.'

Thursday sessions in particular became memorable for the attackers as they would always practise weaving around four mannequins, collecting pinpoint passes from Grealish, McGinn, Hourihane and Lansbury, before shooting. 'Dean was great at getting everyone to know their own role,' recalls winger Andre Green. 'A lot of managers don't do that. They focus on the collective and think it will all come together.'

Terry was already well known and respected by Villa's players but that didn't take away the strange feeling that he was no longer 'one of the lads'. As Grealish says: 'He went from having the banter with us as a player to now telling us what to do, which did take a little bit of time to get used to.'

Terry knew Abraham from their days together at Chelsea. He and the striker would often work after-hours on aerial play in the box and it paid off in Smith's first match in charge when Abraham headed the only goal to earn a 1–0 win over Swansea. It was an emotional day all-round, with the club also marking the passing of former chairman Doug Ellis, who had died the previous week aged 94. Of most obvious note was the crowd. Villa, who had closed the top tier of the Trinity Road Stand following relegation, re-opened it for that match and were duly rewarded with their biggest crowd for years.

Off the field, Sawiris continued to be hands-on and was locked in daily calls with Purslow about how to take the club forward. He had connections in football who were offering advice but he placed trust in Purslow to oversee the changes from Villa Park.

Slowly a new executive team was developing and these were the early foundations of a five-year plan to get back into the top half of the Premier League. With Villa sitting 15th in the Championship at the time Smith took charge, it was a bold and ambitious target.

The win over Swansea was followed by defeats at Norwich and QPR before a 2–0 Friday night win over Bolton Wanderers where Abraham and – most crucially – Grealish showed their class to score early and set Villa on their way. It was Grealish's first goal of the season and, with disappointment over his missed move to Tottenham subsiding, he was quickly taking on board the advice from the new head coach, who demanded he start playing higher up the pitch.

'I'd shown Jack some clips, I think of the Preston game, which showed him dropping deep to get the ball,' says Smith. 'I said: "If I am their coach, I am happy. Why? Because you have a whole team you need to beat to go and create a goal or score. Your game has got to be about creating and scoring."

'Jack's stats at that time were one assist, zero goals. I asked him where he wanted to play. He said he wanted to play at the top of the Premier League and for England. I said: "You won't be with stats like that." I don't think he had ever looked at the game as stats. I said coaches, managers, pundits will look at stats. "At the moment yours aren't good enough."'

If the 2–0 win over the Trotters was a positive, the 3–0 win at Derby which followed felt the moment Smith's tenure really took off. McGinn, Abraham and Hourihane all scored in the final 16 minutes but the scoreline did not flatter the visitors, who should have won by probably double. The trouble was those two clean sheets proved to be too much of a rarity.

Villa's lack of depth at centre-back had been the first thing Smith identified on taking the job. Axel Tuanzebe and captain James Chester were the only two recognised central defenders in the squad. Mile Jedinak, who had played there earlier in the season, missed matches because of a calf injury. For Chester, meanwhile, the win at Derby would prove a significant moment. It was when sitting in his car after the match the skipper would first feel the pain in his right knee which would go on to have a major impact on his Villa career. Though early scans had suggested the issue was not too serious, soon he would be playing through the pain barrier. 'Chezzie was an absolute trooper,' says Smith. 'He was playing through injections galore, just to get through games. But it was a real struggle, centre-back wise.'

Smith's concerns were shared by Suso, with boosting the numbers at centre-back an obvious focus of the forthcoming January transfer window. 'My view was very clear: we were one of the best teams scoring but one of the worst defending,' recalls Suso.

'With Tammy and Jack, we had Premier league attackers. We just needed some changes in defence. I spoke several times with Christian, saying that we have to help Dean because his mentality is always attack, attack and attack, and don't get me wrong, I love this mentality, but we needed balance.

'I said we have to sort out the defence because I'm not sure if my heart will support all this attacking when we are at Villa Park!'

The results which followed proved the point: a 4–2 derby win over Birmingham City in which Grealish scored, an extraordinary 5–5 draw with Nottingham Forest and then a 2–2 draw with West Brom. Villa were on the move, up to eighth in the table but frustration lay in the fact they should have beaten both Forest and Albion.

Entertainment, at least, wasn't a problem. Each game had stand-out moments and those who had lost interest in either supporting or reporting on Villa slowly started to return. If there was one thing guaranteed about Villa games during this period it was that goals would be scored. All types of goals, too – Hourihane fired in a stunning free-kick at Derby, Hutton scored a wonder goal against Birmingham City in which he ran from his own half, while Anwar El Ghazi, who had fallen completely off the radar after being dropped by Bruce, scored against Forest.

He also scored twice at Albion but that night, it transpired, was when the early momentum of Smith's reign would begin to fade. Villa missed a hatful of chances to bury the Baggies in the second half and were then stung at the death when Jay Rodriguez used his hand not once but twice to score. Smith was seething at a moment which quickly became nicknamed the Hand of Rod but even worse news was to come the following morning.

The sight of Grealish limping off late in the match had largely been ignored because of the drama which followed yet soon it would become the story. 'The next morning we were going straight down to London for our Christmas party but I missed the train with the lads because I had to have a scan,' Grealish told *The Athletic*. 'I was in agony. The Doc told me that I could be out for up to four months. I lost my head in the weeks that followed.'

5

THE FIRST MIRACLE

A common game among football journalists is to try and work out how many hours, days or even weeks of their lives have been spent in mixed zones. These are the areas of stadiums which allow access to players after matches. From ground to ground, they vary in location, size and warmth. Many are in nondescript corridors, typically on the route from the dressing rooms to the exits which players must walk along. Others, however, are out in the elements.

The mixed zone at Stoke City's Bet365 stadium falls into the latter category, situated just outside the players' entrance in a corner of the car park. On 23 February 2019, the good news for journalists who congregated there after Villa's 1–1 draw with Stoke was the absence of rain but as is seemingly forever the case at a ground situated on top of a hill, it was brutally chilly. The close proximity to Villa's team coach, engine running, also prompted some dark humour about how many minutes of lives were being lost through inhaling exhaust fumes.

On this occasion the cold and pollution proved more than worth it, as Tommy Elphick delivered an interview which at the time earned respect for its blunt honesty and weeks later would appear so prescient you wondered whether the defender couldn't earn a handy second income from clairvoyance. In the space of around five minutes, Elphick as good as confirmed suspicions not everyone inside the Villa dressing room was pulling in the same direction, while also laying bare what would be required if they were to stand any chance of reviving their play-off ambitions.

A run of just one win in 10 matches since late December had seen them sink to 11th in the table, eight points outside the top six. Almost everyone above them had matches in hand.

'If we all realised that Aston Villa being in the top six is beneficial to everyone, we will start winning games,' remarked Elphick. 'We've got to go on one hell of a run now to put ourselves back in the picture.'

Then he got more specific, adding: 'We've got to believe we can go on a run, win 10 in a row and get ourselves in the play-offs with a bit of momentum.'

No-one present could have foreseen that less than two months later Villa would have done precisely that, setting a new club record for consecutive league matches won and clinching a play-off place with two matches of the season still to play. It was an extraordinary achievement and one which, standing in the cold at Stoke that evening, you simply could not see coming. Even before the draw in the Potteries, those inside the club were already beginning to stress the focus was on next season and the summer rebuilding job required with a host of players due to be out of contract. Smith had drawn up plans to bring the players back early for pre-season in an attempt to hit the ground running in 2019–20, while logistics around summer travel were discussed. Villa's yearly accounts would soon be out and reveal a pre-tax loss of £36 million, a colossal sum for a Championship club.[21] That would lead to obvious questions over the club's ability to comply with PSR, and inside the club there was talk of how best to present the numbers to the media, in order to take hold of the narrative. There was a sense, mentally, of people getting ready to check out of the 2018–19 campaign.

But then Villa's season was about to get a kickstart from a player who for more than two months had been stuck watching from the sidelines. Jack Grealish had not kicked a ball in anger since leaving the field against West Brom but was nearly recovered from the shin injury which had been the cause of so much pain. Even before that night, he had been playing through major discomfort, such was his desperation to fire Villa back to the Premier League, but with every passing game the agony was getting worse.

Finally forced to spend time out, his frustration shifted from the body to mind. Grealish hates not being able to play and is what you might politely call a bad spectator, though those close to him would use a term which could not be printed here. Ever since he was a little boy, eating steak and chips on a Friday night in preparation for playing on a Saturday, right through to this period when he was trying to lead his boyhood club back into the Premier League, it was the matchdays which motivated him.

Smith tried to keep him engaged by including him in team meetings and asking for his opinion on the performances and results. It was also recognised a change of scenery might help and with Smith's blessing it was decided Grealish could spend some time in Dubai recovering. The state-of-the-art facilities and warm weather made it an ideal location and those days were important to take away some of the stresses and strains. It also helped that Oli Stevenson, the head of strength and conditioning at Villa, was a close friend so the pair doubled-down on workouts, often leaving the training ground late into the evening as the weeks progressed.

If Grealish needed picking up, so too did Villa. After being denied so late at The Hawthorns in December, the form of Smith's team had stalled badly. Abraham was continuing to score at such a rate that by early February he was already the first Villa player since

Peter Withe in the Division One title-winning 1980–81 season to hit 20 in a league campaign.

But the goals were not translating into points as Villa's defensive frailties returned to the fore, and without Grealish they were unable to outscore opponents. Jonathan Kodjia came off the bench to rescue a point at home to Stoke but a few days later Villa surrendered a two-goal lead to lose 3–2 to Leeds United, a match notable for the home side fielding three right-backs in the back four as the defensive shortage began to bite. There were 2–2 draws against QPR and Hull, while Villa came from 3–0 down in the final 10 minutes to draw 3–3 with Sheffield United. Yet it was wins Smith's team needed and a personal low point came in a 3–0 defeat at Wigan.

'That was the worst game of my whole time at Villa. We were awful,' Smith recalls. 'My own brother left 10 minutes into the second half, we were that bad! There were other games where we played well enough to win but couldn't get over the line.

'We were giving soft goals away and it was the first period where I felt there could be an anxiety within the players. It is a little bit like Sir Alex Ferguson used to say about playing for Manchester United, you have to have players who can handle that. When things went against us and there was an expectancy in the stands it was tough for a few of the players. I had to work on that on the training ground. The psychology of the game became more important than the actual game at times.'

The January window at least offered the chance to bring in reinforcements and the business Villa did would eventually prove just as crucial to their renaissance as Grealish's return.

Admittedly, that could not be said of the first signing, goalkeeper Lovre Kalinic. Despite having recruited Orjan Nyland just a few months previously, the Norway international's form was already a concern, following some high-profile errors. Nyland had also let in every shot he faced in the 5–5 draw against Forest and there was a sense his performances were contributing to a lack of confidence in defence.

Feelings were mixed because in training the Norwegian was exceptional. He had all the attributes of a top goalkeeper but crumbled too often on a matchday and didn't have the strength of character to thrive in the dressing room among other big personalities.

'We had big, big doubts about Nyland, not because of his quality, but because of the pressure from the crowd,' says Suso. 'But in his support, my view is that any goalkeeper in the world would have had problems at Aston Villa around that time because of the defence.'

Through his contacts across Europe, Suso identified Kalinic, the Croatian international playing at Belgian side Gent, as the answer. Villa had tried to sign the goalkeeper three years previously during their most recent season in the Premier League but missed out because he couldn't get a work permit.[22] The signing felt like a big deal and offered so much hope. This was a player who had just lined up against England for Croatia in the Nations League and at £4 million Villa were sure they had the answer to their problems.

It turned out that the actual answer was much closer to home. Shortly after the Kalinic deal had been agreed, Nyland sustained an Achilles injury that would keep him out for the remainder of the season, so Jed Steer was recalled from a loan spell at Charlton Athletic to cover. Signed on a free transfer from Norwich in 2013, Steer was among the longest-serving players on Villa's books but had made only eight first-team appearances, having spent the majority of his time at the club on loan in the lower leagues. After starting the opening day win at Hull, just his second-ever league appearance for Villa, he had joined League One club Charlton Athletic on loan after Nyland's signing.

'My deal at Villa was up at the end of the season as far as I was concerned, I was going to Charlton to play for my next contract,' explains Steer. In a decision which would have major ramifications down the line for both himself and Villa, Steer had actually turned down the chance to join Bolton on a permanent deal.

'It was a two-year contract and my agent was really keen for me to take it,' he recalls. 'But at the time I thought going on loan to Charlton was a better option. I knew their goalie coach, Andy Marshall, because he'd worked at Villa under Paul Lambert and I just thought I would get more opportunities to play there than at Bolton.'

Nyland's misfortune meant Steer was now needed back at Villa. He was in his home town of Norwich, sat in the house of his wife's parents, when his agent forwarded a text from Christian Purslow explaining he was being recalled. Villa were also giving him a one-year contract extension and he was told he would be playing in the New Year's Day fixture against QPR, while new signing Kalinic waited for international clearance.

'I was not going to play regularly but I had the extension, a bit more security and the chance to work with Dean Smith and Neil Cutler,' explains Steer. 'I was happy to do it. I knew I was going to play in the New Year's Day game so I came back training for a few days, played that.

'Dean then pulled me before we played Swansea in the FA Cup and said, "Look, we have signed Lovre, he is going to take over and he is going to play." I had no issues with that. I knew what I had signed up for.'

Yet by the time of Grealish's return, Steer had been installed as Villa's No. 1 after Smith lost faith in Kalinic after just six weeks. Villa failed to win any of the seven games the Croatian started, conceding 14 goals in the process. In the keeper's defence, it didn't help that he had no functioning defence for much of it. The loss of Axel Tuanzebe to a broken foot in mid-December meant full-backs were having to deputise at centre-back alongside Chester, whose knee issue was beginning to affect his form. Smith acted by recalling Elphick from his loan spell at Hull.

The final straw for Kalinic was in a 2–0 defeat to West Brom at Villa Park in February, where Hal Robson-Kanu sent a looping header over the tall goalkeeper and then Jay Rodriguez scored for the second time that season against Villa, this time with his feet.

To add injury to insult, Kalinic was then forced off with a concussion after taking a boot in the head from Albion midfielder Jake Livermore. The moment would be one of several turning points in Villa's season. Kalinic never played for Villa again, while Steer became No. 1 and a key figure in the march to promotion.

Suso still has some sympathy with his signing. 'We killed and burned Kalinic through our defence,' he says. 'It was an absolute disaster.'

By the time of the defeat to Albion, described that week in the *Express & Star* by the club's European Cup-winning goalkeeper Nigel Spink as the 'lowest of the low points', Villa's back line had been bolstered by two crucial loan signings, Tyrone Mings and Kortney Hause. These were essential arrivals with Chester having battled about as far as he could go. By now the captain was barely training in the week and getting injections before every match.

'I was having a local anaesthetic in my knee, which made me feel great during the 90 minutes,' he says. 'Longer-term? Not so much.

'I was spending a lot of time in the doctor's office, trying to plan a route through it. I remember one day Dean came in and we sat there, looking at the fixtures, seeing how far away January was. I said I didn't mind doing it until you get some cover, really.'

The first player Smith considered was James Collins, a player who represented Villa between 2009 and 2012 but was now a free agent. Terms on a short-term deal were agreed but hours before officially becoming a Villa player for a second time, he sustained an injury and therefore ripped up the contract he had signed out of respect.

Smith and Terry then went on a scouting mission to Bournemouth to decide whether Mings was the right choice. There was no doubting his appetite to join Villa but his durability was a concern. The 25-year-old had made only 23 appearances since joining the Cherries in 2015, having suffered a serious knee injury on his Premier League debut. Though the lack of playing time initially made both Purslow and Suso sceptical about his signing, they were assured he had not missed a single training session that season.

The loan signing of Mings, which eventually went through on deadline day, was another of those occasions when fate fell in Villa's favour. For much of the final week of the window, the defender believed West Brom would be his home for the rest of the season. Yet Baggies boss Darren Moore, who had pipped Smith to the job at The Hawthorns the previous summer, hesitated at the last, allowing Villa to swoop in and complete what would turn out to be a vitally important signing.

'I'd started talking about a move from Bournemouth in October,' Mings says. 'West Brom showed the most interest in me and they were high up in the table and doing well but as it got closer to January their results picked up and they started to get cold feet. They started to say that I would not be guaranteed a start, which felt like a risk to me. Nottingham Forest were also really keen. Martin O'Neill was the manager with Roy Keane as the assistant. It was when Villa came in that I really started to feel the enthusiasm from Dean, JT and Cutts. I was looking for somewhere to be appreciated.'

Mings made a fine impression on reporters during his first interview as he went around the room shaking the hand of every media representative in attendance, and it wasn't long before those in the stands started to appreciate his qualities, too.

Hause, who joined from Wolverhampton Wanderers much earlier in the window, also had injury concerns due to a crack on a bone in one of his feet. But he wasn't suffering any adverse reaction to training and Smith felt alongside Mings the pair would bring quality in both boxes, particularly at set-pieces. In short, they were both risks worth taking.

Inevitably both players needed time to settle in after a lack of playing time at their parent clubs. Hause had featured just two times in the past year for Wolves and was rusty. 'Their first game together was away at Brentford where we lost to a late Neal Maupay goal,' Suso says. 'We were now quite far behind the top six but we felt Mings and Hause would be good together. Actually, if we had this team in place in September, I'm sure we would have won the league.'

The window wasn't all about incomings. Arguably the most important piece of business Villa did that month was keeping hold of Tammy Abraham after the striker emerged as a serious target for Wolverhampton Wanderers. Their Midlands rivals, promoted from the Championship as champions the previous year, were riding high in the top half of the Premier League and viewed Abraham as the ideal foil for their top scorer, Raul Jimenez.

The decision, ultimately, was out of Villa's hands. Abraham's loan agreement contained a January break clause and Chelsea were open to triggering it, should the striker wish to move. Knowing how vital he was to their promotion hopes, Villa were determined to do everything they could to stop that happening. 'I remember for every waking minute that I was told this was a possibility, until the moment he stayed, I relentlessly pulled every single lever,' says Purslow. 'I worked flat out with his agent and Chelsea for four days. When I get the bit between my teeth, there's no stopping me.'

It was all hands on deck. Smith and Terry held a FaceTime meeting with Abraham and his parents in which his importance to Villa was stressed. At that point, the striker was still to hit the mark of 20 league goals. 'We told him he could become the first Villa player since European Cup winner Peter Withe to score 20 goals in a league season and how he would always be held in high esteem at the club,' says Smith. 'What we ended up telling them ended up being true. We felt staying with us would help his career at Chelsea, rather than going to Wolves and having to settle into a new team. We knew it was the Premier League and we knew Wolves, for their part, were confident of getting the deal done. But we told Tammy he had the chance to do something special at Villa, which would hold him in good stead for the rest of his career.'

Grealish, though sidelined, also put in considerable effort to convince his team-mate and friend to stay put. The hard work paid dividends as Abraham did just that. Another critical moment had gone Villa's way.

That afternoon at Stoke did not only become memorable for Elphick's apparent ability to see the future. It was also the day Smith changed tack, showing his players a different, much sharper side of his character.

With Villa trailing at half-time to Sam Vokes' fifth-minute goal and starting to look more and more like a team going through the motions, the normally mild-mannered Smith launched into a rant, telling his players in no uncertain terms that now was the time to sharpen up. He asked individuals if they wanted to stay in the Championship, or achieve their dreams of playing in the Premier League. In short, as Elphick later put it, the head coach had 'delivered some home truths'.

Smith always encouraged open discussion among his players, believing that the best way to get out of a problem was to figure it out together and for them to take responsibility. But on this occasion, it was his voice firmly setting the tone. Players were shocked, partly because they hadn't seen this side of the head coach before, and there were awkward, uncomfortable looks across the dressing room.

'There are points when you have to be a ranter and raver,' says Smith. 'That was one of those. I had seen them training all week and knew we weren't performing the way we should have.

I felt it could change the performance if I lost it a little bit with them.

'I think it shocked quite a lot of them. To be fair we got an outstanding second half performance and could have won the game in the end. I think the dressing room changed that day, a little bit. It was a case of, we're not going to mess with the gaffer!'

At the end of the tirade, a few words from the manager kicked the group into life. 'Be a good team-mate,' he said. Or in other words, help each other out. It was short and simple but it worked. Anwar El Ghazi made amends for an earlier miss by setting up substitute Albert Adomah to score his first goal for almost a year and the supporters reacted positively as Villa left with a valuable point. A 1–1 draw at Stoke was hardly the result to kickstart a season, especially as time was running out. But after the low of losing to West Brom, it at least felt something of a corner had been turned with the second half performance. Even more importantly, Grealish was ready to return and ahead of the following weekend's home match with Derby Smith pulled off a managerial masterstroke.

Grealish was the cheat code for Villa but it was not only on the pitch his influence would help. The 23-year-old's impact on the dressing room was also significant. 'Everyone likes Jack,' observed one of Villa's in-house media team in the week of his return. Intended as a throwaway comment, it was also the complete truth. Into an atmosphere where, as Elphick hinted, thoughts were already turning to the following season, it was Grealish who brought fresh energy. He was the glue which held everything together.

With Chester absent through injury and Alan Hutton, who had taken the captain's armband in recent matches, also unavailable Smith decided he would give Grealish the honour of skippering the side. 'That wasn't as hard a decision as a lot of people think. But it surprised a lot of people at the time,' says Smith. 'I have actually done talks since for pro licences on how you should choose your captain. People always say it has to be a leader, or they have to lead by example or by the way they play.

'The first thing I look for, is who is going to be playing first. If you are going to pick a captain, it is someone who is going to be in the starting XI every week, otherwise there is no point picking him. I looked at our Villa team at the time and five of the players were on loan. Then you had Ahmed Elmohamady, Neil Taylor played regularly. Mile was in and out of the team. John McGinn, it was his first full season at the club. Could I really put that on him with the way he was playing? I didn't want to.

'So it was a process of elimination, coupled with the fact I knew it would help Jack. Having got to know him I knew he would relish being captain. I told JT and Rich [O'Kelly] I was going to do it and at first they said, really? The next day they came back and said: "We really like it."'

Recalling the moment he was told by Smith, Grealish says: 'I couldn't believe it. As soon as I finished training, I called my dad and told him I was going to be the captain. It was an unbelievable feeling.'

It would be fair to say that, from the outside, Smith's decision to select Grealish as captain raised some eyebrows. Despite some traits which suggested he would be great at the job, others hinted he would be better without the armband. Although he has a strong voice, he's not really an organiser or the type to find the motivating words to lift a group when they're down. There is an overlooked kind and caring side to him, though, and he'll step up when needed. He was also an intelligent analyser of the game and not afraid to be demanding in his message for improvement.

'We had a lot of leaders in the dressing room,' says Smith. 'The likes of Glenn, Mile, Elmo and Neil Taylor, they led anyway on the training ground. It just needed a figurehead, who was playing week-in, week-out. I felt it was an easy decision and I knew how much it would mean to Jack.'

'Jack is just someone who everyone gets on with. There is nothing there to not get on with,' says Steer. 'He is such a likeable character. He's funny. He's good with everyone. He is just a people person. Anyone in the team he gets on well with. As a captain, you automatically have respect if everyone likes you.

'Managers have to make big decisions and at that stage something has to change. We had not been on a good run and Jack being fit and back was massive. Making him captain as well was an even bigger buzz for everyone. Everyone is buzzing he is back and it just adds to it. I think it made him go on to another level too.'

Grealish's return could hardly have gone better. Promoted heavily by the club's media team in the build-up to a home match with Derby, all eyes were on him at Villa Park and from the first whistle Villa looked a different team. Hourihane fired them into a ninth-minute lead and grabbed his second of the game after Abraham had already doubled the advantage. Then, seconds before half-time, Grealish crowned his first game as captain in stunning fashion. Whelan floated a corner to the edge of the box from where the new skipper thundered an unstoppable right-footed volley over a crowd of players and into the top corner of the net. For a team in desperate need of a kickstart, there could not have been a more symbolic moment. From a point where they had been drifting toward the finish, Villa had momentum again.

'I probably didn't foresee the impact Jack would have straight away,' says Smith. 'I remember in the Derby game, him playing one-twos on the edge of our box when we were 1–0 up. You just thought, we've missed that composure a bit, the bravery to go and do things like that. That lifted the whole team as well.'

'In years to come I'll look back and realise how lucky I was to play with Jack,' Conor Hourihane would later say when discussing memories of the ten-game winning run.

It's true there were occasional sacrifices the club had to make for Grealish. He certainly wasn't a morning person, and definitely not an early riser, and he absolutely loved to moan in training especially if he was on the losing team, but on a matchday he was always a threat with his driving runs, perfectly-weighted passing and ability to win so many fouls.

McGinn joked that his job in midfield was to 'give the ball to Jack'. Elmohamady and Taylor strategically made runs to free up space for him and Abraham had a lovely connection both on and off the field. 'When he was injured, I spoke to him and he said, "Tam, just wait for me to get back, we'll have that combo again" and he stuck by his word,' Abraham recalls.

Buoyed by the win over Derby, Villa began preparing for their next match, a short trip across Birmingham to face their city rivals Blues, then placed just above them in the Championship table. Grealish was the most talked about man during the build-up but silent himself. Honest to a fault when interviewed, Villa's media team were always careful to keep him away from the press in the weeks before derby games, in the knowledge he would likely give the opposition something to pin on the dressing room noticeboard for motivation. To say there was no love lost between Grealish and Blues supporters would be an understatement, but this would be the day things went too far.

The tone was set in the first few seconds when Birmingham midfielder Maikel Kieftenbeld scythed through Grealish in the centre circle, earning a yellow card. Had VAR been in operation, the challenge might have been deemed worthy of even greater punishment.

Yet a strong challenge was nothing compared to what happened in the 10th minute. With the ball out of play after a Villa attack toward the Tilton End of the stadium broke down, a man ran out from the stands and behind Grealish, knocking the player to the ground with a swinging arm.

Hourihane was among the first on the scene as he, Abraham and Whelan and a steward tackled the assailant, 27-year-old Paul Mitchell, who would later be sentenced to fourteen weeks in jail, ordered to pay £350 in fines and costs and handed a ten-year ban from attending football matches after admitting charges of assault and encroachment on to the pitch.

It was a shocking moment, both for Grealish's family – who had decided not to attend the match such was the hostility toward him – and his team-mates. 'I couldn't believe what happened to Jack and after the game I said to him, "I hope this is the last time I play Birmingham City at their ground,"' El Ghazi told *The Athletic*. 'The hate in their eyes. I would rather not be there. It's the worst rivalry I've ever seen.'

The good news was Grealish was not seriously hurt and he duly got back to his feet before taking revenge in the best way possible, firing home the only goal of the afternoon midway through the second half after Smith had brought on McGinn, absent from the previous two matches after suspension, off the bench.

All the post-match talk obviously centred on the assault but in the context of Villa's season the key statistic was they had recorded consecutive wins for the first time since November. Just three days later, they would make it three in a row with a 3–1 victory at Nottingham Forest before a comfortable 3–0 home triumph over Middlesbrough sent them into the top six heading into the international break. In the space of a fortnight they had gone from being written off to once more being serious contenders in the play-off race.

From there, the wins just kept coming and confidence kept rising. 'When we beat Forest away to make it three on the bounce it was around then people started to think, without getting carried away, this is on,' says Steer.

'At that stage of the season the average points per game for the teams in the top two and the play-offs drop dramatically, because things get so tense. Our points-per-game was going through the roof. We were catching teams at a rapid speed.'

'Day to day, the way we trained was of a high standard,' adds Neil Taylor. 'When I have come across success in my career, there's no surprise that I look back and think "Bloody hell, we had a good training team." There was Mile and Glenn and we'd always try and drive the standards. All the team needed was a few wins to get us going.'

A 2–1 win over Blackburn continued the momentum before a trip to Sheffield Wednesday, where Steve Bruce had taken over as manager, began a pivotal week. Villa were poor at Hillsborough and looked happy to be leaving with a point with the scores tied at 1–1 heading into stoppage time, after Steer had saved a Steven Fletcher penalty. But Smith's team were not to be denied. Grealish, well shackled all game by the hosts, finally found some space on the edge of the box and, though his shot was saved, Adomah fired in the rebound. 'I loved this goal and I remember doing the old man with a walking stick dance,' Adomah says, laughing.

A minute later Villa broke clear again and Abraham slotted home to the delight of the visiting supporters packed behind the goal.

Steer's save had been crucial and owed much to the meticulous preparation he, Neil Cutler and the goalkeeping department carried out ahead of every game. Potential penalty takers in the opposing team were studied in detail. 'A lot of the time when it comes to penalties it is an educated guess,' says Steer. 'You look at diagrams of recent penalties and quite often it is like dot-to-dot around the goal. They can go anywhere.

'But with Fletcher, we noticed he tended to favour the keeper's left most of the time. So I dived that way and thankfully he put it that way. Saving the penalty and going on to win the game was great but it is only now you look back and see it in the context of everything which happened and think, yeah, that was a big moment.'

Having now reeled off six straight wins, Villa were starting to gain an air of invincibility which would be proven in even more emphatic fashion just up the road from Hillsborough a few days later at Rotherham.

This looked like the night the run would surely come to an end after Abraham missed an early penalty and then Mings conceded one for handball, allowing Will Vaulks to instead fire the hosts in front. To make matters worse, Mings was shown a second yellow card for the infringement and dismissed.

But Smith stayed calm and composed and in the moments before half-time put together a bold plan of attack, introducing a second forward in Kodjia to play alongside Abraham and sacrificing a midfielder. It worked a treat, as Kodjia slammed Villa level from the penalty spot and then Grealish got the winner with a goal which would later be voted the club's best of the season, embarking on a jinking run before exchanging passes with Elmohamady and rolling a finish into the bottom corner.

By the final whistle the only surprise was the 10 men had not won by more. McGinn was so good some players in the Rotherham team that night still describe it as the most complete midfield performance they have ever faced. Jedinak, so maligned in the early part of the season, also filled in superbly at centre-back while Tuanzebe was serenaded in the dressing room by the rest of the team with the catchy terrace chant to the tune of 'Lip Up Fatty' by Bad Manners.

Rotherham had been the Manchester United loanee's first start since returning from his foot injury, though it was in place of Hause who had suffered a hip injury which would keep him out of action for several weeks. With Elphick also sidelined with a foot problem, Villa could not be said to be having much luck but their durability was seeing them through. Looking back now, Smith says the win at Rotherham was the first time he felt promotion might be on the cards. 'Going and playing like we did in the second half, that was the moment I thought: "There aren't many teams who can stop us now",' he says.

Grealish was front and centre of the renaissance but the accusation from critics Villa were a 'one-man team' was unfair and would be dispelled just three days later in a home match against Bristol City. Rumours Grealish was not in the team for what was a pivotal match – the visitors sat just a point behind fifth-placed Villa in the table and had a game in hand – had surfaced in the morning. Around 90 minutes before kick-off, they were confirmed. The skipper was suffering with illness and Villa, already missing Mings through suspension, would be without their talisman for what was in every respect a play-off 'six pointer'. But there was no stopping Villa at this stage and only a string of saves from young Robins keeper Max O'Leary kept them at bay before, 10 minutes into the second half, Hourihane was brought down in the box and Abraham fired home the opener from the spot. A short while after Hourihane doubled the advantage and though Fara Diedhiou pulled one back, to set up a tense finish, Villa saw it through.

'Jack's just ill, he had a fever,' Smith later explained. 'Hopefully the monkey's off our back now, we've got a win without him in the team.' Six days later Grealish was back to score the opener in a 2–0 Good Friday win at Bolton and then, on Easter Monday, Kodjia got the only goal as Millwall were beaten 1–0 to secure Villa's top-six finish with two matches still to play. In the space of just 52 days from when Grealish had first made his comeback against Derby, Villa had been transformed from rank outsiders to the team nobody in the play-offs wanted to face. Their run of 10 consecutive league wins broke a club record which had stood since 1910.

'What is crazy is throughout the whole run, no-one got carried away,' says Steer. 'It was almost unheard of, winning ten in a row in the Championship. Obviously, it was a club record.

'But because we knew we were still chasing the play-off spot, it was like: "OK, we want another one."

'We knew we had to keep winning. There was never any thought of: "Bloody hell we are a good side." We knew how bad it had been heading into those 10 games, so no-one took their foot off the gas. No-one believed we were a good team, we just had to keep winning.'

The journey was not over yet. 'If you'd told me eleven games ago we'd go and win the next 10 games, I think I would have said you were crackers,' said Smith, after taking his seat in the post-match press room. 'But there's an awful lot still to do. Our focus is on getting promoted.'

6

PROMOTION

Dean Smith's biggest concern, with Villa's play-off place now secure, was the fitness of Tammy Abraham. The striker had injured his shoulder in the act of scoring his 25th goal of the season in the 2–0 win at Bolton and returned to Chelsea for assessment. Back at Villa, there were genuine fears the Premier League club's medical team would recommend Abraham undergo surgery, ruling him out for the rest of the campaign.

'I'd spoken to our doctor, Ricky Shamji, and he told me Tammy's injury was one which could be sorted quite quickly with surgery,' says Smith. 'My fear was Chelsea would say: "Right, he needs an operation." If that happened he would be out for the season. Fortunately for us, Chelsea looked at it and said they were OK with what we were prescribing. Tammy had to be strapped up and he played through the pain barrier a bit. But as soon as he started training again, he said he was fine with it.'

The good news for Villa was their final two games of the season – against Leeds United and Norwich City, the two teams who along with Sheffield United had been battling it out for automatic promotion – were no longer so important as had looked likely several weeks earlier, so Abraham at least had time to rest before he would be required again.

Indeed, the lunchtime trip to Leeds on the penultimate Sunday of the regular season had all the makings of a damp squib. When broadcaster Sky Sports chose the match for live coverage several weeks before, it had reason to be confident there would be something riding on the result, with Villa chasing a play-off place and Leeds – at that stage – in pole position for a top-two finish and automatic promotion. Yet by the time the match actually took place, things had changed, Villa having already clinched the play-offs, while Leeds had suffered a major implosion, losing three out of five to leave them mathematically out of the automatic promotion race. The noon kick-off, for a contest where the result was effectively meaningless, was therefore the cause for much grumbling among Midlands-based journalists on the road north following a 6 a.m. alarm call. In the end what they witnessed turned out to be more than worth the journey and tiredness.

Much discussion had focused on the strength of the team Smith would select as he looked to maintain momentum heading into the play-offs, while also making sure players came through the game unscathed. The latter were in no doubt how they would approach it. 'We wanted to beat Leeds to put down a marker,' Hourihane recalls of a game which has gone down in football folklore for an incident 18 minutes from time.

With a fiercely competitive but largely chance-free match level at 0–0, Kodjia went down injured as a Villa attack broke down. Leeds winger Tyler Roberts paused for a second and looked like he would kick the ball out of play to allow his rival to receive treatment. Instead, with Villa's players having relaxed, he kicked it down the wing to Mateusz Klich, who cut inside before firing a finish beyond Steer and into the bottom corner.

Villa were enraged. Hourihane, who by this stage was developing a reputation as a player you would want in the trenches with you, squared up to Klich, while El Ghazi scuffled with Patrick Bamford. The Leeds striker fell to the floor and the Villa winger was promptly shown a red card. On the sidelines, Terry led the protests and things were becoming ugly.

Amid extraordinary scenes, Leeds boss Marcelo Bielsa instructed his players to let Villa score from the kick-off to even the scores. At least one member of his team, Pontus Jansson, took umbrage and tried to tackle Adomah as the winger walked the ball in. 'What a mad day that was,' Adomah recalls. 'It was one of the only goals I scored for Villa where I didn't do a dance.'

At that point there was still 13 minutes of normal time remaining and plenty more to be added in stoppages. With nearly 40,000 home fans confused and increasingly angry, Villa faced holding out for a draw with just 10 men, Jedinak having been introduced as an emergency striker with Kodjia also off injured. When the full-time whistle finally went with the scores level at 1–1, it felt as though Smith's men had proven themselves hardened for the play-off battles which lay ahead.

'Can't bully us,' posted Mings on social media shortly after the final whistle. The defender had blocked a stoppage time Roberts shot on the line, while Steer had saved from Pablo Hernandez with virtually the last kick. Most of the post-match talk, understandably, fell on Bielsa's gesture. 'Sportsmanship prevailed,' Smith opined on the incident. Bielsa and his team would later be awarded FIFA's fair play award for their actions.

Smith was less happy with Bamford. El Ghazi's dismissal meant the winger was facing a three-match ban which would rule him out of both legs of the play-off semi-final. It was fortunate for Villa, in that regard, the match was broadcast on live TV. The multiple camera angles clearly showed El Ghazi had made virtually no contact with his opponent and Villa were able to lodge a successful appeal. Instead it was Bamford who was banned for two matches, after the FA charged him retrospectively with deceiving the match officials. Hourihane also escaped censure, much to Leeds' chagrin, after FA officials examined his altercation with Klich and ruled no further action would be taken.

If the Leeds clash gave Villa a taste for the highly-charged atmospheres they would face in the play-offs, then the final game against champions Norwich was a case of what could have been. Smith made changes and a largely second-string Villa team performed well before falling to a 2–1 defeat. Afterwards, the Villa team decided to give the table-toppers a guard of honour to mark their impressive season, although some Villa players felt a little embarrassed because they still had it all to do themselves in the quest for promotion. 'It felt a bit strange because we were desperate to go up but we knew it was totally the right thing to do,' Hourihane says.

Seeing Norwich in such jubilant spirits added fuel to the fire for those in claret and blue. They were desperate to make their own history and with the Championship season complete it was confirmed after 46 fixtures that Villa, by finishing fifth in the table, would take on rivals West Brom in the semi-finals with Leeds lining up against Derby County.

The rivalry between Villa and West Brom is not so vitriolic as that between Villa and Birmingham City. Yet it is still a big deal, the oldest in English football with no shortage of history. The proximity of the two clubs to each other – The Hawthorns sits on the Birmingham/Sandwell border and is just four miles from Villa Park – means there is plenty of crossover between fanbases. Rarely had the rivals met with so much on the line. When Albion had won at Villa Park in February, it had seemed unthinkable the next meeting would be in the play-offs. The Baggies, at that stage, were right in the hunt for automatic promotion but a run of poor results in early March had seen boss Darren Moore dismissed and replaced by Under-21s coach Jimmy Shan. Though Albion had finished a place higher in the table, it was Villa who were perceived to be favourites. Smith certainly saw them as such.

'I genuinely was not worried about playing West Brom,' he says. 'I thought that was good for us. I fancied us over the two legs. I never dreamed they could stop us.'

Semi-finals at Villa Park are special occasions. The previous year's play-off clash with Middlesbrough had produced such a noise inside the ground that Jedinak, who had played in hostile environments all across the world with the Australia national team, described it as one of the loudest noises he'd ever heard.

That game, however, was at night; this was at lunch-time. Such kick-offs rarely generate anything like the levels a spiced-up night match can produce and for much of the early afternoon it appeared the visitors would pull off the perfect smash-and-grab away performance, having taken the lead after Dwight Gayle pounced on Glenn Whelan's first half mistake. The plan from the visitors, to soak up pressure and take the sting out of the game, worked for long periods but Villa had armoury to call upon off the bench and turned the game around in the closing minutes.

Whelan had got the nod to start in midfield ahead of Hourihane and his fellow Irishman, sat on the sidelines, was raging at his exclusion. 'There was a real frustration there because I thought I was in good form,' Hourihane says. Midway through the second half, he got his chance to prove why he should have started. Within eight minutes of coming on, he had drawn Villa level with a trademark piledriver of a shot into the top corner from the edge of the box, after excellent work by Grealish to make the space.

'Honestly, the goal I scored could have gone anywhere,' smiles Hourihane now. 'I just hit it so hard through frustration and luckily enough it flew into the top corner!'

Grealish then won a penalty which Abraham converted and the tie was back in Villa's hands. When Gayle was sent off for two bookings – first for throwing away the ball and then for sliding into Steer when trying to win the ball – ruling him out of the second leg, the stars were starting to align. Abraham, who showed no signs of weakness from the shoulder setback, was lucky not to concede a penalty when he clumsily pulled down Mason Holgate and even with the return match Villa had the spirit and good fortune of unbreakable warriors.

Yet the second leg at The Hawthorns would prove far tougher than anyone expected and Villa's mentality would be tested to the limit.

'I can still picture it all so clear,' Purslow recalls. 'When I walked out of the boardroom to my seat, I remember thinking "this is the real deal."

'This is their equivalent of what we've already had at Villa Park, we're in the lead but my word this feels so fucking big for them. It's going to be a tough night.'

Home supporters gathered outside the players' entrance to rip into the Villa players when they arrived on the coach. They booed, hissed and banged on the side of the team coach in an attempt to intimidate those who had made the short journey through Birmingham. 'The noise from the home supporters was absolutely incredible,' Purslow recalls.

Backed by vociferous support, Albion took an early lead on the night, Craig Dawson heading home to level the tie on aggregate. There was no shortage of suspense, tension and nervousness through a gruelling game, under the lights and in front of a pumped-up crowd as Villa were pushed the distance. Early in the second half, the visitors were seriously wobbling, Mings forced to block a Jacob Murphy effort on the line. The turning point came in the 80th minute. Albion skipper Chris Brunt, already booked for a rash challenge on McGinn, was shown a second yellow card for bringing down the Scot again. Yet even with a man advantage, Villa could find no way through during 30 tense minutes of extra time, Adomah denied a late winner by a flying Sam Johnstone save as the tie went to penalties.

In the away end, season ticket holder Dan Bardell stood with the family of Grealish feeling sick with nerves. 'It was the worst I've ever felt at a football match,' he recalls. 'I'll never forget that game. West Brom made it really intimidating, I thought the Villa players struggled with it and when it went to penalties I was fearing the worst. It's actually one of the most nerve wracking moments of my life. I felt like I was having a panic attack and standing next to Kevan Grealish [Jack's brother] and Sacha [Jack's girlfriend] was tough because I could see the fear in their eyes, too.'

The notion of penalty shoot-outs being a 'lottery' is one of football's most enduring clichés. In the modern game, it is increasingly a fallacy as teams spend hours upon hours on preparation to reduce the element of luck involved. Villa had planned in detail for the occasion, with dress rehearsals on the training ground which included practising the kicks, the walk-up, the order, and how they would handle the pressure. Jedinak, who had never missed a penalty in his professional career and was among the designated takers, was brought off the bench with seconds of extra time remaining and didn't even touch the ball before the shoot-out.

Smith still had to double-check on the designated takers to test their mindset and one player who turned down the chance to join the order was Kodjia, with team-mates describing him as 'nervous'. So the list remained the same as planned: Hourihane to start, followed by Jedinak, Grealish, Adomah and Abraham.

On the other side of the coin, Steer and Cutler had also spent hours studying West Brom's likely takers but as the seconds ticked down at the end of extra time, Villa's goalkeeper noticed there was a potential problem. Over the course of the match the Baggies had lost a host of attacking players with Brunt sent off and Jay Rodriguez and Matt Phillips, another two of their best penalty takers, both substituted having run themselves into the ground.

'I remember toward the end of extra time looking around their team and thinking, I am not sure who is going to take the penalties here,' says Steer. 'Most of the people we had done our work on had gone off, so I thought: "This will be interesting".'

So many turning points over the previous 10 months had led Villa to this moment: The takeover, retaining the services of Grealish, signing and then keeping hold of Abraham, appointing Smith instead of Henry. Yet it remains fair to wonder what might have happened had Nyland not sustained his injury, forcing Villa to recall Steer? He was a quiet, unassuming type who sometimes gave the impression that he never truly believed in his ability. But he more than played his part in the 10-match winning run and here, with Villa's season and so much more on the line, he was about to write himself into club folklore.

Immediately before the shoot-out came a moment which has become among the most iconic in Villa's recent history, Steer staring into the eyes of West Brom's first taker, Mason Holgate, as they walked together toward the penalty box. But as the goalkeeper now explains, the action was by no means premeditated.

'First of all, I was surprised I was walking with Holgate,' he says. 'I am not sure that had ever happened, the goalie walking with the opponent who was about to take the first penalty.

'For any penalty, me and Cuts would write down which way we think they are going to go and I would look over and he would give me a little point. So at the moment I was walking with Holgate, I turned round to look toward the bench to look for the point.

'It was only as we kept walking, I realised Holgate thought I was looking at him. So then, I did start looking at him! He glanced at me and that is when I knew, I've got him here.'

Steer continues: 'That is when I knew I had players coming up here who would not automatically be first choice penalty takers. Straight away I knew I had that on my side.'

It was not only with his eyes that Steer tried to give himself an advantage. Ahead of every Albion penalty, he stood on the edge of the six-yard box, halfway between the penalty spot and the goal, only moving back at the last moment when he felt he had tested the patience of referee Chris Kavanagh to the limit.

'For one thing, it is a delaying tactic,' says Steer. 'As soon as you have thinking time you can start to second guess and your mind takes over. If I can delay the taker while they are waiting to take a penalty it might just put an element of doubt in their mind. That is one thing.

'The other thing is if I'm standing on the six-yard line and they look up, the goal looks smaller. Then I start to go back. I am not the biggest keeper, nor the smallest. But if they put the ball down, see me and the goal looking small behind them, it helps add that bit of doubt. If you have a mind doubting itself, it is only a positive thing for a goalkeeper.'

The pressure proved too much for Holgate, his penalty lacked power and Steer saved diving to his left to give Villa the perfect start. Hourihane then sent Sam Johnstone the wrong way with his kick, before the home side's next penalty taker, Egypt international Ahmed Hegazi, started his walk to the box. Villa's research was about to pay dividends.

'Hegazi had taken one penalty in his career, for Egypt, and I'd seen it,' says Steer. 'He had gone high, to the keeper's right, smashed it into the top corner. I thought I had to go that way and thankfully this time he did not put it as high. It was a nice height for me and I made the save.'

When Jedinak then scored for Villa the visitors were 2–0 up after two penalties and had one foot in the final. Steer's role during the shoot-out was not limited to trying to make saves. Prior to the match, Cutler had read a study which claimed penalty takers were more likely to score if they were handed the ball by their goalkeeper. England had used the tactic in their shoot-out win over Colombia at the previous summer's World Cup. It meant after every Albion penalty, Steer was meeting Villa's next taker to hand them both the ball and a few words of encouragement.

'I have never taken a penalty in a shoot-out,' says Steer, 'but I imagine it must be a lonely place, particularly in a hostile environment as the away team, like we were at The Hawthorns that night. So to then have a familiar face – and what I would also like to think is a friendly face – pass you the ball and say: "You've got this, buddy." If it was me, I would like that.

'You would feel you are not alone and your mate is right next to you. Whether or not that made a big difference I don't know. But it is about the little things you can do to help your mate out and perform the best you can.'

Tosin Adarabioyo and Kieran Gibbs both converted to keep West Brom alive but when Grealish scored for Villa, they were just one kick away. The drama, however, was not quite finished. Adomah missed the chance to seal it when he sent his effort over the bar and when James Morrison blasted home for Albion, all eyes were on Villa's fifth and final taker, Abraham. Score and Villa were at Wembley. Miss and the shoot-out would be back to all-square and into sudden death.

With every Villa supporter across the world holding their breath, Abraham's spot-kick hit the legs of Johnstone but the ball ended up in the corner of the net. The celebrations which followed in front of the away support, involving the entire Villa squad and staff including Purslow and Suso, were wild with a topless Mings at one stage ending up several rows deep in the stands. A delighted Smith remained focused, holding up his index finger to the away end with the message clear. 'One more to go.'

The following night, Derby stunned Leeds by winning 4–2 at Elland Road to clinch a 4–3 aggregate victory.

'I remember the sheer delight of watching the other play-off semi-final without the gut-wrenching emotional stress of being involved,' Purslow says.

'I was gobsmacked that Derby beat Leeds. Leeds were the standout team and I remember saying to Dean, if we had Leeds, we'd have our work cut out, but we're not going to lose to Derby. I went from incredible nervousness, with at best a 50–50 chance, to being absolutely certain that we couldn't lose.'

With thirteen days between Villa's semi-final and the Bank Holiday Monday date at Wembley, Smith recognised his players needed time to get the emotion out of their system before refocusing on the final hurdle. They were granted three days off and initially there wasn't much resting.

This was now a tight-knit group, not only formed by the players but members of the backroom team so a day of celebration was in order.

Henri Lansbury, although a figure largely on the sidelines, played a part in the feelgood factor in the dressing room as he would keep his team-mates entertained throughout the week. 'He used to prank Jack Sharkey, the sports scientist, a lot,' Chester recalls. 'I remember whenever he was taking the warm-ups, Henri would wind him up. One time he had annoyed Henri, so he got 10 boxes of bean bag filler delivered to the training ground and just kept them somewhere until he got the chance to get Sharkey's car keys. When he found that opportunity he filled the car from footwell to ceiling with bean bag filling. That is a story which brings a smile to my face.'

McGinn recalls other funny moments: 'We had such a laugh during the season. Throwing Tommy [Jordan] into the pool was the highlight because he doesn't like water. Glenn Whelan tried to get him in every week and succeeded three or four times which was funny.'

Instead of resting, a boozy lunch in Birmingham turned into an all-day session, fronted of course by Grealish, but ably supported by Chester, Mings, McGinn, Jedinak, Whelan, Hourihane, and some support staff.

The players met in the garden of the Old Joint Stock pub before eating in Fumo and then moving on to a back street karaoke bar in a private room where they sang the night away. 'It was unreal,'

Grealish recalls. 'We had the two masseuses with us – Big Al and Smudge – and that day certainly helped us all going into the final. A part of me thought that something might go wrong because life was just so good at that point that I thought something would come along and ruin it.'

Hourihane, however, was the polar opposite. 'At that point, we felt invincible,' he says, 'Looking back, we shouldn't have been celebrating because we hadn't achieved anything, but we had such a good night – and to make it even better, we caught the end of the Leeds vs Derby game, and Derby winning gave us a boost. There was a softness to them so it left us with no doubt in our head about the final.'

Villa felt they had the advantage due to the results against the Rams earlier in the season. A 3–0 win away and that marvellous 4–0 demolition just a few months earlier at Villa Park raised expectations. Neither encounter had been close.

Smith kept preparations for the final as normal as possible. 'When the players came back in we started working backwards, from when the kick-off time at Wembley would be,' he says. 'We tried to treat it like any other game, as much as we could. We all had tracksuits on when we travelled, as normal. We had been so regular for the last three months and been outstanding. I just wanted to keep the momentum going.'

One difference the players couldn't fail to notice was the arrival, at the side of the main training pitch, of a huge TV screen. Linked up to an analyst's laptop, it allowed the coaching team to explain tactical work in real time. Steer, meanwhile, was limited in the build-up to the final after aggravating a shoulder injury which had kept him out for a chunk of the previous season. But there was never any question of him not playing at Wembley.

'It was the biggest game of my career and I could not really train loads leading up to it,' he says. 'But at that point I was in such a good place, after what had happened at West Brom in the shootout. Everyone's confidence was sky high.'

Smith faced only two selection issues and Hourihane's performance in the semi-final, coupled with an expectation of how the match would go tactically, solved one as he got the nod ahead of Whelan in midfield.

'I didn't think Derby would be that much of a threat for us defensively,' explains Smith. 'Tyrone Mings and Axel Tuanzebe, with the pace they have got, I didn't think they were going to hurt us that much in behind. When you have players who take you that way, it is the space in front which becomes important. Glenn is better at dealing with that because Conor is more of a ball-playing midfielder. He wants to get on the ball and play forward. I didn't think they would give us the problem as much, which is why I played Conor.'

The other was deciding whether to start Green or Adomah on the wing. Smith opted for the older man's experience. 'In the semi-final I played right-wing but I wasn't comfortable there,' Green recalls.

'I felt too much pressure. Purslow said to me before the semi-final, "You need to play well today, this will be the making of you." I didn't handle that well and my performance in the semi-final probably showed Dean that I wasn't ready for it.'

Villa, who had been based at the Landmark Hotel in Marylebone the previous year, this time stayed at the Wembley Hilton as Smith wanted to be close to the stadium. That led to a surreal sight for supporters arriving early on the morning of the match when they spotted Villa's coaching staff, led by Smith, out for what had become a traditional pre-game run.

'There were about five or six of us who after every overnight trip would go and do a run in the morning,' says Smith. 'So as we were staying at the Hilton we went and did four or five laps of Wembley.

'I remember we went and sat down outside Costa Coffee after and JT looked at me and said: "Gaffer. How are you so calm?" My reply was we had done all the work. At Brentford I had got really into the analytics they use and I knew if we played Derby 100 times on a neutral ground, we would win 90 times. I felt our players were better than theirs at that moment. Everything I looked at told me we were ready to go and win. Of course, I knew there was plenty on the line. But my wife will always tell you my favourite word is "cope". Whatever is thrown at you, you have to cope so if it was not to be we would have to cope and get on with it. But I wasn't thinking that way. I just thought it was going to be our day.'

That confident mood, which crucially never crossed over the line into cockiness, radiated around Villa at the time. For players, there was plenty on the line, both collectively individually. Mings knew a win would likely be career-changing. He explains: 'I thought there was probably a very strong chance I would sign at Villa if we got promoted. It was such a crossroads in my career, the play-off final.

'I really needed it to go well, just as much as Villa did because there was a lot riding on it for the trajectory of my career. I didn't want to have a loan spell and then go back to Bournemouth and sit on the bench because I had just tasted playing and being part of a big project.'

Supporters who had turned up to Wembley more in hope 12 months previously now did so with expectation. Among the crowd was the most famous Villa fan of all, Prince William, who sat in a box with his friend and former Villa striker John Carew. To their right, 38,000 supporters coloured one half of the stadium claret and blue. Nearby, meanwhile, were Sawiris and Edens, the latter having picked the play-off final over staying in the US to watch his Milwaukee Bucks who were also at a crucial stage of their season.

Belief inside the dressing room grew further when the teams were announced and Jack Marriott, two-goal hero from Derby's semi-final win over Leeds, was only on the bench. 'That surprised us a little bit,' says Steer. 'There were a couple of players, Marriott being one of them, who we thought would be starting but didn't. I think that gave some of the boys a little bit of a lift too.'

Though respectful of Derby's quality, most of the pre-match discussions in the Villa dressing room focused on how they could hurt their opponent. Since beating the Rams in early March, Villa had become a ruthless, winning machine and they gradually began to take a grip on the game as the first half progressed. Anwar El Ghazi, put them ahead when he headed home an Elmohamady cross just before half-time.

'The goal was a big one. The first one at Wembley. We'd talked about it a lot in the build-up,' says Smith. 'It was about switching play. We talked about going through one eight to the other eight, getting a cross in. We felt Derby didn't defend crosses all that well so it was a focus for us.'

'It was magical to score at Wembley and in such an important game,' El Ghazi adds.

When McGinn got the second just before the hour mark, after pouncing on a mistake by Derby keeper Kelle Roos, Villa were in complete control. Manager Frank Lampard, conservative in his own team selection, made changes and Derby finally began to create chances. Marriott was brought off the bench and with nine minutes to go pulled one back. Mings was injured trying to prevent the goal with Kortney Hause, who had himself not played since the win at Sheffield Wednesday in early April due to injury, coming off the bench.

'At 2–0 up we were cruising. We really looked comfortable,' says Steer. 'Derby didn't threaten that much but then the changes happen, they get the goal, they are shooting toward their fans.

'I remember thinking: "This can't happen. We can't concede again". If they score again and it goes to extra time, their tails are up, we have gone from 2–0 up to 2–2.'

'There was a decision to make for me at the time as Mile Jedinak was warming up, getting ready to come on,' recalls Smith. 'But I just wanted to keep the balance of a left footer, right footer at centre-back so went for Kortney. To be fair, he did OK when he came on.'

'It felt like Kortney headed everything,' continues Steer. 'A couple of crosses came in the box which I was able to keep hold of. The final whistle was one of the most amazing feelings ever.

'I've been really unlucky with injuries in my career, both before and after the play-off run. It is that feeling which you are always chasing.'

In the Royal Box, Purslow was about to let it all out. 'I had a massive emotional breakdown at the final whistle because the Derby chairman, Mel Morris, gave me a congratulatory hug,' he says. 'I mentally processed what we had done and what they hadn't done. I thought it was so classy of him to do that. I felt a combination of joy and sorrow for him. I cried my eyes out. All emotions came out because of everything we had been through in the season. It felt like a complete release.'

He wasn't alone. Tears rolled down Smith's face as it all settled in.

This was a poignant moment for the head coach, who in the build-up to the match had spoken about his father, Ron, who for the past three years had been in a care home, suffering with dementia. It was Ron, who for 30 years worked as a steward at Villa Park and used to follow the team up and down the country, who first instilled Smith's love of Villa. Yet so serious had his illness become, he did not know his son was now manager of the club for whom they both shared such strong passion.

Later, at the post-match press conference, Smith revealed he had visited his father the previous Friday. 'I managed to get his eyes open for two minutes, maximum,' said Smith. 'I told him: "Next time I come and see you, I'll be a Premier League manager". He smiled, if not anything more. Hopefully there was an understanding but it's a terrible illness. For me, that was enough.'

For the players who had experienced defeat on the same turf a year previously, the main emotion was relief. 'It was the perfect way, unbelievable,' full-back Ahmed Elmohamady recalls. 'You could just see how much it meant to the fans but believe me, we felt it, too, because the pressure of getting this club back to the Premier League was massive.'

Grealish was more buoyant, telling Sky Sports on the pitch immediately after the win: 'I thought I was going to leave and 10 months later I'm here. I've led my boyhood club back to the Premier League as captain and scored against Blues twice – perfect season.'

There was a nice touch, too, as Grealish invited James Chester, who had not played since January due to his knee injury, up to lift the play-off winner's trophy with him. Speaking afterward to journalists in the mixed zone, Chester would reveal the true extent of the sacrifice he had made when playing through the pain barrier earlier in the season.

'I have damaged my body indefinitely, really. It is something I am going to have to manage for the rest of my career,' he explained. 'I felt it was my duty to carry on being involved. Once January came around the club were able to bring in some really good players in my position. It allowed me to take some time out and hopefully I'll be ready to go for the start of next season.'

Chester would go on to make just two more appearances for Villa the following season before moving to Stoke, initially on loan. 'Looking back, it was difficult not to be part of that final run, having been so heavily involved up to that point,' reflects Chester now. 'But when I signed it was to get the club promoted, so it still felt I had achieved the goal.

'Even though I did not play, I still felt I had been a big part of getting the club into that position. 'When I see where the club is at now, with the squad they have, I am incredibly proud at having played a small part in getting them back to where I think we all felt the club belongs.'

'Chezzie did unbelievably to hold the fort for as long as he did for us with the injury he had,' says Smith. 'It was his decision to do that. He could very easily have said no, I need to get this sorted now. I sat with him a number of times talking about the injury and how we deal with it. He was quite strong in what he wanted to do, to play as long as he could to help the team before we could get some players in.'

As the celebrations continued on the pitch, meanwhile, a surprise visitor watched on from the stands. Almost a year to the day since he had last been seen in the UK, Tony Xia was back and seemingly determined to try and claim some of the credit.

'I kept my promise,' he later posted on his social media account[23] though, to the disappointment of journalists gathered in the stadium mixed zone, he ignored requests for interviews while making his departure. While still co-chairman, by the time of the play-off final Xia was no longer a person of significant control at Villa. He did not match the cash injections made by NSWE, by way of share issue, meaning his stake had been diluted to less than 20 per cent.

Yet while Wembley would be the last anyone connected with Villa saw of Xia, his time at the club would feature a fittingly bizarre postscript. It can be revealed that, weeks after Villa had secured promotion, Xia submitted a written offer via an intermediary to buy back the club from Sawiris and Edens. Xia was willing to pay £174 million for the full 100 per cent shareholding. Quite how the co-chairman, who had seen his own shareholding diluted since NSWE had rescued the club from financial disaster, had suddenly found the funds for a full takeover, was unclear, although he says it was easier to get approval from the foreign currency controlling authority to allow the funds to invest or buy a company. His offer, rather unsurprisingly, was politely declined by Sawiris and Edens, and things never reached the stage where Xia was required to produce proof of funds.

The extraordinary buy-out offer rejected, Xia's failure to then repay the £20 million loan provided as part of the NSWE takeover the previous summer and settle a £30 million payment owed to Randy Lerner now Villa were promoted, meant his remaining shareholding was diluted. In his response to us, Xia denied that this £20 million was a loan, but in a letter seen by the authors, sent by his representatives to NWSE, express reference is made to 'settlement of convertible £24M loan (£4M interest/return)' as part of an overall offer to buy back the club. Whatever the truth, Xia formally left the club in August.[24]

For a man who had arrived to such fanfare, it was a quiet exit, though within months he would be back in the news. In October, it was reported Chinese authorities had issued a warrant offering a reward for information about Xia's whereabouts, he says in a civil claim relating to unpaid debts.[25] Xia took to Twitter to deny the claims.[26] In early 2021, it was reported he had been arrested, after spending six months in a detention centre on suspicion of harming the interests of a manufacturing company.[27] At the time of writing, his most recent social media post was in April 2020 and even some of his closest aides claim they had not heard from him for over six years.

That was where Xia's story seemed to end. But on the cusp of publication, and after months of trying, the authors were able to make contact with Xia again. After a series of messages on WhatsApp, Xia agreed to a video call to confirm his identity. He wore a cream polo shirt and smiled politely before answering a series of questions in short, broken English but said he could not go into detail on various matters because of 'complications' in his homeland. Xia claimed to be living in Beijing and said that he also spends time in Hong Kong and Taiwan.

In response to a letter sent by the authors, he took issue with some of the more serious accusations concerning his ownership of Villa, and many of his objections have been noted where appropriate.

He admitted to having spent six months in detention in China, 'for some reasons which I cannot speak in detail today' [sic.]. He added: 'As I refused to "cooperate" by doing something which violated my basic moral principles, the relevant authorities decided to find innovative charges to arrest me under the name of economic crimes, namely harming public listed company interests.

'Such matters are not unusual under the present system and many other businessmen have equally been accused and sentenced for such "crimes".

'I have to say, I still love my country after encountering this and even being tortured in the process.'

Xia continued: 'I still love the Villa and have great affection for the people and city of Birmingham.

'Critics are as Oscar Wilde said: "people who know the price of everything and the value of nothing."'

He went on: 'The decisions which I made were always done with the best interests of the club at heart. I am glad to see how the club is doing and proud that I was able to have a part in its journey in getting to this point.

'I never feel regret for what I have tried to achieve for the club. I regret though I may not be able to make Villa achieve what my initial motivation was.

'A club endures not because of the trophies, or [because] they have great star players, not because they own a wonderful stadium, but rather it relies on its fans and followers and can be bound together deeper than winning or losing.

'I was hoping the true meaning of a great football club should be a community that brings people together, across wealth and poverty, cities and villages, and globally British and foreigners alike all bound by love of the game.

'I truly follow what Romain Rolland said: "There is only one heroism in the world, to see the world as it is and to love it."'

* * *

It's no exaggeration to say that the partying on the night of Villa's promotion was wild. The club had booked out the Hilton Hotel and when supporters got wind of the location many headed to see if they could hang out with their heroes. On the streets around the stadium supporters stuck around for hours and they were treated to a singalong from some players who took the party to the balcony so the fans could be involved.

'It was amazing,' Mings recalls. 'It does feel like a cup win even though it doesn't go down as a major trophy and in terms of what the club looks like now compared to Derby, no disrespect, but it cannot be underestimated just what that did for the club.'

'It's still one of my favourite days in football,' adds McGinn. 'The sheer adrenaline of it, the importance of the game was clear for everyone. It was massive, especially after the year before. The pressure was high. Going into it we were confident of getting the job done. It was well deserved on the day.'

Suso, who rarely drinks alcohol, was there with his family and says: 'Let's just say the alcohol in our room was flowing that night.'

He adds: 'I have won the UEFA Cup and La Liga (with Valencia) and for me, it was the most emotional day in my life in football because the challenge was so tough.'

Purslow, so busy and stressed out in the early months as the man overseeing everything, adds: 'I recall feeling so privileged and blessed to have gone to a lunch with not a real chance of going to work at Aston Villa, to almost nine months to the day being a part of the most glorious thing that can happen to you in English football. There's no better feeling than winning the play-offs because of the transformative effect it can have on a club. I was very proud that Deano did it because not many managers come in during a season and win promotion straight away. It shows the scale of his achievement.'

Smith, who had ended up running back to the Hilton with some Villa staff through the crowds due to the team coach getting held up in traffic, ducked out of the party at around midnight and headed into central London to meet with family.

Elsewhere, celebrations carried on late into the night and early through the morning. Even some journalists, including one of this book's co-authors, joined in on the proviso no pictures were taken. It was some night and a rare opportunity for support staff and members of the club's media team to let their hair down with the players. Mings was there, still in his Villa shirt. Pictures of him wearing it the following day on the train ride home to Bournemouth would go viral, but the finer details around the rest of the night shall remain private because, as they say, 'What happens in Soho … stays in Soho!'

It wasn't all smiles. This would be the end of the road for many players with contracts expiring and some popular members of the squad were set to move on. Adomah, in particular, was not in the mood to party.

'I knew I was leaving so I didn't really celebrate,' he says. 'I went to the after-party for like 10 minutes, said "well done" and waved goodbye to everyone. But that was it for me. I knew Dean would call me when I was on holiday which is what happened. It was a mixed feeling, hard to accept that I was not staying. It just felt like "Thanks for your service, and bye."'

Hutton, Elphick, Jedinak and Whelan were not offered extended terms, either. Ritchie De Laet, Mark Bunn, Jordan Lyden and Micah Richards also left as their deals expired while Ross McCormack – whose £30k a week wages were set to double on promotion despite the fact he had not played for the club for nearly two years – was paid off with twelve months of his deal left to run.

Sawiris and Edens congratulated the players in the dressing room and offered to pay for a group holiday that was politely declined as other arrangements had already been made. Instead they bought all the players a commemorative watch, personalised for each individual, as a gift for winning promotion.

The owners were both interviewed by broadcaster Sky Sports after the game, which was also the first time they had spoken publicly to reporters since taking over. Despite so many ups and downs during a turbulent first season, they had achieved the aim of returning to the Premier League faster than anyone had really expected. There was no need to worry about the parachute payments ending because more than £100 million would be heading into the club through Premier League broadcasting revenue.

'The sky is the limit,' declared Sawiris, his comment encapsulating the general mood. Yet there was plenty of hard work to be done.

7

BALANCING THE BOOKS

It wasn't only on the pitch Villa faced a battle during the 2018–19 season. Purslow's tears in the Royal Box after the final whistle at Wembley were the symbol of a man who cared deeply about the club, its future standing and the legacy he would leave behind.

For journalists he was not always the easiest person to deal with because, coming from a background in banking where every bit of information is kept watertight, he could never quite get used to leaks around transfer stories, managerial changes and sensitive club issues. It is not exaggerating the point to say there was something of an obsession about keeping information private and in-house. During a chat with reporters at Smith's unveiling, the first time he had met many of those working the Midlands patch, he infamously threatened to sack any member of staff who he found leaking information to the press. Villa's communications director, Tommy Jordan, had a tough job keeping reporters on the leash. Purslow's dealings with the press were few and far between and he picked his friends carefully.

Experience of working at Chelsea and Liverpool prior to Villa at least meant he knew occasionally stories would slip through. One he did manage to keep quiet for considerable time was how he planned to solve an impending crisis with PSR.

The rules had been introduced in 2013 due to concern too many clubs were spending beyond their means. Under the regulations, clubs in the Premier League are permitted to lose no more than £105 million over a three-season cycle (an average of £35 million a year). Almost every club accepted the need for stricter financial controls. Indeed, it should be noted PSR had been voted in by a majority of Premier League clubs. Yet the manner in which the rules are framed has become an increasing bone of contention, with many arguing they work against those clubs aiming to challenge English football's elite. Under PSR, those clubs with the largest revenues have more scope to spend, giving an advantage to what, in 2013, had become the Premier League's Big Six of Arsenal, Liverpool, Chelsea, Tottenham, Manchester United and Manchester City, the latter of whom had spent close to a billion pounds improving their playing squad since their 2008 takeover by the Abu Dhabi Group. The rules effectively stopped any other club following that same model.

In such context, it is easy to see why PSR was such a frustration for Villa when they were taken over by two billionaires – and why it continues to be an issue for the club to this day. For all the hundreds of millions invested by Sawiris and Edens since 2018, the truth is they would have been happy to spend more had the rules allowed. In a rare interview with the *Financial Times* in 2024, Sawiris blasted the regulations as 'anti-competitive' and revealed he was seeking advice over the prospect of taking legal action against them.

Despite such resentment and despite the challenges they have posed, Villa have remained compliant with PSR under his and Edens' ownership, albeit there have been several close calls. Among the biggest of those occurred in 2019, at almost exactly the same time Villa were securing their passage back to the Premier League. The PSR equation in the Championship was far stricter than in the top flight, with maximum permitted losses of only £39 million over a three-season cycle. Villa had reported combined losses of more than £50 million for the 2016–17 and 2017–18 seasons alone and though certain costs could be deducted from the PSR figure, such as spending on the academy or infrastructure, it was clear Villa would be sailing close to the wind come the end of the 2018–19 campaign.

'When I arrived, without massive improvements, the club would have breached PSR, that was obvious,' Purslow recalls. 'So myself and the finance director put together a wide-ranging plan of six or seven measures to hope to mitigate the PSR position.'

Quite how strict the EFL were in enforcing the rules had been demonstrated earlier in the season, when Villa's city rivals Blues were hit with a nine-point deduction for breaching the limits. Whether they won promotion or not, Villa had to get their figures in order by the end of that year's accounting period on 31 May, or risk a penalty the following season regardless of which division they were playing in. The Premier League would also get to assess the accounts of any promoted club and there were genuine fears within Villa Park they could be denied entry to the top flight if they broke the rules.

The pressure was therefore on Purslow to come up with a solution and, as it transpired, he had several. By far the most effective and lucrative was the sale and lease back of Villa Park, a deal which might more accurately be described as Villa's get out of PSR jail free card. This loophole, since closed, essentially allowed clubs in the EFL to sell their stadium to another company controlled by their owners and book the profit. Without it, Villa would almost certainly have been forced to sell Jack Grealish either in the summer of 2018 or in the January 2019 window in order to avoid a PSR breach.

'The truth is I was surprised when I discovered this, because it wasn't allowed in the Premier League,' says Purslow. 'It's why I wanted the EFL to go through all the conditions first.'

Transparency was always key for Purslow and particularly so when negotiating the Villa Park sale. Villa were not the only Championship club to use the loophole but another of those, Derby County, were charged with a PSR breach retrospectively after the league determined they had over-inflated the cost and gained a larger profit as a result. From the start, Purslow was open with the EFL about Villa's plans. Shortly after he was appointed, he and Villa's chief financial officer Ian Hopson travelled to the league's offices in Preston for face-to-face meetings with their counterparts in which they laid bare the financial situation facing the club following the near insolvency under Xia.

'We had an open-book meeting with the league, shared the exact position we had inherited, what our plans were and said we need to work with you within the rule book,' he explains.

'Our message was that we are happy to finance the club in its recovery and we want to make sure we do everything right.

'One example was that within the Championship we were still able to sell and lease back the stadium, providing it was done on an arms-length basis and at fair value. So it was the league who set out for me and our finance director, Ian, how we should prove that.

'The answer was to have three independent, high valuations done. And that's what we did. Quite literally the league held Ian's hand.

'It's not my job to comment on how other people do it. I'd never seen that rule before, because it wasn't allowed in the Premier League. So the truth is, I was surprised.

'That's why I wanted the EFL to guide us on exactly what we needed to do to adhere to the rules. I wanted the EFL to know exactly what we were doing so that when we submitted the accounts they would be aware of the valuations. Major international property valuers were used, with no links to me or the club, and we still went conservative on it.'

On 21 May, six days before the play-off final at Wembley and just ten before the financial year was due to end, Villa Park was sold to NSWE Stadium Ltd, a company controlled by Sawiris and Edens, for £56.7 million. Villa banked a profit of £36 million from the sale in their accounts.

Though it was this deal more than any other which helped Villa get under the PSR limits, other key moves were also required. The decision, taken early on by Purslow, to re-open the top tier of the Trinity Road Stand – closed since relegation – paid dividends as the surge to promotion during the spring led to the longest string of sold-out matches for decades. Players deemed surplus to requirements, such as Scott Hogan, had also been loaned out to ease the wage bill.

Yet despite that Villa still entered the final days of May dangerously close to the limits and it would need one more deal to ensure they were compliant. Ironically, it was their greatest rivals who came to their rescue.

The previous summer Villa had allowed Gary Gardner, a product of their youth system once touted as a future England international before two serious knee injuries scuppered his progress, to join the Blues on loan. Their rivals were now keen to sign the midfielder permanently but money was a problem. Villa valued Gardner at £4 million and they could not afford it. Yet there was a player in the Blues ranks who also interested Villa. Spanish winger Jota had played for Smith at Brentford and was considered a useful squad addition for a team heading into the Premier League. So to help their rivals afford Gardner, Villa agreed to pay £6 million for Jota in a separate deal.

In PSR terms, this worked perfectly. The £4 million received for Gardner would be immediately banked in the 2018–19 accounts as profit, with the £6 million outlay for Jota spread over the length of the player's contract. All that mattered was ensuring the deals were completed before the accounting deadline, which Villa just about achieved.

'For Christian to get this done on the last day was amazing,' Suso says. 'We couldn't suffer any more heart attacks at Villa Park. We couldn't lose our life through this!

'Can you imagine if we had been promoted and then relegated because of PSR?'

It was in early June, while driving up to the Premier League shareholders meeting in Harrogate, Purslow was informed Villa's accounts had been signed off by both the EFL and Premier League.

'It was a great relief,' he says. 'I pulled into the hotel where the Premier League shareholders meeting happened and was told Villa's PSR accounts were in good order and we were being admitted into the Premier League. That's how tight it was.'

8

'DOING A FULHAM'

Less than 48 hours after securing promotion to the Premier League – and with heads still a little sore from celebrating – Nassef Sawiris called a meeting in his Mayfair office.

Going up via the play-offs had been thrilling but the downside was it left relatively little time to prepare for the following season. Just 11 weeks after winning at Wembley, Villa would be kicking off at Tottenham in their first match back in the top flight.

For months, discussions had centred around two recruitment plans – one in the Championship if Villa were unsuccessful in the play-offs and another if they got promoted. Deciding the future of the out-of-contract players in advance was essential because transfer business, regardless of which division Villa were operating in, was going to be a little rushed.

Time was of the essence and Sawiris was a man in a hurry so he called Suso and Smith, who had stayed nearby at The Connaught Hotel, to join him and Purslow in talks to plot a way forward. 'Plan A' targets – turning the loan moves of Abraham, Mings and El Ghazi into permanent deals – were identified as a priority but only two of the three would be completed.

After tearing up the Championship, Abraham decided that he wanted to stay and fight for his place at Chelsea. The London club, usually big spenders in the market, had been hit with a transfer ban meaning there would be more opportunities for their younger players. When club legend Frank Lampard, fresh from losing the play-off final to Villa, was appointed Chelsea's new head coach it gave Abraham even more encouragement. The striker scored 19 goals over 49 games in all competitions the following season. Villa had to move on.

Signing El Ghazi and Hause, at least, was more straightforward. Villa had options to make both loan deals permanent and duly did so, with El Ghazi signing a four-year contract. Getting Mings, a hugely popular figure with fans, would not be so easy because, as much as he was a priority, Villa were not in a position to overspend.

Rebuilding the squad with both quality and quantity was essential, as was staying within the parameters of PSR. Just 11 players remained under contract following the play-off win but after coming so close to falling foul of the rules the previous season – and after finally starting to put the club back into a more secure position – Purslow stressed the need to box clever. As much as the owners wanted to spend heavily on improving the squad, there were restrictions from the start. A big-money bid for Abraham, for example, even if only to get Chelsea thinking about a sale, was not an option because a successful offer would have blown a large chunk of the budget.

Ideally, Villa would have signed four or five players with the qualities to jump straight into the starting line-up, yet that wasn't an option because the squad was seriously short on numbers. At the London meeting Sawiris, Purslow, Suso and Smith thrashed out a strategy to reduce the average age, wage and increase the quality of the squad. An initial £45k-a-week limit was placed on wages. Prized asset Grealish was already earning considerably more than that but was the only exception.

Pulling off such an approach would be easier said than done and Villa's hierarchy knew they would be spreading themselves relatively thin. The average Premier League wage was around £65k a week but Villa had to be creative. They had little help from within as the scouting and research department was so thin that most of the work was left to Suso who was working through an agent-led process.

'We finished three weeks later than others so they started making moves before us,' Suso recalls. 'Preparing the team for the Premier League, where every club has a squad that is already stronger than ours, and then knowing that we still haven't got enough top players to stay in the Premier League, is such a challenge.'

Purslow adds: 'Everyone in football knows how crazily intense transfer windows are. This first one was really difficult because we only had six weeks until pre-season, then a few more weeks after, to build a team with a shot of staying in the Premier League with very, very high PSR constraints. Spending too much money and then pumping up the wages was almost impossible because our PSR loss-allowance was half of that of the other Premier League clubs. I was telling everybody that I've got owners who want to conquer the world but I can't spend the money on wages because we won't comply.'

A move Villa were able to secure early – and firmly with one eye on the future – was the hire of Mark Harrison from West Bromwich Albion as the new academy manager. This move would be a game-changer for Villa in the years to come as Harrison was able to identify and lure top young talent from his former club, once recognised as having the strongest youth set-up in the West Midlands. An aggressive recruitment drive from Villa, now with engaged and enthusiastic owners, would see a shift in direction and help transform the academy.

Supporting Purslow at Villa Park was his experienced assistant, Paul Tyrrell, who worked almost as a vice-CEO. Nicola Ibbetson, formerly of Chelsea, settled in well as chief commercial officer and another backroom target was identified after a successful pre-season tour to the USA.

Rochdale-born Matt Bennett, the player liaison officer at Minnesota United FC, had impressed Villa so much when they visited the club that he was offered a position as first team operations manager.

Steadily, each department at Villa was strengthened.

At first team level, an early bid of £12 million went in for Bristol City's Adam Webster but Villa were quoted double by the Championship club so they had to look for defenders elsewhere. Suso was desperate to sign Kalvin Phillips from Leeds United and had the full backing of Smith. At this stage Villa were the only Premier League club showing a serious interest and there was confidence in getting the deal done, but the midfielder pledged his future to the losing play-off semi-finalists after showdown talks. Villa also bid for winger Said Benrahma but were not prepared to match Brentford's £20 million valuation.

After the early arrivals of Jota, El Ghazi, Hause, and eventually Mings, Villa went on to complete a total of 12 signings at a total cost of around £130 million. It was a splurge which would draw criticism from some outside the club and comparisons to Fulham, who had spent a similar amount after beating Villa in the previous year's play-off final only to be relegated back to the Championship. Indeed, the claim Villa were 'Doing a Fulham' was one heard regularly from rival fans during a season they would spend battling against the drop.

Yet as everyone at Villa would be quick to point out, the rebuild was entirely necessary and the spend not exactly egregious considering the number of deals involved. 'When you look at some of the other deals which were going on in the Premier League at the time, I think the average fee for a top-half signing was £20 million,' says Smith. 'We signed Wesley Moraes for £21 million and he became our record signing. We had such a huge turnaround with players who had been on loan going back to their parent clubs and others being released.'

'Some of the players we signed were because we needed numbers,' Suso recalls. 'We knew they could be with us for just one or two years because we didn't have the freedom to sign the other players we wanted.'

It was truly a collaborative effort with Suso and Smith both picking out individuals and discussing between themselves the benefits each would bring. Purslow also contributed and Sawiris even decided in the case of the winger Trezeguet that his fellow Egyptian would be a good fit for Villa, as they attempted to add some flair to the team after missing out on Benrahma.

Suso and Smith travelled to the Africa Cup of Nations to watch the player in action before completing the deal. A year later, the signing would look inspired as Trezeguet played a huge part in Villa retaining their top-flight status.

By and large, though, this was Suso's summer, and a chance for him to identify the talent to take Villa onto a new level. Although all signings were signed off in joint agreement, it's widely recognised that most of the overseas arrivals – many with links to Belgium – were pushed by the sporting director.

'Suso was excellent. His knowledge and his contacts,' recalls Smith. 'We had obviously spoken and had two separate scouting avenues, one for the Premier League and another for the Championship. We had two different ideas of where we were going to go.

'I always wanted to speak to players before we signed them, just to get a feel for them and make sure they were the right character, the right personality, whether they would fit in the dressing room. Whether they wanted to come. Suso would be the one who would make the contact with the agent. Christian and Suso would then speak to get the financing agreed.'

Trezeguet, who arrived from Turkish club Kasimpasa for £8.75 million, was seen as relatively low risk. So was Bjorn Engels, a centre-back signed from Reims for a similar fee. Smith had scouted the Belgian while with Brentford and believed he had the quality to perform in the Premier League. The head coach also pushed for the signing of another defender, Ezri Konsa, from his former club. Villa knew Konsa's contract had a £12 million buy-out clause.

Smith says: 'We knew there was a buy-out which had to be triggered at a certain time. I was one who pushed and said: "Listen, he will be a really good player for us."'

Left-back Matt Targett, signed from Southampton for an initial £11 million, was also identified by Suso as a player who could grow in both quality and value. Midfielder Marvelous Nakamba arrived from Club Brugge for a similar fee. But it was another signing from Brugge who would capture most of the headlines. At £21 million, Wesley became the club's first-ever Brazilian player and record signing. The 22-year-old had a remarkable life story. Wesley, whose right leg is three centimetres shorter than his left, lost his father when he was nine and had a son at the age of 15 and a daughter a year later. He worked in a factory sorting screws before making it as a footballer, first in Slovakia with Trencin, then at Brugge in Belgium where Villa watched him play.

Having signed one Brazilian, Villa promptly went out and got another in the shape of midfielder Douglas Luiz from Manchester City. The 21-year-old had never kicked a ball for City having failed to get a work permit after signing from Vasco da Gama two years previously. He had since been sent on loan to City's sister club Girona, where Suso had watched him and become a huge fan. After showing clips to Smith, who was also impressed, Villa's sporting director moved quickly to complete a complex £15 million deal which included the option of a buy-back clause for City.

'I loved the player, his potential, the capacity of the player,' says Suso. 'I travelled to Brazil, a 14-hour journey, then I met him and his father and his agent in the airport for six hours, and I convinced him to come back with us.

'On the same day, I came back to Birmingham to prepare all the documents with City and the player accepted to come with us. It was an amazing decision for him and also it was an amazing decision for us.'

Luiz would go on to be one of Villa's best signings in recent history, though initially communication was a problem and a couple of months after his move the club hired a translator to help him understand his team-mates and staff. 'After a month or two I could tell Dougie was not learning English as quickly as we would like,' recalls Smith. 'I remember leaving him out of the team for one game and I brought Suso into the room so he could translate for me. That is why we ended up getting a translator in to work for the club. That worked really well. A few of the meetings he would be whispering in Dougie's ear as I was talking, which I think caused some amusement for his team-mates!'

By far the most complicated negotiations surrounded Mings, as Bournemouth were playing hardball. The defender had made pretty plain his desire to make the move when he travelled back to the south coast by train the day after the play-off final, still wearing full Villa kit. Yet initially, the two clubs were some distance apart on the price. After Villa initially offered £15 million, an agreement was eventually struck at £20 million, rising to £26 million.

'Cementing Tyrone was important,' Purslow recalls. 'I spent a lot of time on that. It was never in doubt. It was all about the price. He came to my home in Portugal because it was taking so long. After the loan ended, he left us in no doubt that his heart was with Villa, but when it wasn't done by the end of June and we were into July, he came to ask me if there was anything he could do to help. I was just trying to be disciplined on the price.'

Mings explains his thought process at the time, saying: 'I was keen to do it before the club went on our pre-season tour. I felt the tour would be such a big part of understanding the manager's plans for the season so when pre-season started and I still hadn't signed, there was a bit of frustration because there was never any doubt in my mind that Villa was the club I wanted to join.'

The famous episode of wearing his Villa kit on the train back home to Bournemouth the day after the play-off final now draws a slightly embarrassed look from the defender as he says: 'To be honest, I was really just too hungover to contemplate changing! My mentality is that I'm just a normal geezer so that was the mentality I had when I jumped on the train. I wasn't thinking about people taking pictures of me. Of course people would have put two-and-two together, but if you think of the fact I got in a taxi from the hotel in London, made it all the way to Bournemouth and then it was only a ticket inspector in Bournemouth who asked for a picture – I nearly made it home without anyone batting an eyelid. Maybe it was just naivety but maybe also a little bit of euphoria as well in terms of one of the best things I achieved in my career.'

Completing the new-look side was Tom Heaton, an England international goalkeeper, who signed for £8 million from Burnley. While Steer had been rewarded for his heroics in the promotion run with a new, four-year contract, Smith recognised his squad also needed more Premier League experience. At 33-years-old, Heaton was the father of the group – a tried and tested performer at the top level who would act as a calming presence when the going got tough.

'When you are bringing all these players in, there is a human side to it as well,' says Smith. 'For instance, I spoke to Jed Steer and told him I was bringing in Tom Heaton. Jed had been unbelievable at the end of the season and I wanted to make sure he felt part of it. I just felt we needed some Premier League experience and Tom gave us that.'

'I liked that we still had the foundations of our team,' Grealish recalls. 'Myself, Ginny, Tyrone, Conor – it was the spine from the

Championship – but building from there was always going to be difficult. For any Championship club it's difficult. The main objective for us was to stay in the league.'

Smith agreed with the survival mission but was also determined to stick by his principles of playing exciting, attacking football and the arrival of the two Brazilians was part of a pledge to change the identity.

'We needed quality players to be in the Premier League and I wanted our style of football to be different than it had been previously,' Suso adds. 'It wasn't just about the atmosphere, about feelings, about playing long ball or about character and personality. We had to mix all of these with quality.'

Villa played with a freedom and spirit on the opening day away at the Tottenham Hotspur Stadium and went ahead through John McGinn. The wild scenes in the away end marked a changing of the times. After three years in the Championship it was uplifting for the travelling supporters to be up against top-quality opposition once again, and it didn't get much tougher than facing the Champions League finalists who had a squad packed with quality.

In what would become a similar pattern as the season developed, Villa were unable to hold onto a lead and conceded three times late on to fall to defeat. While their performance attracted plaudits from many observers, Smith noted his team had faced 23 efforts on goal. 'We knew we could not keep doing that, or we were going to be in trouble,' he says. 'I knew every point was going to be important to us.'

A 2–0 win over Everton at Villa Park just two weeks later helped get the season up and running. New signings Jota and Wesley showed early promise and linked up for the opening goal. By October, and after a scintillating 5–1 win at Norwich City, Wesley had scored four goals in his opening eight games, and although already coming under some criticism for his sluggish performances, there were signs he was growing into his role. Smith told him privately that he would not be judged solely on his goals, which helped as they dried up considerably in the months ahead. In November, he received a call-up to the Brazil national squad for the first time, which is no mean feat. 'You don't do that unless you have talent,' Suso recalls.

A last-gasp winner from Targett against Brighton helped Villa up to 11th in the table just past the midway point of October, but from there results began to turn. Smith points to a 2–1 home defeat to Liverpool in early November as an important moment. Villa were leading 1–0 through Trezeguet's first goal for the club only to concede twice in the closing stages.

'It would have been a huge statement had we held on and won that game,' he says. 'There are moments like that which I just think can fill the dressing room with a bit of confidence. Jurgen Klopp later said it was that afternoon which propelled Liverpool on to win the title. To concede those two late goals, for us, really hurt.'

Despite the indifferent form, Smith was handed a new four-year contract late in November, the deal signed following a 2–0 home win over Newcastle. He was then visited by Sawiris and Edens in the dressing room ahead of Villa's next game, a 2–2 draw at Manchester United memorable for a sublime Grealish goal. Smith thanked both of them for his new deal and says Sawiris replied: 'Dean, even if we get relegated this year, who better to get us back up than you?'

Though that might have convinced Villa's head coach his job was not under any serious threat, the truth was results were causing concern in the boardroom. A run of six defeats in eight led into a home match against Southampton which started in nightmare fashion when McGinn suffered a broken ankle. The subsequent 3–1 loss left Villa in the bottom three at Christmas and though a Hourihane goal earned an unconvincing 1–0 Boxing Day win over Norwich, the respite lasted 48 hours as a nightmare 3–0 defeat at

Watford left no doubt they were in a relegation battle. Troy Deeney, a lifelong Blues supporter, scored twice for the Hornets. Behind the scenes Sawiris was losing faith in Smith and giving serious consideration to making a change.

Sacking a head coach who had so much credit in the bank for his efforts the previous season would have been a bad look, especially after backing him with a new deal only a month before. But these were testing times with McGinn facing a lengthy lay-off and big questions now being asked of the summer business.

Any promise shown by Jota in the early weeks of the season had now disappeared, Wesley and Luiz were struggling, Konsa and Engels were error-prone and Targett had endured a miserable afternoon up against the Watford winger and future Villa nemesis Ismaila Sarr who left him seeing stars after a dazzling display. Villa had not kept a clean sheet away from home all season and had conceded the most goals of any professional team in England. There was also an over-reliance on Grealish to work some magic and he just couldn't do it all alone.

Ahead of the New Year's Day trip to Burnley, Purslow called a meeting which included Smith, Suso and performance director Jeremy Oliver. 'I remember thinking, why are we having this meeting?' says Smith. 'We don't normally do this. I remember being in there and coming out fighting a little bit. I said hold on, this has happened, that has happened. I fought my corner very well. I came out of it and never thought any more of it. The meeting was all about where are we at and what do we need to improve on? I'm guessing Christian would then have gone and reported to the owners about what we were doing going forward.'

Smith was about to get a timely boost with the return of Mings, who had missed almost a month through injury. The defender went straight back into the starting XI at Burnley, with Smith opting to change tactics by fielding a three-man central defence. Villa promptly produced their most cohesive performance for some time, with Wesley and Grealish scoring in a 2–1 win which immediately lifted the scrutiny on the head coach.

Yet the victory came at a huge cost. Midway through the second half, Wesley sustained a serious knee injury after being tackled by Ben Mee. With 10 minutes to go, Heaton was also stretchered off, having also injured his knee when trying to keep out a Chris Wood header. Both players required surgery on damaged knee ligaments. Heaton would never make another first-team appearance for the club. Wesley would be sidelined for nearly 15 months. With McGinn already out it meant Villa had lost their player of their season from the previous year, their experienced goalkeeper and record signing in the space of a fortnight. A January transfer window which was supposed to be about adding quality and strength in depth now became all about sourcing replacements. 'These two injuries nearly killed us,' Suso recalls.

Sawiris and Edens, already over £200 million into their adventure as Villa owners, made it clear that funds would be available for replacements, but Purslow again had to remind them of the PSR constraints. If Villa were tight over the summer, then another big spend in the winter window would cause further problems down the line.

Kalvin Phillips, the Leeds midfielder tracked over the summer, was no longer an option so others were considered. Suso wanted to bring in Steven N'Zonzi, the French midfielder who was ending a loan spell at Galatasaray from Roma, however his wages were too high.

Villa's perilous position in the table made it difficult. Not only were they unable to buy their way out of trouble, but there was also the challenge of convincing players that joining a club seriously threatened by relegation was a good career move.

The target was to bring in players with more Premier League experience, with an acknowledgement this was something the summer spend had not focused on enough. One player who needed a fresh start was the Chelsea midfielder, Danny Drinkwater, having struggled for minutes since joining from the 2016 Premier League champions, Leicester City. His £120k-a-week wages were an issue but Villa agreed to pay half in the hope he would cover sufficiently for McGinn.

Suso had nothing to do with this particular signing – in perhaps a sign things were starting to unravel behind the scenes – as it was put together by Smith, Terry and Purslow, the latter two who had strong connections to Chelsea, helping get the deal over the line.

Two other positions still needed to be filled. Heaton's injury had left Villa seriously short in the goalkeeping department. Steer, hero of the promotion push the previous season, had already been sidelined a couple of months before when he suffered a calf injury just minutes into a 2–1 defeat at Wolves. With Heaton now also out for the long term, it left Nyland as the only fit, senior shot-stopper. Villa needed to bring in both competition and an experienced head to make up for the loss of Heaton's voice in the dressing room. Former Liverpool keeper Pepe Reina, then aged 37, fit the bill and was signed on loan from AC Milan, making a return to the Premier League after more than five-and-a-half years' playing in Italy. He was immediately installed as Villa's new number one.

The other pressing concern was at the other end of the pitch. Unlike in the Championship, where Kodjia filled in reliably when the main striker in Abraham was not around, the same could not be said of the Ivorian in the Premier League. Not only was the step up in quality too much for Kodjia, who Grealish claims was, at times, 'away with the fairies', but the desire to work hard and fight for the team was lacking, too.

In a 2–1 FA Cup third round defeat to Championship side Fulham on 4 January, where the ball-boys worked harder than the man asked to lead the line for Villa, it was clear his time was up. A lucrative offer to play for Al-Gharafa in the Qatar Premier League had turned the player's head. Such was the emptiness in his stare at Craven Cottage, it appeared mentally he was already on the flight to the Middle East.

Smith had no choice but to turn to the next in line for the run of games ahead as Kodjia finalised his move. With Keinan Davis also out injured, that man was El Ghazi, the winger switching to a central attacking role. That 18-year-old academy graduate Indiana Vassilev was the next option from the bench indicated how stretched the forward line had become.

Every day that passed without Villa signing a striker only added to the stress though, at the time, results on the pitch were just about holding up. Grealish netted an important equaliser in a 1–1 draw at Brighton and when Mings scored the winner with virtually the last touch against Watford four days later, Villa were out of the drop zone.

Suso eventually turned to his contacts in Belgium again to solve the striker crisis, bringing in Mbwana Samatta for £9.5 million from Genk but says: 'He was the only striker who wanted to come to us, nobody else would sign.'

It wasn't for a lack of trying. Villa looked at Hwang Hee-Chan as he impressed for RB Salzburg and worked on signing Michy Batshuayi on loan from Chelsea but he wasn't interested. An even harder push was made for his team-mate, Olivier Giroud, but the French World Cup winner didn't fancy a move either.

'Neither of them wanted it,' Suso recalls. 'Christian and myself went and met with Giroud and he said "no". I then travelled to Monaco and met with Islam Slimani several times, but in the end Monaco asked for £15 million and we didn't have money to do that, so the only striker we could get was Samatta.'

To say that pressure was on the 27-year-old was an understatement. As well as needing to score the goals to keep Villa in the division, he also arrived with the weight of a nation on his shoulders. As the first ever Tanzanian to play in the Premier League, there was incredible hype in the East African country where he was both an icon and inspiration, as well as a footballer.

Villa's official Instagram page added 150,000 followers on the day he arrived and although he was a little rusty on his debut, it was a night to remember as his new team beat Leicester City at Villa Park in the second leg of the Carabao Cup semi-final to squeeze through and set up a final showdown back at Wembley with Manchester City.

Villa had benefited from Brighton and Liverpool fielding effectively youth teams in earlier rounds as they made their way to the last four. Yet the 3–2 aggregate win over a Leicester team then riding high in the Premier League was seriously impressive.

Trezeguet was the hero on the night, scoring a stoppage time winner that sparked wild scenes and a pitch invasion. Another player who deserved more adulation for his performance was Nyland, who made a hat-trick of stunning and important saves to keep Villa in the tie.

With the new-look three-man defence of Mings, Hause and Konsa, Smith appeared to have found a winning formula. Specific instructions to restrict the amount of space for Leicester's forwards Jamie Vardy and Kelechi Iheanacho, a striker Villa had turned down the chance to sign in the summer, were executed perfectly. When Hause later claimed Villa's defence had utilised the game's 'dark arts' to get over the line through tactical fouling, it felt like the team were starting to become more streetwise. Yet consistency in the league was still a big problem.

Samatta scored on his Premier League debut away at fellow strugglers Bournemouth which sent social media into meltdown as Tanzanians lauded their 'Champion Boy' who had now officially made it. But the goal meant very little to Villa as it was a consolation in a 2–1 defeat and for whatever fun the team were having in the Carabao Cup, this was the start of a decline in the league that would leave Smith fighting for his job once again.

Hourihane, who by this stage was in and out of the team, admits he was struggling with the step-up in quality: 'I wanted to rise to the challenge but this was new territory and the physicality, speed and technical level was a big shock for me. We had some other players who had been in the Premier League before but our results were just so up and down. It was beginning to get really difficult.'

Villa lost all three of the games leading up to the Wembley final with emergency deadline day signing, Borja Baston, cementing his status as one of the strangest signings in the club's history during two substitute appearances and 18 uneventful minutes of action. Championship club, Swansea City, agreed to rip up the Spanish forward's contract to let him join Villa, who needed an experienced head to make up the numbers. Perhaps unsurprisingly, he failed to make an impact. Suso believes there was a bigger reason for the drop off in form, as the team were too focused on Wembley.

'It was the biggest distraction for us, and it's always the same when one small team with not enough big players is in two competitions and you are close to the final in one competition,' he explains. 'Everybody wants to play in the final so I felt like we lost our concentration and that cost us a few points. The players were thinking more about the final.'

Smith, for one, disagrees with that assessment. 'If I had my time again I would want that run because I think it kept a lot of the players buoyed,' he says. 'The fact we had a Wembley final, it also keeps the supporters onside. To them it is all about winning trophies. I remember wanting Manchester United to beat Manchester City in the other semi-final because I thought we had a better chance against them.'

The reality was Villa, while huge underdogs against a City team who had thumped them 6–1 in the league just a month before, were potentially just 90 minutes away from winning their first major trophy in 24 years. When the big day came, both Sawiris and Edens were back in attendance while Smith again referenced his father and how he wanted to win for him.

Grealish and Elmohamady were the only two players in the starting line-up to have played in both of Villa's play-off Wembley outings and they were pumped up. 'It's a chance to show the world how good I am,' Grealish said in the matchday programme but there would not be a repeat of the success in the national stadium nine months earlier.

City, managed by Pep Guardiola, had beaten Real Madrid in the Champions League four days earlier and even with changes to the line-up they were still a cut above Villa. Goals from Sergio Aguero and Rodri put City ahead and a bullet header from Samatta, while another big moment for Tanzania, again proved only a consolation.

Describing the personal pride at scoring at Wembley, Samatta says: 'Everything about the final was just amazing. The goal. The atmosphere. The opponent. It was fantastic. I couldn't believe that I was the one to score that goal in the middle of Wembley.'

'It was a great day, just a tough game against Man City,' recalls Smith. 'There was a moment on the sideline which JT always talks about. He came out to me on 65 minutes to talk about subs and all of a sudden I have said: "Oh shit". He asked me what was wrong and I said De Bruyne was coming on for them. He just started laughing.'

Villa by no means played badly. Engels did have a late chance to level but drew a brilliant save out of City keeper Claudio Bravo and Smith's players felt hard done-by on the final whistle, especially as there was controversy around the awarding of the corner that led to Rodri's match-winning goal.

Beaten but not defeated, Smith organised a huddle in the middle of the pitch to encourage his players now all the focus was on the relegation battle. He believed that if his side could run the champions this close, they were still in with a chance.

Optimism proved short-lived. Just eight days later, Villa were thumped 4–0 at Leicester, their fifth straight defeat in all competitions. With his team back in the relegation zone, Smith was once again under pressure, a home match against Chelsea the following Saturday appearing a pivotal moment for the head coach. And yet his fate, along with the lives of everyone else on the planet, was about to be changed in a manner which seemed barely imaginable.

9

THE GREAT ESCAPE

'There's no doubt that Covid saved us,' Conor Hourihane says. 'Without it we were dead and buried.'

After the wet and windy night at Leicester's King Power Stadium, there was an overriding sense of doom seeping into the team. Everyone involved at Villa had accepted the season would be tough, particularly with the scale of the previous summer's squad restructure. Yet the theory had been the team would get better as the season progressed, as the new group of players became more used to each other. Instead, they were getting worse. John McGinn had been a huge miss and with the midfielder almost recovered from a broken ankle a huge amount of faith was being placed on his ability to hit the ground running.

There were now fears the squad simply wasn't strong enough to pull through and for the first time reports surfaced in the press claiming Smith was on the brink.

'It was so hard,' Samatta recalls. 'We were struggling, the pressure was high and we had to stay in the league. We know the strikers were supposed to do more but look at the statistics, it was hard for every player.'

The biggest concern was Villa's defence, having conceded 56 goals up to this point, the most in the league. Training sessions at Bodymoor Heath were slowly becoming laborious as the defeats hit hard. As often tends to happen with struggling teams, arguments were building and a day after the defeat at Leicester things got heated in a small-sided training game among the players who had not been involved in the action the previous night.

Danny Drinkwater, a huge disappointment since joining on loan in January, lost his cool after finding himself stuck on the bench against his former club and filled with humiliation. He planned to speak with Smith after training but ended up taking his frustration out on Jota by headbutting him after an altercation on the practice pitches.

Discussing the incident with the *Telegraph* two years later, the midfielder put it down to years of built-up anger as well as embarrassment. 'The fans were waiting for Danny Drinkwater and this loaf of bread turned up in midfield,' he said in reference to his fitness and physique.

Jota quickly moved on, as he recalls: 'Of course I was angry at first, even if these things happen a lot in football. But Danny called me straight after and apologised. I could see that he felt so, so sorry about it.'

News of the incident broke that night and there was speculation Villa might try to cut short Drinkwater's loan stay from Chelsea. Yet that story and everything else was about to be overtaken by the huge elephant that had been sitting in the room of everyday life for several weeks. The spread of the Covid-19 pandemic had already seen matches in Spain and Italy suspended and it seemed like only a matter of time before England would have to follow suit. The only question was when?

On the Thursday, 48 hours before Villa were due to host Chelsea in a match which was potentially must-win for Smith, the Premier League released a statement declaring it would be business as usual that weekend. Yet within hours, the outlook had changed. Late that evening, news broke that Arsenal boss Mikel Arteta had tested positive for the virus. The following morning, Chelsea winger Callum Hudson-Odoi was another confirmed case and by Friday lunchtime the Premier League had finally been forced to accept the inevitable. Football was suspended until further notice.

'I don't think any of us really knew how to approach it,' says Smith, who recalls how the unpredictable nature of the time was summed up in one meeting at Bodymoor Heath involving himself, performance director Jeremy Oliver and club doctor Ricky Shamji. 'We knew a lockdown was coming and we were sat there discussing our plans and how best to deal with it as a club,' he says. 'About 15 minutes in, Ricky said he wasn't feeling well and decided it best he left and continued the meeting from his car. A short while later he called back to say he had Covid. He had to go and lock himself in his bedroom for a week!'

For several weeks the fate of clubs and their managers felt rather irrelevant in the face of a national health crisis and lockdown. That said, the Premier League still had to decide the best way to conclude a season which was not going to be finished on time. The cancellation of the European Championships, scheduled for the summer, at least bought leagues around the continent a little more leeway.

A number of scenarios were discussed, some of them beneficial to Villa, others less so. Sitting 19th in the table when the season was halted, declaring it finished there and then would have been the nightmare scenario and seen them relegated back to the Championship. Yet that immediately seemed unfair, considering Smith's team had a game in hand on those around them in the table. Deciding the final table on points-per-game would have worked in Villa's favour, as would declaring the whole campaign null and void, though there was obviously large opposition to the latter, considering it was at that point three-quarters complete. Suso suffered something of a PR gaffe when he claimed null and void was the best option during an interview with the Spanish press.

Villa, mindful of the suffering which was taking place across the nation, were conscious of how callous discussing football outcomes in public seemed. No-one in society was immune to the crisis, Premier League football clubs included.

Club masseur Alex Butler, known better as 'Big Al', was hospitalised and hooked up to a machine that would assist his breathing. He thought he was heading into a coma and even messaged loved ones in case he didn't make it out the other side.[28]

Goalkeeper Pepe Reina also fell ill and said he couldn't breathe for around 30 minutes after 'running out of oxygen' and spent over a week inside his family home recovering after testing positive. Others suffered mild symptoms but the more people who contracted it, the more the virus became real.

In late March, Grealish would create unwanted headlines when he crashed his Range Rover, having gone to visit former Villa teammate Ross McCormack, just hours after posting an online video urging the public to respect lockdown rules and stay at home to protect the NHS. Photos and a video emerged of the incident, which happened in the car park of a Solihull apartment block. Grealish issued an apology and said he was 'deeply embarrassed' by the incident. He was disciplined by the club and reprimanded by Smith.

'It was a tough one to deal with because you were dealing with it remotely,' says Smith. 'No-one was allowed out. It was not like I could sit down and have a chat with him.

'The conversation was essentially "Listen, you are the captain of the club and you have to be better." But I think a lot of the players at the time were like caged animals. They had nothing to do, nowhere to go.

'With Jack it was just about talking about his responsibilities. He is always the most apologetic and he understands and takes responsibility for it as well. That is the loving part you have for him because he will say "shit, I've fucked up".

'I remember another time he messed up and I pulled him in and said: "Jack, all the players are looking at me now to see how I am going to deal with you. How would you deal with you?"

'He asked what I meant and I said: "Well, would you fine you, would you not play you, drop you out of the squad? How do you think it is going to work?"

'He said: "Fine me, gaffer," and then said: "No, I tell you what, I will take the whole squad out for dinner." So that is what he did. All of a sudden the rest of the players are thinking yeah, he has been punished but he has taken us out for dinner as well. I thought it was a good way of dealing with it.'

Grealish, who would donate £150,000 to a local hospital during the pandemic and raised more than £50,000 for the NHS by auctioning off a signed shirt, would later be fined, made to pay costs and banned from driving for nine months after admitting a charge of driving without due care, related to the incident.

It was not just health which was a concern during that time. Jobs were on the line with the country's service industry shut down and Rishi Sunak, the Chancellor of the Exchequer, announced that a furlough scheme would also be introduced to support employers to retain and continue to pay staff while businesses were closed. Villa decided not to participate and instead continued to pay staff in full through their own funding. Other clubs weren't so forthcoming: Newcastle United, Tottenham Hotspur, Bournemouth and Norwich City all announced they would furlough some non-playing staff, as did Liverpool, but after a fierce backlash the latter reversed the decision.

Behind the scenes, meanwhile, Purslow was a leading voice in talks with his fellow Premier League executives over a plan which became known as Project Restart. Playing matches at neutral venues was an issue on which Villa were pushing back, even though it was acknowledged the sport would almost certainly resume behind closed doors. This was one subject on which Purslow was prepared to talk in public, warning during a series of interviews in early May how clubs at the bottom end of the table were facing a '£200 million catastrophe' if relegated.

Preparations for the season's resumption, for Smith, would take place amid deep personal anguish when, in late May, his father Ron passed away at the age of 79. Ron had been living in a care home since 2018. He had contracted Covid earlier in the month.

'It was tough,' Smith says. 'My dad had been ill for a while and it was not necessarily Covid which killed him. He'd had dementia for five years. He had been deteriorating all that time. The way I am, I had probably processed we were going to lose him soon when he went into a home two years earlier.

'The tough part is when he passes. Mom wanted to go past Villa Park with the coffin and everyone lined up outside. I remember the hearse drove to my mom's and the whole of the road was lined with people, with scarves. It was tough but it was one of those things you have to get through, everyone has got personal lives which are going on. There were a lot of people who supported each other in that period.'

Ron's funeral took place after the season had resumed and Smith, who spoke at the service, remembers a brief moment of humour when he told the mainly Villa-supporting mourners he would be keeping his words brief as he was busy trying to keep the club in the top flight.

When the campaign had been halted, the head coach had thrown himself into work, watching back every single game to see where his team had been going wrong. The number of big chances they were conceding immediately jumped out and the focus became reducing those. Treadmills and other gym equipment were sent out to players who did not already have the provision at home. Players were also encouraged to exercise in their back garden, or during the one hour of open air time they and every other member of the public were permitted by the government each day.

Video calls through the Zoom platform were vitally important. Smith set up individual meetings with each player to debrief the season so far. He asked for open and honest reflections from his players and identified strengths and weaknesses in their game.

'To be fair to Dean, he made the most of Covid,' Hourihane recalls. 'He didn't use it as an excuse that we couldn't meet up and train. Instead he made us all log on for daily and weekly videos to show how we were going to get better as a team.'

Clips of how Liverpool – the best team in the Premier League and Champions League winners – and Lazio – the team who had conceded the fewest amount of goals in Italy – defended were shown to the players as case studies. Smith wanted a new focus for Villa: to become harder to beat, to reduce the amount of chances they conceded and ultimately to get enough points to stay in the division.

Gradually, as infection rates lowered, Premier League clubs were allowed back to training, initially in small groups. 'You could only work with three or four players at a time but I loved that,' said Smith. 'It was great working individually with the players and chatting with them. I think we got a lot of good work done which set us up nicely when the season came back.

'We could well have got relegated had the season just continued. There is no pause button normally. But after the Leicester game, we did get our pause button and had the chance to reflect and react to it.'

The halt to the season also meant Villa would have McGinn available for the run-in. Having been on the brink of returning from his broken ankle for the Chelsea match, the Scot had suffered a stress fracture in his shin which would have ruled him out for the rest of the campaign, had it continued as normal. The break allowed him time to recover.

'It was down to trying to get back too soon to help the team,' says McGinn. 'I was gutted but the silver lining was that I wasn't going to be missing any games during that time. I stumbled my way back to fitness for the restart but I was massively out of shape. It was out of necessity more than anything.'

'John was still coming into the last 10 games not where we wanted him to be,' adds Smith. 'But he was so important to the dressing room at that time, we needed him.'

Smith's plan, in agreement with Purslow and Suso, was to effectively treat the final 10 matches as a World Cup-style tournament. The club struck an agreement with The Belfry Hotel, located close to Bodymoor Heath, which allowed them to stay both the night before and after home matches. Players would later claim that move helped bring the squad closer together.

'We stayed in hotels as a team to build that togetherness,' recalls Ezri Konsa. 'Sometimes after the games we'd stay in a hotel as well. It was nice to have that family feeling and I feel like we were really close as a team.'

Smith had planned out the final 10 matches, including details on each opponent and how Villa planned to set up in each match and presented it to Sawiris and Edens. 'We were in a controlled environment where we could break down the game, reflect on the game and do the video work and then train,' adds Smith. 'We were pretty much living out of the Belfry for those 10 games and I think it helped us a lot, in terms of building the narrative to the players of what we were trying to do.'

When the season eventually resumed on 17 June, Villa were straight back in action, hosting Sheffield United in the first behind closed doors fixture. Due to the unpredictable nature of the pandemic, the Premier League had decided to play matches in hand first, so teams would at least be level on the number of games played should the season need to be halted again.

This was football like no-one had experienced before and though it would be another 10 months before fans were allowed back in, it never quite felt normal. Media passes were restricted as was the use of facilities within Villa Park. The press room became the opposition changing room and proof of a negative Covid test was required to enter the ground as well as a temperature check on arrival.

Perhaps the biggest takeaway from the first game was just how vocal Tyrone Mings tends to be on a matchday. In many ways it was a privilege to be able to attend these games while others watched at home, not only to continue working, but to gain insights that would have otherwise been impossible.

The first match would deliver controversy with one of the most memorable moments in Premier League history. Smith had made a big call in his team selection, dropping the experienced Reina and replacing him in goal with Orjan Nyland. Shortly before half-time, the Norway international went to claim Oliver Norwood's free-kick under pressure and inexplicably carried it over the line. Even journalists stationed toward the other end of the pitch could see both the keeper and the ball had ended up in the net but the Hawkeye goal-line technology system, having never knowingly failed before, did so on this occasion. Referee Michael Oliver's watch, which should have buzzed to alert the official when the ball crossed the line, didn't and his assistants also failed to trust their eyes as Villa survived.

'We got away with one there, it was five yards over the line,' Grealish said to Chris Wilder as he walked off the pitch at half-time. Wilder told *The Athletic* in an interview three years later: 'We knew straight away because the goalkeeper was standing in the Holte End when he palmed the ball out!'

Smith had a different, more poignant theory as to what had happened. Unbeknown to the head coach, a member of the club staff had draped a steward's jacket over a seat in the Holte End prior to kick-off in tribute to his father Ron. 'The thing was, my dad was into his watches,' he says. 'He had about 30 of them, all different types. My brother and family were saying he was behind the goal, fiddling with the ref's watch. That's why it didn't work!'

The match finished 0–0 and Villa claimed a point which would eventually prove crucial in their battle against the drop. It is, of course, impossible to know how the game would have played out in the second half had the goal been correctly awarded. Smith and his players could also point to an incident much earlier in the season, in a 1–0 defeat at Crystal Palace, when an early referee's whistle had denied them a perfectly legitimate goal and a point. Whether this was simply luck balancing itself out or not, this felt another crucial moment when the fates seemed to have aligned in Villa's favour.

The clean sheet, even though not technically legitimate, helped build some confidence but Suso, who had spent the lockdown back in Spain with his 90-year-old mother, feared the absence of supporters at home games would turn out to be damaging. 'The strangest thing was not having fans inside Villa Park,' he says. 'Imagine if when you are the strongest you cannot play with your supporters in Villa Park. It's an amazing place to reverse games with the people supporting the team. I started to think, "Oh my God, maybe we could go down."'

Some of the players weren't enjoying the lack of atmosphere either, most notably Grealish. 'Jack thrives on atmosphere so it was a little bit different for him,' says Smith. 'I remember talking to him after two or three games behind closed doors and he said he was not quite there, he could not quite feel it at that moment.'

Villa were beaten by Chelsea the following weekend but then

picked up another point at Newcastle United through a late Elmohamady equaliser. The frustration was it should have been all three but for a mistake by Konsa which led to the Magpies opening the scoring.

Terry helped Smith put together a plan to become more secure during the final fixtures and reiterated two key messages: The first to improve communication between the back line and the other to always focus on the distances between each player.

Villa's defensive statistics prior to the season's pause had made for grim reading. Their expected goals (xG) figure, which measures the quality of chances a team gives up to an opponent, was the worst in the top flight. Teams facing Villa had been expected to score an average of 2.1 goals a game. Even worse was the number of shots they were facing. The average of 18.1 shots per match was also a Premier League worst. Both of these were drastically reduced following the restart, and the Newcastle game, despite the lack of a clean sheet, was a sign of how different the approach would be until the end of the season.

The trouble was an improved defence was not translating into results. Villa were beaten 1–0 at home by Wolves and, despite conceding just three goals in four matches following the season's resumption, had scored only twice themselves. Neither was the fixture list providing many favours. Back-to-back matches against Liverpool and Manchester United brought good performances yet ultimately defeat. The home game against United was particularly galling. Villa started well, almost took the lead when Trezeguet thumped a shot against the post but then went behind when the visitors were awarded a penalty despite Konsa appearing to be the man fouled in the box. The subsequent 3–0 defeat left Villa without a win in 11 matches dating back to January and seven points adrift of safety with just four matches left to play. 'The belief is still there, that is for sure,' Smith told the press. But it was getting harder to believe him.

Behind the scenes, a feeling of unrest had also developed as Suso recalls: 'During Project Restart, I was thinking about other things because I felt something would happen with Dean, with me or with both. We were no longer travelling with Christian because of Covid so we didn't have the same relationship and we were all feeling the pressure; myself, Dean, Christian, the players. All of us, for sure.'

Disagreements between Suso and Purslow had started to increase. Purslow speaks Spanish and would often argue with his sporting director in the language when things got heated. Suso believed that his CEO became too involved with footballing duties and therefore undermined some of his suggestions to Sawiris. Purslow, however, wanted to be all-in on everything and was not going to change.

The issue on the pitch was more straightforward but far from easily solved: Villa simply needed to find a way to score goals. Incredibly, the team had gone nearly 14 hours without a goal from an attacking player with Samatta and Keinan Davis, the only two available strikers, now void of any confidence.

'Honestly, I thought we were going to get relegated,' Grealish now says, looking back. 'With four games to go I thought it was going to happen. I thought we were gone. We had lost too many of those early games in Project Restart and we had lost our big advantage – playing in front of fans at Villa Park which was massive for us.'

All the effort of the previous 12 months was in danger of going to waste. Villa needed someone to grasp the goal-scoring mantle and an unlikely hero was about to emerge. Trezeguet, a man who had a street named after him in Egypt after playing a leading role in helping his country qualify for the World Cup, had waited long enough to step up but was now about to deliver when it mattered.

The 25-year-old scored both goals in a crucial 2–0 win against Crystal Palace, a match in which the bad luck Villa felt they had suffered against United was repaid when Mamadou Sakho saw an early goal for the visitors ruled out for handball, despite replays showing the ball had clearly struck his shoulder.

'The brilliant thing about Trez was his running stats,' says Smith. 'It didn't matter whether there was a crowd there or not. We were always going to get someone who ran 14 km in the game, with about 1,800 high speed metres. He was phenomenal and he deserved those goals.'

The win over Palace cut the gap to safety to four points and Villa looked set to reduce it further when Konsa gave them a 1–0 lead late on at Everton the following Thursday. But El Ghazi missed the chance to seal the points when he blazed over from a yard out with Reina, who had by then reclaimed the No. 1 jersey from the shaky Nyland, then misjudging an 87th minute Theo Walcott header as the game finished 1–1.

Matt Targett struggled to hold back the tears during a post-match interview with club media, while Hourihane remembers feeling defeated: 'That was a quiet coach home,' he says. 'We all thought it was over.'

El Ghazi felt personally to blame, saying: 'I wasn't in great form, so to get a big chance like that and miss it was really hard. I thought that we might not stay up because of me. It was so hard to take, especially with the stick I was getting from the fans. But I was pissed with myself so I could understand why people were pissed with me.'

Events elsewhere, however, were about to help Villa's cause. West Ham and Watford, both three points above them in the standings, played each other the following night and a 3–1 defeat for the latter resulted in them sacking boss Nigel Pearson and his assistant Craig Shakespeare with just a week of the season to go.

'That was brilliant for us,' recalls Smith.

When the Hornets, under the caretaker charge of Hayden Mullins, suffered a 4–0 defeat against Manchester City, it meant

Villa entered their penultimate match of the season at home to Arsenal with a chance to go above their rivals and climb out of the drop zone on goal difference with a win.

'We watched the game just before we went out to play against Arsenal and it made us think "Hang on, maybe the door is slightly ajar,"' Mings recalls. 'Now would we have had that mentality if Watford hadn't played before us, who knows? These are the fine margins when you're battling to stay up.'

With the momentum swinging in their favour, Trezeguet was again the hero, volleying home what would prove the only goal of the game from a 27th minute corner. Arsenal were sitting ninth in the table, their lowest position in years, and the first half of the match was notable for a plane being flown over the stadium trailing a banner protesting against the London club's owners. Yet there was still serious talent in their ranks with the likes of Pierre Emerick Aubameyang, Bukayo Saka and Alexandre Lacazette. As the clock ticked down, the more it became a backs to the wall effort for Villa and in the final minutes came another of those sliding doors moments. A minute after Davis had missed a good chance to make the game safe, Eddie Nketiah rose to meet a Nicolas Pepe corner and sent a header against the far post, the ball bouncing right back at home keeper Reina, who eventually grasped it before giving it a kiss.

The Spaniard had been recalled after Nyland had endured a nervy performance in the defeat to Wolves. Smith says: 'At that point I decided I needed Pepe's personality and experience. We were unbelievable against Arsenal at home. We never conceded a shot on goal in that game. The way we worked, we had two banks of four, Jack playing behind the striker. I'd told both of the forwards, Ally Samatta and Keinan Davis, they would have to share the workload through the run-in and both of them did really well.'

When the final whistle sounded, Villa had gone from being dead and buried to having their fate in their own hands, all in the space of ten days. Reina would later tell Smith the match was among the most emotional of his career and during the debrief he was almost in tears. Finally, it looked as though all the hard work was paying off. All those Zoom calls and long days working on defensive structure had reaped dividends. The new-found resistance and willingness to keep the ball out of the net, coupled with just enough attacking threat, had turned the season around in the nick of time.

Yet the job was not yet finished and, just as in the previous 37 matches, nothing about the final day trip to West Ham would feel easy. On the coach to the London Stadium there was tension as nerves started to kick in. El Ghazi lightened the mood with a joke about his wife's choice of handbags, saying that next season she might be back shopping on the high street rather than at designer outlets as relegation would mean wage cuts all around.

'It was a very similar feeling to a play-off final, although with no fans inside the stadium, we didn't get that buzz and anxiety from the crowd,' Hourihane says. 'We knew there was so much riding on it and I'd only been in the Premier League for a year so I didn't want to get relegated. In all my career, I had never been relegated so I definitely didn't want that on my CV.'

The atmosphere around the stadium was eerie. A smattering of Villa supporters had made their way to East London, despite knowing they had no chance of actually getting into the stadium.

For Mo Razzaq, watching from home with his two daughters, it was a surreal experience. 'It was bizarre because it is not as though people are at the match and you are not. Nobody is at the match!' he says. 'The behind closed doors games had already thrown up a few strange results so we really didn't know what to expect. The heart rate was through the roof.'

The strange pre-match silence which greeted every behind closed doors fixture seemed entirely inappropriate for an afternoon where so much was on the line. 'There were so many emotions going into that game,' Konsa recalls. 'So much was on the line and we knew as players that we had to go there and win because a draw would mean relying on other results. I was nervous and so was everyone else.'

In the stands Purslow cut a worried figure. The '£200 million catastrophe' was running through his head and there was no way to hide his concern. 'Karren Brady (the vice chair of West Ham) says she's never seen a more stressed face in her life,' he recalls.

Even Smith, so calm at Wembley 14 months earlier, was feeling it this time around. 'I think I was more nervous before West Ham because it was in our own hands,' he says. 'I don't think I showed it much, to be fair. We made sure we had people wired into the other games so we could follow what was going on. The message to the players was to simply carry on what we have been doing, follow the process and play the game.'

Villa began nervously. The hosts were now safe from relegation themselves and hearts were in mouths when Konsa misjudged a long ball and Michail Antonio shot wide. News that Watford were already 3–0 down at Arsenal lifted the mood yet Bournemouth, three points behind Villa but with a better goal difference, were winning at Everton. Smith's men could not afford defeat and their Premier League fate remained on a knife edge.

Then, with six minutes to go, the tension evaporated. Grealish cut in from the left and the power on his shot was enough to beat Lukasz Fabianksi in the West Ham goal. Villa's players and bench celebrated as one. Grealish, the hometown hero and saviour. The script was perfect, surely?

Within a minute, the mood had changed. Andriy Yarmolenko's shot took a huge deflection off Grealish. Reina somehow could not keep it out. Villa were back to a position where one more goal conceded would see them down and Watford were also adding to the nerves, having pulled things back to 3–2 at Arsenal.

'When Arsenal were 3–0 up, it felt good,' Purslow recalls. 'But when West Ham equalised and Watford pulled it back to 3–2, I felt like we were really exposed. It was like the other side of the play-off coin where everything hinges on one match. The most dramatic thing I've ever been involved in and I was just thinking all the good work we have done would have been written off, and we would have been back to square one if we went down.'

When the full-time whistle blew it was all eyes on events at the Emirates Stadium. Villa's players and staff gathered round an iPad in the centre circle. Up in the press box, journalists did the same. Confirmation came from a yell down on the grass and the sight of Trezeguet breaking away from the group and running with delight before the emotion got too much for him and he fell to the ground.

'I was so, so nervous,' Jota, sitting on the sidelines, recalls. 'I felt like I was having a heart attack in those final few minutes because I knew how sad relegation would be.'

'I've never played under such pressure in my life,' said McGinn during post-match interviews. Somehow, Villa had survived. Staring down the barrel in early March, the onset of a pandemic had bought them valuable time and just when all looked lost they had reeled off their longest unbeaten run of the season to stay up by a point. One of the toughest steps in the journey under Sawiris and Edens had been completed in the most surreal of circumstances.

'I feel that was a better achievement, staying up that year with everything which had been thrown at us, than going up the previous year,' says Smith. 'When we got on to that run in the Championship, five or six games into it you always felt there was a good chance we were going up at the end of the season. With the players we had compared to a lot of the other teams, we should have done too. Whereas in the first Premier League season we had a lot of things thrown at us, players getting injured, the positions we had been in. I thought it was a better achievement than the year before.'

Mings agrees, adding: 'I don't think it gets spoken about enough. Because if you are seven points adrift with four to play with such an horrendous goal difference swing as well. Everyone who contributed to that season can take great pride in what we ultimately managed to achieve because gosh, it is so hard.'

Questions in the post-match press conference immediately turned to the future of Grealish, already believed to be a serious target for Manchester United.

'What happens next with Jack? He goes out and gets drunk with me!' smiled Smith.

The Villa boss, who walked back into the dressing room to find Reina smoking a huge cigar in triumph, was good to his word. Villa's team returned to Birmingham and with lockdown restrictions having been lifted a few weeks earlier, partied until the early hours, if not longer.

'We had a party in Snobs which was fun and then I went straight to Ibiza the next day,' Grealish recalls. 'It's all a bit of a blur now. When I think back to all the really big games I've played throughout my life, I can't remember too much about the day or the game. I just know that I was confident on the day – much more confident than in the weeks before when I thought we were going down.'

Smith would later reveal he spent the night sleeping in his office at Bodymoor Heath.[29]

There was still time for the day to gain an unusual postscript. With the Villa squad almost back in the Midlands, news broke in Portugal that Smith would be sacked and replaced by former Benfica boss Bruno Lage. Immediately shot down by Villa's communications team, the reports nevertheless carried a grain of truth. Lage had been identified by Villa as a likely successor, should they have been relegated and the decision taken to move on from

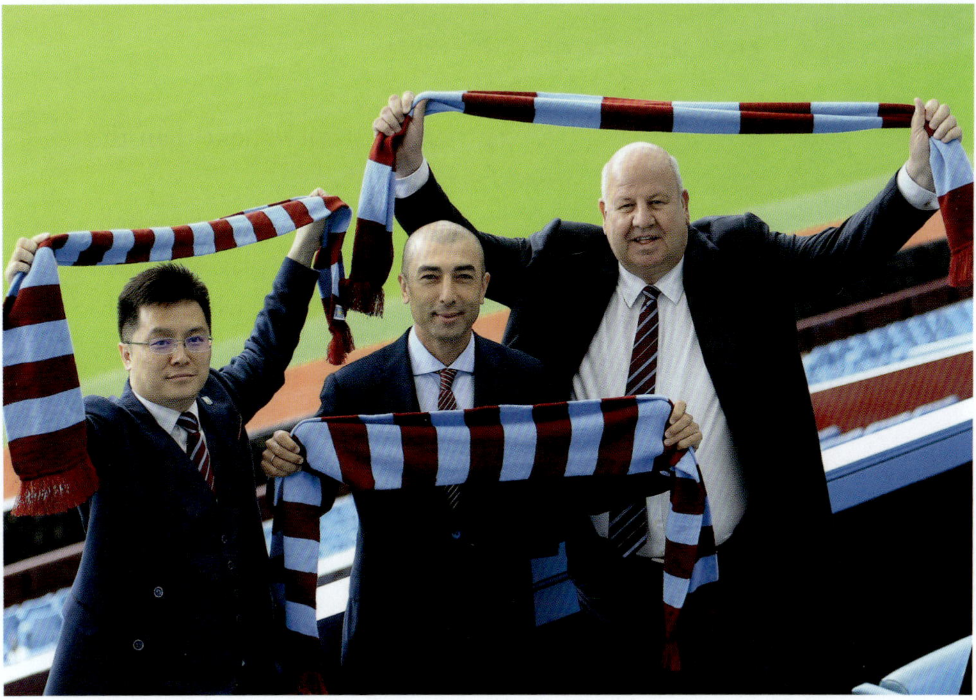

PA Images / Alamy Stock Photo

Above: Aston Villa chairman Dr Tony Xia, manager Roberto Di Matteo and chief executive Keith Wyness.

Below: Steve Bruce talks to Wes Edens and Nassef Sawiris at Villa Park, 25 August 2018.

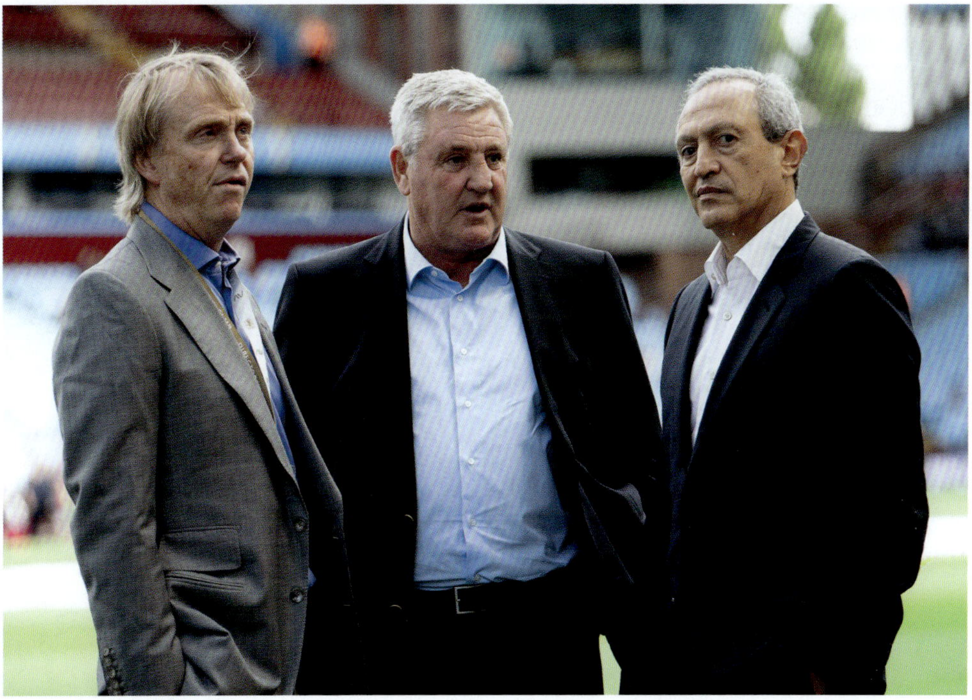

Neville Williams/Aston Villa FC via Getty Images

Neville Williams/Aston Villa FC via Getty Images

Above: Tammy Abraham scores against Nottingham Forest at Villa Park, 28 November 2018.

Below: Jed Steer makes crucial save in the Championship Play Off Semi Final first leg match against West Bromwich Albion at Villa Park, 11 May 2019.

Lena Coker / MI News/NurPhoto via Getty Images

Aston Villa's Jack Grealish and manager Dean Smith celebrate lifting the Championship Play-off Final Trophy, May 2019.

PA Images / Alamy Stock Photo

Egyptian midfielder Trézéguet celebrates scoring the opening goal against Arsenal, 21 July 2020.

Paul Terry/Sportimage

Above: Dean Smith and assistant John Terry celebrate the draw against West Ham that keeps them from relegation from the Premier League, 26 July 2020.

Below: Ollie Watkins holding his 3 fingers up after scoring a hat-trick against Liverpool in the 7-2 win in October 2020.

Steven Gerrard looks dejected following his side's defeat at Fulham, 20 October 2022.

Ryan Pierse/Getty Images

CEO Christian Purslow with Unai Emery during a press conference at Villa Park, 4 November 2022.

Aston Villa/Aston Villa FC via Getty Images

Matthew Ashton - AMA/Getty Images

Above: Emi Martínez kisses the World Cup trophy after beating France the 2022 World Cup final at Lusail Stadium, Qatar, 18 December 2022.

Below: Unai Emery celebrates his side's second goal against Manchester United at Villa Park, 6 November 2022.

PA Images / Alamy Stock Photo

John McGinn and Tyrone Mings at Villa Park, 4 March 2023.

Marc Atkins/Getty Images

Jhon Duran scores the opening goal of the Champions League game against Bayern Munich, 2 October 2024.

Neville Williams/Aston Villa FC via Getty Images

Jhon Duran signs a new contract pictured with Damien Vidagany, Unai Emery and Monchi at Bodymoor Heath training ground, 7 October 2024.

John McGinn leads his team out to face Bologna FC 1909, 22 October 2024.

Simon Stacpoole/Offside/Offside via Getty Images

Smith. Survival meant there was no longer any chance of that happening. In masterminding the greatest of great escapes, the Villa boss had done enough to keep his job. Others, however, would not be so fortunate.

10

KEY WINDOW

While the dramatic manner in which Villa had achieved survival was worthy of celebration, few at the club were in doubt that serious work was needed to avoid the next season being another of struggle.

Within an hour of the final whistle sounding at the London Stadium, John McGinn was laying the situation bare during a Zoom call with journalists still sat in the press box. McGinn has a wonderful knack of cutting through the noise and telling it like it is and there wasn't much of what he said which could be argued with.

'I think everyone is aware we need quality added,' he began. 'We can't get complacent and think everything is alright now. It was a poor season overall, we know that – us as players and I am sure everyone upstairs is fully aware of that.

'There is no way we should be celebrating finishing 17th with the size and stature of this place and the money we have spent.'

In a moment which quickly came to appear prescient, McGinn also said: 'There will be changes, I am sure of that.'

Just a day later came a big one, when Suso was told his services were no longer required. Rumours the sporting director was set to be sacked had surfaced during the party which took place in Birmingham hours after the West Ham match. The Spaniard had missed out on the celebrations at the stadium after a strange incident when he was not allowed into the 'Red Zone' area by the dressing rooms. True enough, the uneasy feeling he had felt in the closing weeks of the campaign came true as Purslow told him he would be paid up and moved on. Suso now admits the decision didn't come as a huge surprise, considering how his relationship with the chief executive had become. 'I was never given an exact reason which was disappointing,' Suso says. At the very least, he expected a frank discussion over the way forward. 'But Nassef and Christian both thanked me for the work that I did.'

Suso met Smith on the Monday night for dinner after being told the news. 'My wife and daughter joined us because they both loved Suso as well,' says Smith. 'I was really sad he was going because I had worked really well with him. I enjoyed his company and his knowledge of players. He could be fiery at times but he was also, with me, quite calming. He knew the game and we would talk about it a lot. I was sad to see him go but football happens like that.'

To sum up the brutal nature of the sport and how fortunes are so dictated by results, Suso had been involved in discussions over a possible replacement for Smith had Villa been relegated and a change wanted. In addition to Lage, former Brighton boss Chris Hughton was considered while Purslow had also put forward Steven Gerrard, then managing at Rangers, as a possibility. The Great Escape, however, killed any immediate appetite for change in the dugout.

Instead, it was in the sporting director department where Villa decided they needed a switch. If the business over the previous summer was designed to give the team a fighting chance of survival, then this period of trading was needed to help the club become established back in the Premier League. Nailing the recruitment in the forthcoming window was going to be vital.

'The way I looked at it is, when we went into the Premier League, our job was to stay up,' says Smith. 'That is the hardest part for any team which comes up. Then you can go and build. I always felt if we stayed up and brought in reinforcements we could quite easily climb five or six places because of the size of our club and what we could bring in, the squad we had. There were teams you could very quickly go ahead of.'

Even before Suso's exit, transfer targets had already been lined up. Sawiris feared the long-term future of Grealish would lie elsewhere so he asked Suso what he would do to replace him.

Suso says: 'I said, you'd need to get in two or three players to find the same skills really quickly because Jack is a complex player, an amazing player. I didn't know any English player who was able to provide all the skills he had.'

In his final reports, Suso therefore recommended Emile Smith Rowe of Arsenal followed by Chelsea's Conor Gallagher. Both had recently spent time in the Championship on loan and were players with high potential.

Aurelien Tchouameni had previously been pinpointed as a young player with talent but Suso knew Villa had missed the boat when Monaco signed him from Bordeaux in January 2020. The French midfielder would go on to join Real Madrid for a deal worth up to £100 million two years later.

Mason Greenwood of Manchester United was another but the challenge of bringing him in was understandably difficult as he was highly rated and playing regularly for the club who had developed him from the age of six. Suso liked the 17-year-old Uruguayan star Matias Arezo, who had been scoring heavily for River Plate Montevideo and was keen on discussing a move to Villa. The player eventually moved to Spanish club Granada.

Brentford striker Ollie Watkins was also on the list and it would become the job of Suso's successor, Johan Lange, to get that deal and others over the line. There was no time to waste. The delayed finish to the season meant a shorter break. There were just seven weeks between the final day at West Ham and the start of the next campaign, which would be the most congested in the history of English football. With the pandemic showing few signs of abating, matches would again take place behind closed doors.

The speed of Lange's appointment, just three days after Suso's exit, left little doubt this was a change the club had been planning for some time. Villa used a headhunting firm to identify a series of young and talented candidates who were available and after a round of interviews selected Lange as the standout choice. He went through a series of discussions, first with Purslow and then Sawiris and Edens, impressing with a presentation that laid out clearly the impact he would have on helping the club grow. Lange was joining from FC Copenhagen, where in his six years as technical director the Danish club had earned a reputation for identifying young talent and selling those players on at a healthy profit.

The official announcement of his appointment included a rare statement from Sawiris and Edens in which the owners stated they were 'happy' with staying up but added: 'We will not be satisfied until we achieve our goal of bringing sustainable success to Aston Villa at the top tier of European football.' The owners described Lange's hiring as the next step in 'building a world class organisation'.

'Suso had a very difficult task to put a squad together for the Premier League when we had really significant PSR constraints,' Purslow says. 'Johan became a technical director. He took over at Bodymoor Heath by building the training ground capability. We improved our recruitment and became stronger in performance, nutrition, research, data and administration.'

Lange's financial reporting skills were also an upgrade and seen as essential for the future. The club would spend another £100 million on transfers in the weeks ahead despite all the uncertainty and loss of income through Covid, but now the goal had changed.

The aim was to finish around the middle of the table and Lange got to work on the search for five new players.

First, he hired Rob Mackenzie as the new head of recruitment from Belgian club OH Leuven, as he felt he needed an English right-hand man who knew the Premier League and Championship inside out. Mackenzie had worked at Tottenham Hotspur where he signed Son Heung-min and Toby Alderweireld, and then Leicester City where he identified Riyad Mahrez and Ngolo Kante among others ahead of the title-winning year. His eye for talent and skill in video scouting appealed and alongside Lange he would become a key part of a successful window which would help lay foundations for future success.

The final game of the Championship season – the play-off final between Fulham and Brentford on 4 August – would be the cause of a nervy first week in the job for the pair as they watched on knowing that if Brentford were to win there would be no chance of signing Ollie Watkins, their top striker target. Five other clubs were keen including Leeds United but Villa felt they had a strong hand with Smith, who had a good relationship with the player from his time managing the Bees.

Before pursuing Watkins, a £14 million deal was arranged with Nottingham Forest for right-back Matty Cash. Mackenzie liked Cash's versatility and his ability to also play in midfield if needed. 'I remember Johan actually brought Cash to me,' says Smith. 'He was aware he had been made available and we could get him. I said he was a converted full-back. When he played against us in the 5–5 draw in 2018 he played wide right. I went away and watched a few Forest games with him at right-back and liked him. So I said yeah, let's do it. Between Johan and Christian they went and got the deal done.'

Lange quickly found himself spinning many plates during a period where Covid was still making daily interactions, especially in the world of recruitment, particularly difficult. Working out of a cramped office where water was leaking from the air conditioning unit was hardly the ideal set-up for a technical director with big plans to build a data and research department. Villa didn't even have a registered club account with popular data providers at the time of his arrival, as scouts used usernames and passwords from friends at rival clubs to gain access.

This was how far the club had slipped behind in the Championship years, but changes were on the way. Joe Bucknall, the first-team data analyst, began to look deeper into signings for the future while Bryn Davies and Ben Hackney – two members of the scouting operations team – were able to improve the scouting set-up as Mackenzie and Lange placed trust in their work.

Getting the Watkins deal over the line was not easy. Brentford were notoriously tough negotiators and ultimately it was Villa's willingness to pay a fee which looked a little over the odds at the time, £28 million rising to £33 million, which put them in pole position. 'I knew Ollie would be a difficult one because I obviously knew Brentford owner Matthew Benham and their sporting director Phil Giles,' says Smith. 'I knew the valuation we had was going to be different to what theirs was.

'We were thinking we would get him for £23–24 million but I said no. I said if you want me to get involved, I will speak to Matthew and see where he is at because we still have a really good relationship. I phoned him and asked what would get the deal done. He said: "Listen, if Ollie goes to Villa, he will be your best player," to which I replied: "I think Jack Grealish might have something to say about that!" He told me he was telling me what their stats were saying. I said if he is your best player, it is going to take at least 30, isn't it? I reported back and said that is the number we are looking at.'

Villa's desire to land Watkins was further heightened by a failed attempt to sign Callum Wilson from Bournemouth. The striker had instead chosen to join Newcastle, and in no mood to suffer a further setback Villa promptly blew every rival for Watkins out of the water with their offer. 'Me and Johan met Ollie and sold him the plan, how we saw him and what he was going to do,' says Smith. 'He was coming in as the No. 9. I think he had other clubs in for him as well, but he liked the fact he had worked with me before. We had a good relationship. Part of the presentation we gave explained how we would get him in the England squad, funnily enough.'

The initial plan was to sign both strikers and phase out Samatta and Davis, but missing out on Wilson would, as it transpired, work out rather well in the long run. Had a £21 million deal for the forward gone through, Villa may have reconsidered moves for some of the signings that followed, including goalkeeper Emi Martinez.

Villa were in the market for a keeper with Reina having departed at the end of his loan and Nyland deemed not good enough. But moving for Martinez, who would want to come in as No. 1, was not a straightforward deal for Villa because of the respect they had towards Tom Heaton, a leader of the team and most experienced member of the dressing room. Still sidelined from the serious knee injury suffered on New Year's Day, the keeper was expected back later in the year and the timeline was important. Should Heaton be ready just a few weeks into the season, Villa would have been happy to ride with Jed Steer for a few weeks.

Lange and Smith were torn on the decision, yet when it became clear Heaton would not be back in action until December Villa decided to firm up their interest in Martinez. The Argentine had been with Arsenal for nearly a decade and spent most of those years out on loan. But an injury to Gunners No. 1 Bernd Leno shortly after the previous season had restarted had finally given him a chance and he had proved something of a revelation, starring as Mikel Arteta's team beat Chelsea to win the FA Cup.

There was a sense, however, that Arteta was yet to be fully convinced and Villa eyed an opportunity. Goalkeeping coach, Neil

Cutler, had built up a relationship with Martinez as he looked for a move away and was a key voice in the deal, while Smith had also received good reviews from former Arsenal goalkeeping coach Sal Bibbo. Lange met with Martinez's representatives in his first week at the club alongside Cutler and formed a bond that helped pave the way for his arrival. Martinez was pushy with the pair and emphasised how much he wanted to join Villa. From that point, it was all about the fee. Villa agreed to pay £17 million rising to £20 million and after signing Cash and Watkins the ability to take a man who had just won the FA Cup with Arsenal was seen as a big statement.

'Emi had a massive influence on everyone and made an instant impact,' Purslow recalls. 'We all felt like we were going to climb the ladder now. We were buying players that other clubs wanted and spending big money on fees and wages.'

'He was a great signing,' says Smith. 'A confident lad from day one and he has lived up to that with what he has done now.'

A joint signing day was arranged for Cash and Watkins – who are now great friends – to mark their step up from the Championship.

'It was one of my favourite days in football,' Purslow says. 'A lovely moment because Ollie and Matt came with a large group of family members and they were so proud and pleased to be signing for the great Aston Villa. The way they turned up to training from that moment was incredible. They were just so happy to be with us and that also had a huge effect on everybody.'

Villa's transfer window was now fully up and running and for some of the longer-serving staff this felt like the first window where the club were finally starting to flex their muscles. Lange put in processes that would help shape the future of the club and make recruitment more data-driven rather than agent-led.

The bold and ambitious moves continued but arguably the biggest deal of the window was for a player already on the books.

Despite genuine interest from Manchester United, Jack Grealish agreed to sign a new five-year contract, again on enhanced terms and now including a confidential £100 million release clause. Purslow promised him that further signings would arrive and reiterated the desire from Sawiris and Edens to take Villa into the higher reaches of the Premier League in the years ahead.

'The owners have made it very clear to me how ambitious they are and how they want to build Aston Villa,' said Grealish in a statement. 'There are exciting times ahead and I am very glad to be part of it. This is my club, my home and I am very happy here.'

Securing the future of Grealish was huge but Smith and Terry felt it was important to bring in more attacking players to help take the pressure off the star man. Bertrand Traoré joined soon after for £17 million from Lyon as a recommendation from Lange. Smith and Terry were excited, and the latter knew his qualities from his earlier years at Chelsea. The plan was to use Traoré on the right wing in an attempt to free up Grealish on the left, who was often man-marked or doubled up on because of his qualities. Traoré, an explosive if unpredictable winger, could also play as a striker if needed so that appealed to Villa, too.

The final piece of the jigsaw was to bring in Ross Barkley on loan from Chelsea, which felt like another statement signing. Grealish pestered the England midfielder, who was eager for more playing time, for three weeks to join. Purslow even invited him into his house to lay out the grand plans for the season ahead and explain how a move to Villa would help his chances of making the Three Lions squad for the European Championships that had been moved back to 2021. Smith, Lange and Terry all attended the meeting at Purslow's house to help convince Barkley that Villa was the place to be.

'My daughter made him and his agent some carrot cake which also helped,' Purslow says, laughing.

This new-look team had all the makings of an attack-minded outfit ready to ruffle a few feathers and upset some of the big boys in the division.

The additions were not only confined to the playing staff. In early August, Smith brought in his long-time friend Craig Shakespeare as assistant boss. While the head coach was happy with his current staff, Terry was still learning as a coach while O'Kelly, aged 63, was at the opposite end and without any elite-level experience to turn on prior to joining Villa.

Bringing in someone with more Premier League experience was seen as key. Shakespeare, the man recognised as 'the glue' that kept the Leicester City dressing room together during the 2015–16 title-winning season under Claudio Ranieri, added a new dimension to matchdays and in training. He had the experience of working in testing situations at Leicester and then again with England and at Everton under Sam Allardyce.

Bodymoor Heath was also undergoing a huge transformation and by the turn of the year Lange and Smith were both working out of new offices as the rebuild started.

The fact Villa would be a very different proposition this season was quickly evident as they won their first four matches of a league campaign for the first time in 90 years.

With the season opener at Manchester City postponed, due to the latter having been involved in the Champions League until mid-August, Villa's first league match – just as it had been when the previous season restarted – was at home to Sheffield United.

All the pre-match talk was of 'ghost goals' but it was Martinez who took the headlines, saving John Lundstram's first half penalty on his debut before Ezri Konsa got the only goal of the game in the second half.

'Emi had a similar impact to when JT arrived in 2017 in the way he re-energised the group,' Conor Hourihane recalls. 'Coming from a big club like Arsenal he had a vision of Aston Villa heading in the same direction. He put big demands on his defenders to keep clean sheets and then demands on the team to improve. He was a big driver for change.'

Goals from Grealish, Hourihane and Mings, who had also signed a new contract on the eve of the season, then helped Villa sweep Fulham aside in a 3–0 win at Craven Cottage. What followed in the third game of the season was a victory so spectacular and surprising that it sent shockwaves through the division.

Incredibly, Villa beat the champions Liverpool 7–2 in a performance of perfection that even earned applause from the opposition manager Jurgen Klopp. This was the night Watkins announced himself as a Premier League striker, scoring a wonderful hat-trick as Smith put together a plan to target Liverpool's high line. The aim was to press high and block off the passing lanes, a mission made considerably easier by the lack of composure of Adrian, the stand-in goalkeeper replacing the usually-reliable Alisson Becker, who was out injured.

Still, Liverpool had Virgil van Dijk, the best defender in the world, playing and a wealth of attacking riches. The best player on the pitch, though, was Grealish who set a record for five Premier League goal contributions in a game with two strikes and three assists. 'What is going on?' Villa's No. 10 roared as the fifth went in, and that's exactly what the few people fortunate to be inside the stadium were thinking as McGinn and Barkley added to the scoreline.

After all the work Villa had done on strengthening the defence during lockdown – and using Liverpool as the ideal case study – it was incredible that they were able to pick holes in that system with such ease. As was the image of the scoreboard on a night where it felt so cruel that supporters were kept out.

After a two-week international break, Villa went to Leicester and won again, this time through a last-minute winner from Barkley.

Two defeats followed, to Leeds and Southampton, but Villa then won 3–0 at Arsenal, Watkins scoring twice on a Sunday night in which he and Grealish stole the show.

'I loved playing with Jack because he's so unselfish and he wants to create goals more than he wants to score himself,' Watkins says. 'Whenever he got the ball he was always looking to find me because he wanted to see me score, as the striker, and that was amazing to have a team-mate like that.'

Martinez, put up for post-match media duties after the return to his former club, claimed Villa could target European football that season. Villa's style of play was winning plaudits. 'If Villa were walking down the road, they would be John Travolta from *Saturday Night Fever*,' proclaimed former Arsenal striker Ian Wright, analysing the game on the BBC's *Match of the Day*.

By the turn of the year Villa had already won nearly as many matches as they had in the whole of the previous season and sat sixth in the table, right in the thick of the race for European football. But the pandemic, now at its height, was about to have a serious impact on their progress. On 7 January, the club were forced to close their training ground after a significant outbreak saw nine players and five members of staff test positive for Covid-19. Despite all the strict protocols introduced by the Premier League, who were determined to keep their season running at a time the rest of the country had shut down, Villa's bubble had been breached. League matches against Tottenham and Everton were postponed, while the club was left with no option but to field their youth team in an FA Cup third round tie against Liverpool.

Mark Delaney, the Under-23s manager, had just 24 hours to prepare for what became one of the strangest games in Villa's long history. The team had an average age of just 18 and every player who featured was making their senior debut, against Liverpool's strongest XI. Parents dropped the players off at the stadium and a minibus was provided to take them all home. The youngsters performed admirably with Louie Barry providing one of the season's most memorable moments when he scored four minutes before half-time to cancel out Sadio Mane's opener. Liverpool's class, pressure and physical presence eventually told after the break with three goals in the space of five minutes but the 4–1 defeat still felt like a positive for Villa.

When the league season resumed on 20 January, Villa faced playing their final 23 Premier League matches of the season in the space of 123 days. It was a schedule which ultimately proved too much as their form began to tail off. Smith changed training time to allow players a later start, sensing that it may help, and there were still good results, including a 1–0 home win over Arsenal which completed the season double over the Gunners. But Smith's men were becoming far more inconsistent, losing 3–1 at home to West Ham in a match where the head coach described their defending as 'horrendous'.

'David Moyes said to me up until 1 January we were the best team in the league and I would agree with him,' says Smith. 'Whoever we played, it didn't matter. But then we had the Covid break, which messed it all about. I still have a defeat against Liverpool on my record and I watched it in my house!'

In mid-February came the ultimate hammer blow. Grealish sustained a shin injury and though Smith kept everyone guessing on the severity, Villa would not see their star man again until the final week of the campaign. A run of just two wins in 12 matches put paid to any European hopes.

Grealish's future was now becoming the subject of serious scrutiny. In many senses this was nothing new. Villa had long accepted it was impossible for a transfer window to go by without their captain being linked with a move elsewhere. Yet there was now a sense that some of his suitors were ready to firm up their interest. Manchester United were big admirers but also had Donny van de Beek and Jadon Sancho on their radar. The interest from rivals

Manchester City had grown, too, and during a Nations League game between England and Belgium in November, City midfielder Kevin De Bruyne told Grealish how much he rated his qualities and how his performances were attracting widespread praise.

The £100 million release clause in Grealish's contract at least offered Villa some protection. Of more immediate concern was City's interest in Douglas Luiz, the midfielder now vastly improved following a slow start the previous year. The Manchester club had a buy-back option valid until July 2021 on Luiz, who had been sold to Villa for £15 million in 2019. Villa's belief was the option would be exercised that summer so they decided to move fast in the January window by signing Morgan Sanson from Marseille as a Luiz replacement.

On paper, the deal looked an excellent one. Sanson, who Marseille had valued at £30 million the previous summer, was snared for just £13 million. As a player he ticked all the boxes on the data checks which were overseen by Lange and Mackenzie. After five seasons in Ligue 1 where he had performed to a high level and hardly missed a game, he appeared to be a safe bet.

But injuries and a difficulty adapting to life in the Premier League made it tough for the Frenchman and he was unable to recover from a slow start. It was a major blot on Lange's card and when Manchester City's football director, Txiki Begiristain, informed Villa after a game between the two teams in April that his manager, Pep Guardiola, would be extending the contract of the veteran midfielder, Fernandinho, and no longer taking up the option on Luiz, the move for Sanson began to look a waste of money. Accounts released in March would reveal Villa had lost £99 million during their first season back in the Premier League, so balancing the books would again become an issue.

After a successful loan at Doncaster Rovers in the previous season, Jacob Ramsey was emerging as a player with big potential and that would impact other more senior members of the squad.

Smith and Lange discussed the situation around Henri Lansbury, a midfielder who had struggled to find any real momentum since joining from Nottingham Forest in 2017, but was very popular in the dressing room with key players like Grealish and McGinn. It was decided that Lansbury must be moved on to free up space for Ramsey and by January 2021 his contract was mutually terminated, a little later than hoped.

Hourihane's time was also coming to an end as Ramsey slowly edged ahead of him in the pecking order. Smith was in no rush to let the Irishman go but such was his hunger to play regularly that he asked for a loan to Swansea City in the Championship where he would go on to make 18 appearances and score five goals.

One player who continued to impress was Ezri Konsa and he was rewarded with a new deal. Carney Chukwuemeka, meanwhile, emerged as the standout talent from a development team that would win the Youth Cup and go some way to justifying the huge spend on improving the academy under Mark Harrison. The 18-year-old was included in the first-team set-up in the closing stages which helped build positivity in Grealish's absence.

Martinez also equalled the club's Premier League record of 15 clean sheets in a season and would go on to star for Argentina in the Copa America win over the summer. What made the achievement even more impressive was the fact the goalkeeper had written down both targets on a sheet of paper at the start of the season, which he kept in his locker as a daily reminder and source of motivation.

The final two games of the season proved just how important the real star man, Grealish – described by Martinez as 'Messi with a right foot' – was to this team, as he returned to help see off Tottenham and Chelsea in a rousing end of season finish. For the first time in more than 14 months, supporters were permitted back into stadiums, with 10,000 attending the latter fixture at Villa Park. The 2–1 victory, over a team which would win the Champions

League the following weekend, saw Villa finish 11th in the table, their haul of 55 points the most by any team to ever finish in the bottom half of a 20-team Premier League table.

'We probably should have finished higher,' says Smith. 'But I wasn't too disappointed because the following season it gave us the opportunity to climb again. People forget once you get to 11th or 10th in the league the next step is the hardest step. Now you have to pass established European teams as well.'

Grealish agrees with Smith, adding: 'It was probably the best football I've ever played in my whole career.

'I was the fittest, strongest and fastest I have ever been, and obviously the most confident.

'I loved that season and I really thought we had a great balance in the team. The only thing that stopped us were the injuries and the Covid setbacks. I remember one point we were near the top and then after a lot of games we were still fourth and we deserved it. I genuinely think if me and Ross had stayed fit for the whole season we could have finished sixth or even a little bit higher.

'But I was so gutted that there were no supporters inside because that would have been amazing to have them with us when we were playing so well.'

Grealish's season was far from finished, though. That summer he would go on to play a key role in the England team which reached the final of a major international tournament for the first time since 1966, losing to Italy on penalties.

Manchester City were ready to move. The only question was whether they were prepared to pay the £100 million needed to get Grealish out of Villa.

11

SELLING JACK

'There's times now where I think what might have happened if I had stayed at Villa, it would have been nice to stay there for my whole career,' Grealish explains.

'But I know there would have been regrets about not playing Champions League football, not playing under Pep Guardiola and not playing with my idol Kevin De Bruyne. I just hope everyone understands that now.'

Grealish is speaking from the heart and revealing exactly what convinced him to join Manchester City in the summer of 2021 in a £100 million British record transfer deal.

'It wasn't that Villa didn't match my ambitions,' he says. 'I just felt like it was the perfect time for me to move on. I was coming off the back of the season where I had played my best ever football.

'I had a once in a lifetime opportunity to go and join what was easily the best team in England and what I thought was a top-two team in the world.

'It was a no-brainer, to go and work with a manager like Pep and see what he was all about. I couldn't turn it down because I didn't know if it would ever come again.'

For so long in his life, Grealish's dreams centred around Villa. He wanted to play alongside his hero, Gabriel Agbonlahor and celebrate in front of the Holte End. As a child he used to mimic doing the latter in the garden of his Solihull home, jumping into the bush pretending he was jumping into the stands. Another target was to score against rivals Birmingham City and he had ambitions to wear the armband and lead out his side.

After promising to be a part of the future when he signed a contract extension 12 months before City came calling, Grealish was focused on firing Villa up the Premier League and he loved his final season at the club more than any other.

Yet it was only a matter of time before professional ambition would take over those boyhood dreams, as he continued to meet every challenge he faced in claret and blue. Those inside the club knew it too. 'I always said we were probably a year, 18 months behind where we needed to be to keep Jack,' reflects Dean Smith. 'He needed to go to compete in Europe and for titles.'

Missing out on a move to Tottenham in the summer of 2018 had hurt Grealish but that feeling didn't last long, as he helped Villa win promotion and then scored the goal that kept his team in the Premier League on the final day of the following season. His performances were also the main reason why Villa were able to establish themselves back in the top flight.

Nagging away at him, though, was the chance to win trophies. The interest from City appealed so much because of their success in the Premier League. Guardiola's team had just been crowned Premier League champions for the third time in four years. Grealish wanted his skills to be recognised through titles and had seen how his friend and England team-mate, Harry Kane, also a City target that summer, had become frustrated at leading the way for so long at Tottenham but failing to convert any of that into silverware.

The fact City, beaten a few months earlier by Chelsea in the Champions League final, were yet to turn their domestic dominance into success on the continent also helped. Grealish wanted to be in the team that delivered European club football's biggest prize.

Moving to Manchester was life-changing and it wasn't far away from happening a year earlier for a fraction of the price. People within Grealish's inner circle were told City were ready to lodge a bid for him if Villa had been relegated in July 2020.

Guardiola praised his performances in previous games between the two sides, saying publicly: 'He's an exceptional player,' and admitting that he 'had a lot of information' on the attacker's qualities.

Manchester United had a similar plan but decided Ajax midfielder Donny van de Beek, with his experience of playing Champions League football, represented better value-for-money at just £35 million. How wrong that decision turned out to be. By the end of the 2020–21 season Grealish had become, undisputedly, the real deal, and was now worth significantly more than a year earlier.

The interest from United in the previous summer had proven distracting. During a training camp in Wales ahead of the 2020–21 season, Smith sensed Grealish wasn't 'quite mentally there' and decided to speak with his skipper when the squad returned to the Midlands.

'When we got back to Bodymoor I had a big, long chat with him and said: "Remember you are still captain,"' explains Smith. 'I told him whatever was going on in his head, to remember people were still looking up to him and to remember what he is to Villa.

'Those chats worked really well for Jack, I think. I am quite relaxed in my nature and I think it relaxed him more. The message was whatever will be, will be. Just stay relaxed.'

Grealish committed to Villa by signing his new deal, ironically on the day they played United in a pre-season friendly. Yet toward the end of the campaign, Smith sensed the mood had changed. 'We played Man City at home toward the end of April and before the game I was in the tunnel chatting to Pep [Guardiola] and their director of football Txiki Begiristain,' says Smith. 'Jack walked past and they said hello. Pep turned to me after and said: "I like him." I just smiled and said: "I know you do, but please leave him!" I always had the sense something was going on.'

It was not only at Villa that Grealish was now loved. He was also one of the most talked about players in the England setup and that summer would play his part in the Three Lions reaching the final of the European Championships.

Grealish's journey to England's senior team had been a lengthy one. Capped seven times for the Under-21s, having switched allegiance from the Republic of Ireland in 2015, he did not receive his first senior call-up until August 2020 and even that was due to Marcus Rashford pulling out of the squad due to injury. There was an unmistakable sense England boss Gareth Southgate wasn't so convinced about Grealish as many others were.

Despite nearly every television and radio pundit putting him in their preferred starting line-up for England's opening match of the Euros against Croatia, Grealish had to make do with a place on the bench. In truth, Southgate's decision to stick with Raheem Sterling was justified as the latter scored three times in the opening four matches of the tournament.

Yet it was Grealish, finally given his first taste of the action in the final group stage match against the Czech Republic, who would play a vital role in the last-16 triumph over Germany. With England struggling to break their opponents down, it was Grealish's name the Wembley crowd started chanting. This was a clear sign of just how popular Grealish, nicknamed England's Golden Boy in one *New York Times* article, had become. Bowing to the pressure from the stands, Southgate introduced Grealish off the bench and within a few minutes he played a part in the move that set up

Sterling for the opener and not long after that he crossed for Kane to double England's lead.

It was at this point when City's focus began to sharpen. Guardiola was well briefed on his qualities and excited at the thought of adding Grealish to an already talented squad. City liked his commercial appeal and pictured having this handsome, engaging and authentic star at the heart of their operation.

Grealish used the Euros to quiz City's England players, Sterling, Phil Foden and Kyle Walker about the intricacies of playing for Guardiola. He received positive feedback from each and began imagining life at the best-performing club in the country.

Encouraging words from his representatives followed as they were sure a huge money bid from City would be forthcoming. When England lost the final to Italy on 11 July – a game Grealish didn't even feature in – things began to gather pace.

Villa, having recorded their highest Premier League points total for 12 years, were not going to let their best player leave without a fight and had already rejected one offer from City earlier in the summer. Just as the previous year they had been proactive in the window, fending off competition from Arsenal to sign Emi Buendia from Norwich City in a club record deal worth a potential £38 million. Buendia was told he would be joining Villa to play alongside Grealish and not replace him. Villa also pushed to sign another attacking midfielder, Emile Smith Rowe, from Arsenal but were unable to match the salary increase he was offered at The Emirates. They came close to signing Michael Olise from Reading but he opted for Crystal Palace instead and one old face returned as Ashley Young, a player who made almost 200 appearances for the club between 2007 and 2011, re-signed from Inter Milan.

Finally, on 29 July, City submitted a bid of £100 million, hitting the release clause in Grealish's contract. Yet because the clause was confidential, City did not realise it and Villa were able, initially, to stall their response.

The prospect of giving Grealish, already the highest-paid player on the club's books, another pay rise was discussed. Purslow, who began to take centre stage as he desperately tried to keep Grealish at the club, set up a lengthy video call with the player and his parents in which he reminded them all of the No. 10's star quality and status at Villa. It was emotional and he questioned whether the timing was right for Grealish and if he would be given the same leading role at City with so much competition in his position.

It was all to no avail. Grealish's mind was long made up and City were not backing down, with their chairman Khaldoon Al Mubarak even discussing the bid on a telephone call with his Villa counterpart and long-time friend Nassef Sawiris.

Members of Grealish's inner circle, who knew about the £100 million clause, became increasingly perplexed when four days passed and the offer still hadn't been formally accepted. At the same time, they were reluctant to consider legal action as it was a route Grealish was desperate to avoid. With so much love and affection for Villa, he wanted his departure to be handled smoothly. Never once did he ask for Villa to lower their asking price despite City testing the water with a number of lower bids.

From Purslow's perspective, the delaying tactic was not to spite a player he loved watching and being in the company of, or even to extract more money out of City. The priority was always to keep Grealish and during a final push there was an offer to match his personal terms at City, yet the financial package, as rewarding as it would be, was never the motivating factor for the player. It was all about playing in the Champions League.

A key moment came when Grealish's father, Kevin, contacted Sawiris directly to explain how much his son wanted the move. Now the focus became rebuilding the squad in the wake of his impending exit with Villa keen to announce new signings before Grealish's sale went through, in part to ease the huge sense of disappointment which would be felt through the club's fanbase.

'I was flat out from the second Jack said he wanted his clause to be activated,' Purslow recalls. 'I was trying to process the sale and make sure that the incomings would be as contemporaneous as possible.'

It's why swift deals to bring in striker Danny Ings from Southampton and winger Leon Bailey from Bayer Leverkusen for a combined fee of £55 million would follow. Lange and his recruitment team had studied multiple players and initially liked Moussa Diaby – a team-mate of Bailey's at Leverkusen – but the asking price was too high. Wolverhampton Wanderers' Pedro Neto was the other option but when the Portugal international suffered a serious knee injury in April, his name was reluctantly scratched off the list.

In the meantime, for both Grealish and Villa, things were becoming a little awkward. With Covid restrictions still preventing most foreign travel, the squad was based at the Lensbury Club in Teddington for a pre-season training camp, and as talks over his move to City continued behind the scenes Grealish agreed to attend and even took part in a training session.

'I was asking Jack how close the move was and he said very close,' says Smith. 'I was speaking to Christian and Johan too so I knew the state of play. We certainly weren't pushing him too hard in training because we didn't want to risk injury. He did some technical stuff but otherwise we made sure he was a bit part player.'

Though everyone inside the club was now well aware the move was happening, photographs of Grealish in training raised false hope among supporters their hero might be staying. Grealish stayed tight-lipped when signing autographs for fans who had found the location of Villa's training camp before finally, on the evening of 3 August and with deals for Bailey and Ings virtually done, Purslow accepted City's offer.

The following day offered Grealish the chance to say farewell to his team-mates and club staff but even then there was an element of confusion. Smith had set up a meeting which would include a video call to staff back at Bodymoor Heath but at the last moment was pulled aside by the club's head of communications, Tommy Jordan. Purslow had been in touch to say the deal was not yet 100 per cent rubber stamped but with a room full of players in front of him and others watching from afar the head coach proceeded in any case.

'There were a few calls before saying we can't do it because it isn't done, but my response was: "We've done it. Don't worry,"' laughs Smith. 'I wanted Jack to have the opportunity to say goodbye to everyone at the club. He meant so much to the players but also the staff as well. The doctors and masseurs who had worked with him much longer than me. We had a video room at the hotel and he came in and spoke to everyone. I spoke about him and then he came and spoke and thanked everyone.'

Grealish broke down in tears when he addressed the team to say thank you and goodbye. After the meeting, he then killed time by playing a crossbar challenge with support staff as he waited for his official release and the green light to head north to Manchester for his medical the following morning. Eager to look his best in the promotion photos, he booked a haircut for later in the day and bought a new suit for his unveiling. Villa also had things to announce with the signings of Bailey and Ings now over the line.

Finally, at 8 p.m. on 5 August, Grealish's sale to City was confirmed. From Villa's end, it was done in extraordinary fashion in the form of a five-minute, almost presidential-style address in which Purslow spoke directly into a camera and explained, in almost unprecedented detail, the events which had led up to the sale, including the release clause and the club's efforts to keep their star man on board. There was also an insistence Grealish's exit had been mitigated by the signings of Buendia, Bailey and Ings, three players who combined would replace the skipper's 'creativity, assists and goals'.

'I want you all to be reassured that the board, Dean Smith, Johan Lange and I obviously knew this day might come and have planned accordingly,' said Purslow.

Even so, Grealish's exit was a difficult one for many supporters to take. The human qualities which made him so popular and seem more accessible than your average professional footballer in this case worked against him. For many fans, unable to separate Grealish the Villa fan from Grealish the ambitious footballer, it was as though their own son or brother had turned their back on the club.

'I remember my mom being a bit like that,' smiles Smith. 'She absolutely loves Jack and was asking me: "Why is he going?"

'He is an incredible guy. You can't not like him when you meet him. He is so humble. He still texts my kids on their birthdays. It is just the way he is. He is a top guy.'

Weeks after his exit, Grealish returned to Bodymoor Heath to present expensive gifts to a handful of staff members who helped him along the way. Some members, on modest salaries in comparison to those they work alongside, were shocked and almost reduced to tears themselves.

His departure wasn't easy for those at the club as McGinn recalls. 'I'll never forget the day I signed for Villa (in 2018), Jack was on the yellow bar (on SkySports), with the news that he wasn't going to Spurs. He didn't have a clue who I was but he was really supportive, other than on the first away game where we were rooming together and he requested to move! Now he's somebody I speak to pretty much every day.'

For Smith he was not only losing his best player but also his captain and a friend, with the pair of lifelong Villa supporters having developed a close bond which endures to this day. But he could also empathise with his player and understood entirely why he had to make the move. 'Ultimately you're a professional with a career to consider,' he says. 'It had been the same for me in 2018.

I'm a Villa fan but if I thought the club were in bad shape I would not have gone there. I would not have gone there if I thought: "Nah, I'm not going to last nine months with these guys."

'My disappointment was when Jack came back to Villa with City he did not get a good reception. That hurt me. They should have a statue outside the academy building for Jack. A British record signing for £100 million who came through our academy and supports the club? He was an incredible player for us.'

12

DEAN'S DREAM IS OVER

25 September 2021. It felt like a seismic day in the immediate post-Jack Grealish era for Villa.

A 1–0 win at Manchester United, just their second Premier League win over the Red Devils in a quarter of a century, sent Dean Smith's team into the top half of the table. Emi Martinez danced in front of the Stretford End after Bruno Fernandes blazed a stoppage-time penalty over the bar with Kortney Hause Villa's unlikely match-winner, having headed home an 88th minute corner. There are few other results which can convince Villa supporters their team is in a good place like beating United, such has been the latter's dominance in the fixture over recent decades. After a difficult start to the season plagued by injury, illness and international disputes, there was now a sense Smith's new-look side had turned a corner. There was life after Jack, after all.

And yet just six weeks later it would all be over, Smith sacked after a run of five straight defeats sent Villa plunging down the standings. Barely three months after one hero of the club's resurgence had departed in the shape of Grealish, so would another, only not in the way he desired.

'It just seemed to come from nowhere,' says Smith. Three years on, that feels a fair assessment. Yet in truth, the seeds of his demise were sown months before.

It was in early September, shortly after the closure of the transfer window, that Smith first sensed he and Villa's owners might have differing expectations for the season ahead. Though both Nassef Sawiris and Wes Edens had made clear on several occasions their long-term ambition to take the club back to the top table of European football, they did not set their head coach specific targets for an individual campaign.

'The target was always to improve, to progress,' explains Smith. It is why despite Villa being unlucky to miss out on a top half finish the previous season, the head coach wasn't too upset. 'It gave us opportunity to climb again,' he says. 'People forget once you get to 11th, 10th in the league the next step is the hardest step. Now you have to pass established European teams as well. We'd sold Jack, brought in three big signings. It was always going to take a bit of time to get to that next level.'

Smith had pretty much delivered the above message in public, during a Zoom call with journalists set up by Villa's communications department shortly after the end of the previous season. As one club insider put it at the time: 'The fans are expecting us to go and qualify for Europe next season. That is going to be a lot harder than people think.' The early summer press call was, essentially, an exercise in expectation management.

It was only when speaking to Sawiris and Edens, during a board meeting three matches into the campaign, that Smith realised the target the owners had in mind might be a little higher than his own. Villa's hierarchy, it is understood, felt that even after the sale of Grealish they now had a squad capable of challenging for a top-eight position.

'We used to have regular board meetings,' says Smith. 'I had gone away with my wife and I remember sitting there speaking to the owners. Christian (Purslow) and Johan (Lange) were on there as well. We had four points from the first three games. But because our opponents had been Watford, who had just come up, Brentford who had just come up and Newcastle, I knew straight away the owners expected nine points. I could hear it in the tone of their voices. I said to my wife after this is going to be a tough season, because I know now what they are looking for.'

Grealish's sale might have been the most high-profile departure of the summer but it was not the only significant exit. There had also been a big change on the coaching staff with both John Terry and Richard O'Kelly departing and Aaron Danks and Austin MacPhee, a specialist set-piece coach, arriving. Some form of reshuffle had long been mooted but ended up being much bigger than anticipated. Smith had been told, after successfully lobbying to bring Craig Shakespeare on board the previous summer, that he would have to restructure his coaching staff 12 months later.

'The club felt four, with me, Shakey, JT and Rich was too many,' he explains. 'It was a case of them saying OK to having one season with four and then one of them has to move. So there was a bit of pressure on me.'

For much of the season, there had been a belief the problem would solve itself. After more than two years as assistant head coach, there was an expectation Terry would soon strike out on his own and become a boss in his own right. He had previously been linked with the vacant job at Bristol City in 2020 and insiders at Villa thought it was only a matter of time before he left to pursue his long-stated ambition of becoming a manager. But for whatever reason, the opportunity he was seeking never materialised.

Even then, there was a sense Terry would be leaving in any case. His family were still based in Surrey and he had never bought a place of his own in the Midlands, instead choosing to stay at the Belfry Hotel for four or five nights a week since first joining Villa as a player in 2017. This arrangement actually led to one comical incident early in the pandemic when, with the hotel closed, the former Chelsea and England captain briefly lived in his wife Toni's horse transporter on the Bodymoor Heath car park.

'He and his brother drove it up from his house and JT ended up living in it for a bit when we returned to training,' laughs Smith. 'To be honest, I wouldn't have minded living in it. It wasn't your normal horsebox. It was more like a Winnebago!'

Having spent so long away from his family in the past four years, Terry had told Smith he was considering leaving as the 2020–21 season drew to a close. Ultimately, he decided to carry on for another season but this left Smith searching for a new role for his long-time assistant O'Kelly. A new post was created which would see him work as a link between the first team and the Under-21s.

This was the setup heading into pre-season but very soon there were problems. Smith, for one thing, contracted Covid and missed warm-up matches against Walsall and Stoke. Terry was also absent and very quickly the reason became clear. Despite initially deciding to stay on, Terry had undergone a change of heart.

'I want to be as respectful to the manager and everyone at Aston Villa as I can and, having given my future serious consideration over the summer, I genuinely don't feel it is fair to move into a new season without being certain of seeing that through,' he explained in a statement.

This posed a problem as O'Kelly had already been moved into his new role and – as it quickly transpired – wasn't particularly enjoying it. He visited Smith after Villa's final pre-season match, a 3–1 friendly win against Italian club Salernitana, to explain his feelings.

'Rich said: "I'm not sure I can do this." He was not sure he could be a bit-part player because previously he had been all-in,' says Smith. 'It was a really tough conversation but I told him only he could make the decision.'

From a position where he expected to lose one coach, Smith had now lost two and though Birmingham-born Danks, then assistant to Vincent Kompany at Anderlecht, was identified by Villa as a young, up and coming coach who could add a new dimension to the backroom team, he did not join until September. That meant fans who arrived early for the opening day match at Watford were greeted with the sight of Smith, who usually watched warm-ups from the tunnel, cup of tea in hand, running the shooting drills, such was the temporary lack of coaching staff.

There had been other issues in the build-up to the opening game too. Grealish's sale and the arrival of both Danny Ings and Leon Bailey had gone through just 10 days before the start of the season, leaving little time for the pair to get accustomed to their new surroundings. Axel Tuanzebe, who returned for a third loan, was not as sharp as when he went back to Manchester United two years earlier, and Bailey's efforts were not helped when, almost immediately after signing, he contracted Covid and had to isolate. When Ollie Watkins sustained a knee injury in the friendly against Salernitana, ruling him out of the season's opening weeks, it meant Smith had to fast track Ings into the starting XI quicker than planned.

Ings' signing, which was a surprise to many supporters, although not the handful of journalists who knew in advance of the rushed announcement on 4 August, was regarded as something of a coup. The 29-year-old had scored 35 Premier League goals in three seasons at Southampton and earned a recall to the England squad the previous year. Villa were not sure he would even be available to sign until late on. Instead, the majority of their effort to that point had been focused on bringing back Tammy Abraham on a permanent deal. Smith had met with the striker, one of the heroes of the 2019 promotion and still hugely popular with supporters, to discuss the move. The difficulty came in negotiating a deal with Chelsea, who wanted to insert a buy-back clause.

'That was the sticking point for us,' says Smith. 'We wanted Tammy to be our player. We didn't want them to have the opportunity to buy him back if he scored 25 goals. We'd also been working on Danny but weren't sure we could get him. That one became Christian's baby. He kept it so quiet and was so proud of that.'

Some media outlets, including *The Athletic*, were preparing to run the story before it was revealed by the club, in what became the peak period of paranoia for Purslow as he tried to prevent leaks around transfer stories.

Smith saw the experienced Ings, who joined in a deal worth £30 million, as the ideal competition for Watkins. Yet there was also an acknowledgement the new arrival would need time getting up to speed. Watkins' injury, however, meant he could not be afforded it and by this point it became clear that Wesley, now a shadow of the player Villa signed two years earlier, would no longer be able to cut it in the Premier League following his horrific injury.

'Danny was not up to doing 90 minutes at that time,' says Smith. 'He'd had a few injuries in his career and got managed differently at Southampton to how we wanted to manage him. I remember his first session we did a shooting drill and he said he hadn't done that for three years. He was coming from a certain way of training to a different way of training. We were building him up but he had to play straight away.'

Even with the disruption, Smith expected a better performance than he got at Watford against the newly-promoted Hornets, in what was the first game Villa had played in a full stadium since the 4–0 defeat at Leicester nearly 18 months previously. Villa, who had record buy Emi Buendia in the starting XI, never got going in the first half and were 2–0 down at the break. Matt Targett, who had endured a nightmare against winger Ismaila Sarr in the club's last visit to Vicarage Road, suffered a déjà vu experience and was taken off at half-time. The left-back had been so poor he apologised to

Smith in the dressing room. A stunning goal from Chuco Hernandez then put the hosts three to the good and though Villa did rally late, with Ings scoring his first goal for the club from the penalty spot after John McGinn had pulled one back, Smith left his players in no doubt the performance had been well below expectations.

Bailey, who came on at the hour mark, provided some positives with his performance but then suffered an injury during training the following week. So too did his fellow winger Bertrand Traoré and misfortune, leading to constant changes to the starting line-up, became a feature of the early weeks.

Though no-one could have known it at the time, the second half at Watford was one of just two occasions Buendia, Ings and Bailey, the three players intended to replace Grealish, would be seen on the pitch together under Smith. It was rarely a decision the head coach made through choice.

The manner of the performance at Vicarage Road led to inevitable questions as to whether Villa were suffering from a hangover following the loss of their talisman. It was a narrative which was impossible to escape. In an interview with the *Express & Star* on the eve of the season, Ezri Konsa had expressed a desire to prove wrong the 'doubters' who accused Villa of having been a one-man team. On that score, it had not been a great start.

Ings at least lifted the mood with a superb acrobatic volley to set Villa on their way to victory over Newcastle the following weekend. But the build-up to the next match against Brentford proved something of a nightmare. Tyrone Mings, who Smith had selected as captain following Grealish's departure, missed out with a rib injury while John McGinn, the other man who had been in contention for the armband, went down with Covid on the eve of the game. So too did Jacob Ramsey. Buendia, who had struggled in his first two matches, earned Villa a point with a superb goal but then saw his progress stall after both he and Martinez were called up to the Argentina squad.

Though the pandemic was easing, restrictions on international travel remained strict. By travelling back home, both players would be entering a 'red zone' country, where cases of the virus remained high according to the UK government. That would require them to isolate for 10 days in a hotel upon their return or, as they and Villa chose, travel back via a green zone country where they could train for 10 days. It meant that, after a farcical trip which saw Argentina's World Cup qualifier against Brazil postponed when Martinez was among several players accused of not having followed Covid protocols, the Villa pair spent more than a week in Croatia training alone at the facilities of Hajduk Split. Both missed the 3–0 defeat at Chelsea after the international break, a match in which Villa performed well and recorded 18 shots on goal with six on target, only for Mings to make a major error when they were on top. They eventually landed back in the UK on the morning of the next game, at home to Everton. Though Martinez played, Buendia was only on the bench having missed out on all the tactical planning.

'It was a nightmare period,' recalls Smith.

The Everton match perhaps summed up Villa's luck at that point, with Bailey inspiring them to a 3–0 win after coming off the bench but then being forced off before the final whistle, having suffered a hamstring injury which would keep him out for nearly a month. Then came the win at United, a huge one for supporters and a special day for Smith, even though he did his best to play it down in the pre-match press conference.

'I knew how much that result meant to our fans,' says Smith. 'They'd had so many bad days at Old Trafford so to win there felt really good.'

Villa went to Tottenham for the final match before the next international break in confident mood, knowing victory would likely put them into the top six. But they could not follow up the Old Trafford display, falling to a 2–1 defeat in a match only memorable for Watkins finally getting off the mark for the season.

The biggest blow, certainly in terms of the team's psychology, came in the next game at home to Wolverhampton Wanderers. Leading 2–0 and apparently in control with 10 minutes remaining against their Midlands rivals, Villa contrived to concede three times and fall to defeat. Smith left the players alone for 15 minutes as he studied the closing stages of the game before sharing his thoughts. It was an angry dressing room because of the manner of Villa's downfall. Fingers were pointed at individuals who made costly mistakes. Morgan Sanson, who ripped off his training bib on the sidelines and sat sulking in the dugout when he was overlooked by Smith as the third and final substitute, had reached the nadir. Smith would describe the defeat as a 'travesty'. Inside he was raging, his mood not helped by a rare appearance from Edens who had already made it clear just weeks earlier that high standards were expected this season.

Villa still looked shell-shocked the following Friday night, when a first half no-show set them on route to a 3–1 defeat at Arsenal. That result made it three Premier League losses in a row for the first time since before the pandemic and heading into the next fixture, at home to West Ham, Smith made a big call.

Since Watkins had returned to fitness, Villa had been playing with three central defenders to make it easier to include two strikers in the line-up. Yet Smith had started to feel his team had become too passive as a result and too happy to sit back. At half-time at Arsenal he switched to a back four and decided he would keep that system against the Hammers. That meant dropping a defender and to the surprise of many arriving at Villa Park for the Sunday evening kick-off, the man to make way was Mings.

There was no doubt the England international had been some way below his best and in many ways he could have few complaints with the head coach's decision. But dropping the captain was still a big call and Smith needed it to work. Instead, Villa were beaten 4–1 in a match which saw Ezri Konsa, who partnered Kortney Hause at the back, sent off.

'When you have lost four on the spin you suddenly think, where has that come from?' says Smith. 'We were just trying to get people back fit. Leon had only just come back from injury, while Emi Buendia had been in and out.'

The run of four straight defeats, ahead of another Friday night away match, this time at Southampton, led to reports Smith's position was under threat. Another international break was on the horizon, a dangerous moment for struggling managers due to the extra time it provides clubs to find a successor. Smith himself felt secure until, just a few hours before kick-off at St Mary's, he bumped into a trusted member of staff at the team hotel.

He explains: 'I had someone at the club to whom I once said: "Listen, if you ever hear anything make sure you let me know. I would rather it came from you." Everything was fine. Then four or five hours before the game, I saw him and he says: "I've been told if you don't win tonight, there's a chance you could go." When you know that, your mind is like right, OK.'

The night could not have got off to a worse start. Less than three minutes were on the clock when Matty Cash misjudged a long ball and Adam Armstrong, who had not scored with any of his previous 25 shots on target, thumped a finish into the top corner. Villa were poor for the rest of the half and though they rallied after the break the goal remained elusive. Ings, by now, had joined the list of absent players, along with midfielder Douglas Luiz, both having suffered soft tissue injuries. Smith's final two substitutions as Villa boss would be to bring young strikers Cameron Archer and Keinan Davis off the bench. This was certainly not the strike force Villa had envisioned when they sold Grealish, but for all the mitigation and the fact the travelling supporters at St Mary's Stadium gave the head coach a decent reception at the finish, there was a sense it would not matter. Defeat left Villa sitting 15th in the Premier League table.

Matt Targett pushed the case for the defence in his post-match interview when he declared: 'There's only so much a manager can do.' Others were not so supportive as one player was heard close to the dressing room saying: 'Hopefully that's him done.'

Smith, meanwhile, called Purslow, as he did after every match. 'He said they had a board meeting on the Saturday and when I asked if he wanted me on it, he said no,' says Smith. 'I asked if everything was OK, do I need any backing? He said it was a normal board meeting. But I knew in the back of my mind what was happening.'

Smith's instincts were correct. At the board meeting on Saturday evening, it was decided a change was required. At that point, Smith was sat at home, hoping for the best but in his heart resigned to the inevitable. 'My two best mates came round and we had a few drinks,' he says. 'We were celebrating what was Villa because I knew it was going to happen.'

At around 9.30 on the Sunday morning, the text from Purslow arrived. It read: 'I am at Bodymoor Heath. Can you come and see me? I'm here alone.'

'I spoke to the kids first,' says Smith. 'I said to my wife: "Phone Jamie, I'm just going in to get sacked." There are definitely emotions but I have been in the game too long to know it is just the way it is.'

The official announcement, when it came, was greeted with sadness by supporters, in stark contrast to almost every managerial exit from Villa arguably dating back to Brian Little nearly a quarter of a century earlier. Even those fans who felt it was time for change recognised a cherished era had ended. There were countless social media posts from players, including one from Grealish, in which he called Smith the 'real GOAT'.

Even Purslow was cut up, saying now: 'On a personal level it was incredibly hard. Dean is the nicest guy I've met in football. By the time he left I considered him an extremely good friend which is always difficult when someone works for you, but it was strictly business. It was an easy decision professionally but extremely difficult personally. It was helped by the fact that his place in the club's history was guaranteed.'

Smith had walked into a club at risk of tearing itself apart in October 2018 and brought unity, promotion and consolidation back in the Premier League. At least twice previously in his reign he had been on the brink and on both occasions turned it round. This time he would not be given the chance. In a statement released by the League Managers' Association the following day, he expressed his gratitude to Sawiris and Edens and thanks to Purslow, Suso and Lange for the support they had provided during his tenure.

'I thought really hard about what I was going to put in my statement,' says Smith. 'I believe we would have turned it round. But they decided otherwise.

'I just felt there had been a lot of turnaround at the club in the previous six to nine months. In terms of coaching staff, playing staff. Trying to move to the next level takes time. We'd lost a talismanic player too in Jack. There will always be the people who say it was only because of Jack Grealish. But it doesn't bother me. He would be the first to say I helped him as much as he helped me. We will be friends for all time.'

It's rare that a club sells its best player and improves. Villa were one of only a handful of clubs in Europe who relied so heavily on an individual. When Tottenham Hotspur sold Gareth Bale in 2013 they struggled. At the point of writing, Barcelona have never scored more goals in a season since Lionel Messi left in 2021. The club needed time to adjust but the cut-throat nature of the Premier League rarely allows that.

Villa's statement referenced a record of 18 defeats in 35 Premier League matches since the start of the calendar year. While that statistic was undoubtedly poor, there was also a sense that ever since the club had been forced to close its training ground in January due to the Covid outbreak, at a time when the team was riding high in the league, Smith had barely caught a break. For a lifelong Villa supporter, the most important thing was being able to leave with his head held high.

'I've always said that I was simply a custodian of this great club and my aim was to leave it in a better place than I found it,' he wrote in his statement. 'I believe that together we have achieved that.'

There could be no arguing that point. For Villa's board, the onus was on finding a successor with the skills to build on Smith's fine work. Whoever they chose was going to have the unusual challenge for an incoming Villa boss of having a difficult act to follow.

13

THE GERRARD EXPERIMENT

It was Steven Gerrard's hunger which helped him land his first job as a manager in the Premier League. Rather than staying at Rangers, where he had just won the Scottish title in his third season as head coach, the 41-year-old saw Villa as the perfect next step in a managerial career he hoped would be just as successful as the one he enjoyed as a player.

When Gerrard hung up his boots in 2016 he did so as a legend of the modern game, with more than 700 appearances for Liverpool under his belt, most of them as captain, along with being one of the select group to collect more than 100 caps for England. There was a Champions League winners medal in his cabinet, together with a host of other achievements and accolades.

A move into management seemed inevitable and Gerrard turned down his first offer within days of his retirement, admitting the opportunity to take charge of MK Dons, a club in English football's third tier, had arrived a 'bit too soon'.

Instead, he returned to Liverpool, accepting the role of coach in the club's academy to build experience while completing the UEFA A Licence course. When he became the Liverpool Under-18s manager it was clear he was serious about working his way up. The long-term ambition was to one day manage the team for whom he had played almost his entire club career.

Accepting the job at Rangers in 2018 had proved a shrewd move. The Scottish giants, who had gone through a financial crisis earlier in the decade which had seen them relegated to the bottom division, were lagging well behind their Glasgow rivals Celtic. Over the course of three seasons, Gerrard righted the ship and eventually claimed the title which prevented Celtic winning what would have been a record 10th championship in a row. That same season there had been a deep run into the knockout rounds of the Europa League. Gradually, Gerrard was building a reputation as a promising young manager. He'd already turned down a handful of opportunities in the Premier League and the Championship and by the time Villa decided to move on from Smith he was firmly on their radar.

An existing relationship with Purslow, from the latter's time as Liverpool's managing director, certainly helped. Gerrard and his Reds team-mate Jamie Carragher had attended Purslow's 50th birthday party. They trusted each other.

Yet while to the outside world his appointment, just four days after Smith was sacked, seemed swift, it was no coronation. Other candidates were interviewed at length. Admittedly, Villa's pursuit of Graham Potter barely got off the ground when it became clear that Brighton wanted around £18 million in compensation and the owners were not prepared to spend anywhere near that. But Thomas Frank, the manager of Brentford, and Southampton boss Ralph Hasenhüttl had qualities that also appealed. However, Gerrard, when interviewed, set a very high standard.

Villa sporting director Johan Lange posed Gerrard a series of testing questions, wanting to know how he would respond in certain situations. In return, Gerrard put together a presentation lasting five hours where he pinpointed exactly what he would do with each player, how he would help the team progress, and what he would bring if appointed. 'It was an outstanding interview and left us in no doubt that we were on with the right man,' Purslow would later claim.

The manner in which Gerrard had handled the pressure at Rangers, a club where the scrutiny is so great managers can feel as though they are living in a goldfish bowl, had also impressed Villa's hierarchy. Purslow and Lange quickly came to the view this was a man with big potential, primed to return to the Premier League sooner rather than later. If Villa didn't make the move, it might be one they would live to regret.

As part of the negotiations, Villa agreed to pay the release clause in Gerrard's contract at Rangers of just under £3 million. A similar clause inserted in the three-and-a-half year deal he signed at Villa was set at a far higher bar – £25 million to be precise. Purslow's reasoning was if Gerrard dragged the club away from the relegation zone and into the top half, and other bigger clubs were interested in hiring him, they would have to stump up a huge amount to prise him away. Both Purslow and Lange were excited by the appointment. There was a sense Villa's chief executive was slightly overdoing it, however, when he described Gerrard's appointment as a 'fantastic moment' in Villa's history at the new head coach's unveiling. Within the space of a year they were words which would come back to haunt him.

Central to Gerrard's plans was Michael Beale, his tried-and-trusted first-team coach who had great responsibility at Rangers and would assume a similar big role at Villa. A highly-rated coach, Beale had turned down offers to manage in the Championship himself just weeks earlier. He agreed to join Villa and place his own personal ambitions to one side because Gerrard was so excited about the project. With the freedom to bring their entire backroom team from Rangers, the belief in their way of working was such they were confident success in Scotland could be replicated in England.

While Gerrard would be the face, leader and standard-setter, with Gary McAllister – previously assistant to Gerard Houllier at Villa a decade previously – returning to the club in the same role, Beale would do virtually all the coaching and take most team meetings too, which Villa were comfortable with.

Tom Culshaw (technical coach), Scott Mason (lead analyst) and Jordan Milsom (head of fitness and conditioning) also moved south but Villa wanted to keep coach Aaron Danks, set-piece specialist Austin MacPhee and goalkeeping coach Neil Cutler, something which caused a little friction and left some staff members feeling disconnected. From the start, the coaching team felt too big and no longer would every voice be heard.

The loudest and most prominent voice was Beale. He had first built his reputation working in the Chelsea academy and then moved to Liverpool as Under-23s manager, where he met Gerrard, before spending a short period in Brazil as the first-team coach at São Paulo. Well-travelled and strong in his beliefs, Beale was not afraid to take the wheel at Villa. He had a clear methodology and though players felt the level of coaching went up considerably upon his arrival, his frankness of personality occasionally ruffled feathers. Some players and staff members felt, at times, he would be too demanding. Even in the early stages he was not afraid to single out players if he felt they weren't pulling their weight. Compared to what had come before under Smith and Shakespeare, when such conversations would generally be held in private, it was a big shake-up.

Initially, the methods worked well. Villa's new coaching staff had just three days of full training at the end of the international break to prepare for the visit of Brighton, where they would be looking to end a run of five straight defeats. They spent one day working on a shape out of possession, another focusing on the system in possession, then specific match-related movements for the game at Villa Park.

The club needed a lift because there was a feeling of sadness following Smith's departure and Gerrard could sense that from within. He spoke passionately about getting off to a good start in a team meeting and told all the staff at Bodymoor Heath that he would do his best to make the training ground a positive place, and that on matchday if his mood changed it would be because it was time for business. Every department felt his energy and enthusiasm. At the press conference for his unveiling – the first in-person briefing at Villa Park for nearly two years as Covid restrictions eased – he also said all the right things and handled the tough questions with class and composure. 'This is not going to be about changing things overnight,' he admitted. Perhaps, then, the transformation arrived quicker than expected.

Villa beat Brighton 2–0 thanks to late goals from Ollie Watkins and Tyrone Mings. The game plan of being more solid, compact, and blocking off central areas worked well and, while the match could hardly be described as a thriller, Watkins' excellent 84th minute goal prompted the new head coach to celebrate wildly with his coaching staff. After Mings grabbed the second soon after, Gerrard marched down the touchline, pumping his fists in delight.

A 2–1 win away at Crystal Palace was impressive the following weekend and a feelgood factor was returning to Bodymoor Heath. Gerrard made subtle changes around the training ground, removing sauces from the menu in the canteen and slightly amending the travel arrangements before games. While his standing in the game gave him an aura which meant players immediately looked up to him, the new boss also had a softer, considered side.

Training ground staff initially approached interactions with him carefully, not fully understanding his personality and how he would respond. It didn't take long to see there were no real barriers. Gerrard was as fun and engaging to be around as he was inspiring. He had light-hearted banter with support staff to make them feel at ease and took an open and honest approach with the media.

The early fixtures presented some tough examinations on paper and though there were defeats to Manchester City and Liverpool, the latter at Anfield where Gerrard handled the return to his former club about as well as possible, both were by a single-goal margin. Youngster Carney Chukwuemeka missed a great chance to equalise against City and a win over Leicester, which made it three wins from Gerrard's opening five games, still represented a good start.

It became four wins from six when Villa won 2–0 at Norwich in an early reunion with former boss Smith, who had taken charge at Carrow Road. The appointment was earning widespread praise in the mainstream media and Gerrard began to lift Villa's profile.

'I think when any manager gets sacked and a new manager comes in there's always a new lease of life,' Matty Cash explains. 'Gerrard was great for me because I like to get forward and attack as much as I can and in that season I did it really well. I was playing with freedom and no fear and I feel like we started off really well under him.'

Watkins, who scored in the first two home games under Gerrard, recalls the main difference. He explains: 'We got off to a really good start, he showed us that our running stats were the lowest in the Premier League, so he made us run a lot harder and work harder. That in itself helped us win more games and create a togetherness to fight for each other.'

The first hiccup arrived when midfielder Marvelous Nakamba suffered a serious knee injury. Described to Gerrard upon his arrival at Villa as 'limited', the Zimbabwe international, who had often struggled to hold down a regular starting place since joining from Club Brugge in 2019, had nevertheless established himself as a key component in the new head coach's team. The coaching staff thought Nakamba was outstanding and loved his attitude, application and how willing he was to execute the specific instructions he was given.

In the first five games he became one of Villa's most consistent performers, benefiting greatly from playing in a narrow formation with a shorter distance between team-mates. His passing accuracy improved and his presence in front of the defence allowed Douglas Luiz, a more naturally gifted midfielder, to play further forward.

Another player who stepped up in the early weeks of Gerrard's reign was Ashley Young. Though signed by Smith to primarily play full-back, Gerrard often used his former England team-mate in an advanced position, replicating the 'Christmas Tree' formation he used at Rangers which essentially consists of four defenders, three central midfielders, two inverted wingers and a striker. Young immediately became a key figure as Gerrard and Beale leaned on his experience and winning mentality. They wanted the 36-year-old to be a conduit between the coaches and the players as he was the only member of the team who had performed at the highest level and fought regularly for top honours with both Manchester United and Inter Milan. Gerrard had many discussions with Young about the motivation of the players and how in an elite environment, with state-of-the-art facilities, there should be more elite players on board. 'There will be a no-excuse culture here,' Gerrard said early into his time, and supporters were buying into the change. 'I liked his swagger and I liked the way he talked,' recalls Mo Razzaq.

The initial upturn in results had lifted the club away from the relegation places but momentum began to stall around Christmas. A home match with Burnley was postponed after several players contracted Covid, while Gerrard himself missed a 3–1 Boxing Day defeat to Chelsea after himself coming down with the virus. The head coach returned in the New Year but could do nothing to prevent Villa tumbling to a 2–1 defeat at Brentford, before they were then knocked out of the FA Cup at Manchester United, on a night when Gerrard – never a popular figure at Old Trafford

– turned to face the abuse from the Stretford End as he walked to the dugout.

By then the transfer window was open and Villa were about to make a major splash by signing one of the most high-profile players in world football. Philippe Coutinho had become the second most expensive player of all time when he moved from Liverpool to Barcelona for £141 million in 2018. While he had struggled for consistency at the Nou Camp, the notion of him joining Villa, a mid-table Premier League club, still seemed rather far-fetched even if they did have his former Liverpool team-mate in charge.

But Villa and Gerrard were serious. The Brazilian's name had first cropped up during conversations between the head coach, Purslow and Lange in the weeks leading up to Christmas. Gerrard insisted it was a move which should be explored, largely because he wanted more 'proven winners' at the club. Coutinho certainly ticked that box, having won trophies at Barcelona and the Champions League while on loan at Bayern Munich.

The prospect of signing Coutinho also excited Villa's ownership. Sawiris, it's understood, took immediate interest after learning Gerrard had held a positive Zoom call with the player. Coutinho was willing to join Villa on loan, at first solely because of Gerrard, but then because he started to believe in the sporting project he was being presented. Purslow, a fluent Spanish speaker, was tasked with negotiating a deal with Barcelona, who were keen to get a chunk of the 29-year-old's £25 million-a-year salary off their books in order to comply with the Spanish league's salary cap. An option to make the deal permanent in the summer for a fee of £33 million was included.

Coutinho's signing undoubtedly raised Villa's profile and excited the dressing room. Many of the English-speaking players asked his fellow countryman, Luiz, for updates to see if it was true and were genuinely surprised at the news. It felt fair to describe the signing as something of a coup. The fact Coutinho was only being signed on loan also made the move relatively low risk, if a little expensive.

Villa could argue it also demonstrated ambition and Coutinho's signing did help convince the French left-back, Lucas Digne, to join from Everton for £25 million. This signing, more than any other, marked a shift in policy away from the 'young and hungry' mantra preached under Smith. Like Coutinho, Digne was in his late twenties and signed a deal which would make him one of the highest earners at the club.

Gerrard wanted another midfielder and identified Rodrigo Bentancur of Juventus as a good option but the Uruguay international instead moved to Tottenham Hotspur. Atletico Madrid's Geoffrey Kondogbia was another top target, while Villa failed in a last-minute £25 million bid for Brighton's Yves Bissouma after the Seagulls told them they valued the Mali international at twice that amount.

'If a move is not right we will not become desperate and make decisions we don't think are right,' said Gerrard. 'If it's not right at the time, we might have to be patient.' Already, Villa were making overtures to the representatives of Boubacar Kamara, a midfielder at Marseille due to be out of contract and available for free in the summer. Villa, meanwhile, rejected tentative approaches for Luiz. Though the Brazilian was struggling for consistency, Gerrard and his coaching staff were convinced he could still be a major asset in their team.

Arguably the most important signing of the window was of a player already at the club. Emi Martinez, now the most high-profile player at Villa following his superb first season and exploits at the Copa America, agreed a new five-and-a-half year contract, the value of which would only grow later in the year when he would help Argentina win the World Cup. Gerrard and Beale played a huge role in convincing Martinez, who had a growing list of suitors, Villa was the place to be and the shot-stopper provided some notable insight into the pair's working relationship during an interview with Amazon Prime.

'It's the first time in 14 to 15 years of my career that the assistant coach does all the talking,' he said. 'With Michael, we feel him and Stevie G are both the managers.'

Coutinho and Digne were clearly Gerrard's signings, though the loan arrival of Sweden international goalkeeper Robin Olsen from FC Copenhagen was a Lange deal. The new head coach also allowed Matt Targett to leave for Newcastle on loan while Axel Tuanzebe, who had made just two brief substitute appearances under Gerrard, went back to Manchester United so he could join Italian side Napoli. Villa's final signing of the window came completely out of the blue as Calum Chambers arrived from Arsenal on a free transfer. Gerrard liked the 27-year-old's ability to play in both defence and midfield and described Villa's overall business in the window as 'extremely strong'.

Coutinho was clearly the star attraction and the Brazilian, who had not played for more than a month, made an impressive start by coming off the bench and scoring the equaliser in a 2–2 draw with Manchester United. His complete lack of ego, despite his fame, meant he quickly became a popular figure at the training ground. Coutinho's respect for the coaching staff – he called every one of them 'Mister' – rubbed off on his team-mates, who were also struck by his immense quality. So good was Coutinho on one occasion in training that fellow players started applauding him off the pitch. Yet for a player who possessed just flair on the pitch, off it he was quiet and humble. When he was unveiled to the Villa Park crowd before kick-off it was clear he was uncomfortable with all the attention.

The trouble was the impact his arrival had on Emi Buendia. Having struggled in the early months following his club record move from Norwich, the Argentine was beginning to find his feet, scoring the only goal in a 1–0 win at Everton. Gerrard admired his hunger and publicly praised his winning attitude, even if he wasn't always able to keep a lid on his emotions. 'He is a little competitor, he is tenacious but I don't mind any of that,' he said. 'That's the mentality I want in all of my players. If we can get everyone in the same place as Emi, controlled, we will be alright.'

Yet while Buendia and Coutinho had a strong relationship off the pitch, efforts to pair them effectively together as a creative 'dream team' proved fruitless. The win at Goodison Park was the only time Villa won a match they both started and after two straight defeats, to Newcastle and then at home to Watford, an afternoon which saw the team booed off, it was abundantly clear Gerrard and Beale needed to pick between the two.

It was Coutinho who got the nod for the following week's trip to Brighton and he played his part as Villa won 2–0 to stop the rot. Gerrard had urged his players to 'wake up fast' after the dire Watford defeat and in the days before the trip to the Amex Stadium a team-bonding session of social activities and a meal was held in a bid to boost morale.

It was an opportunity to switch off and hit the restart button. Tweaks were made to the gameplan, an acceptance that attempts to be more dominant in possession were not working as well as initially hoped. The build-up to the match was chaotic. Villa were staying 40 minutes from the stadium but turned up late due to a crash on a nearby road that forced a delayed kick-off. It was a logistical nightmare but amid the disruption Gerrard found inspiring words in a team talk players now reflect on as one of his best.

Sometimes the head coach would write motivating words or reminders of their duties underneath the names on the team sheet. This time he told the players to think about their families and whether they would be proud of the way they performed, and encouraged each individual to earn the right to enjoy a Saturday night as many of the previous weekends had fallen flat.

Matty Cash got Villa off to the perfect start when he scored early and Ollie Watkins then made the game safe with the second after half-time. It was Watkins' first goal in more than two months, a loss of form which had seen him dropped for the first time since joining Villa.

He netted again the following weekend in a 4–0 win over Southampton, set up by Danny Ings in the first time the strikers had combined for a goal since the latter's arrival the previous summer. Coutinho was also excellent against the Saints and when he scored again in a 3–0 win over Leeds five days later, a victory capped by a goal of the season contender from the unlikely figure of Chambers, Villa were into the top half. Gerrard appeared to have overcome his first blip and there was a sense his reign was now properly up and running. That night at Elland Road, however, would eventually be remembered as its high point.

14

DOWNFALL

Steven Gerrard's downfall at Aston Villa didn't begin or end with Bournemouth. The 2–0 defeat on the south coast on the opening day of the 2022–23 season was, however, the moment it became clear to pretty much everyone connected with the club that something wasn't right. Villa had travelled to the Vitality Stadium huge favourites against a newly-promoted Cherries side who had endured something of a nightmare in their summer recruitment and were everyone's tip to go straight back down to the Championship.

The visitors, by contrast, were entering the season on a wave of optimism powered by what appeared a strong close-season, in which they had been bold and proactive in the transfer market. Wes Edens flew in from the USA to join co-owner Nassef Sawiris at the match. Both shared a sense of excitement for the nine-month campaign ahead. Just 90 minutes was all it took for that to be extinguished and replaced by a mood of unease and a host of questions.

Villa were well beaten, while a clumsily-handled post-match interview turned a recent decision by Gerrard to change the club captaincy into a major controversy. The manner of the defeat and the fallout hit the club like a sledgehammer. No-one at Villa had seen it coming. Perhaps, admittedly with the benefit of hindsight, they should.

Warning signs had emerged in the final months of the previous campaign. Not even a rousing speech from a member of the royal family could pull Villa out of a slump which meant Gerrard entered the summer with the jury still firmly out.

Prince William picks his moments carefully at Villa, combining a busy schedule with visits for pleasure. It's widely agreed that if his royal duties were not so demanding, he would spend far more time attending games. The Prince of Wales is certainly no casual supporter. He has in-depth knowledge of every squad member, so much so that he once surprised an Under-21 player during a visit to Bodymoor Heath with words of encouragement after watching him in action through an official club stream the week before.

If the future King of England watching Villa's Under-21s on a Friday night sounds amusing then picture the faces of the players when he pitched up to the training ground to tell them how he would regularly mimic their style when playing himself.

After winning at Leeds in early March, Villa had suffered four straight defeats to West Ham, Arsenal, Wolves and Tottenham – the latter a 4–0 thumping in which the team had unravelled in the second half after making a promising start.

An insipid goalless draw at Leicester at least stopped the rot but did little to lift the mood and with six games to go Villa were down in 15th place, all but safe from relegation but with optimism once again draining.

It was around that time William made one of his occasional visits to the training ground and addressed the players with a speech for the ages. He joked about running down the wing like Matty Cash and then mimicked the right-back by flicking back his hair. Then he pretended to be John McGinn and arched his back in the same way as the Scot does to maintain possession. To finish he re-enacted a typical Ollie Watkins celebration, leaving the players in fits of laughter. It was all light-hearted stuff but part of a bigger message to show the impact the players had on people who support the club.

Throughout Gerrard's time as manager, William offered words of support through messages to the club or during visits. In difficult times, he has been a reassuring voice, once writing a letter to Grealish when he was punched in the face by the Birmingham City spectator, and also appearing as a guest in the dressing room when the team needed a lift. Yet his words, passionate and inspiring as they were, couldn't fire the team up and the season fizzled out.

Villa beat Norwich on the day Dean Smith returned to the club and also suffered the first relegation of his managerial career. A 3–1 win over Burnley the next weekend was also encouraging but was followed by defeat to Liverpool and two uninspiring home draws against Crystal Palace and Burnley – where wins had been expected – heading into a final-day trip to Manchester City.

'It was a bit strange,' Razzaq recalls. 'As supporters we wanted it to work. But maybe we were buying into Gerrard the player, rather than Gerrard the manager. As time went on you started to wonder whether he really had a clue what he was doing. There were glimpses but not enough glimpses.'

The game at City was the stuff of dreams for newspapers. Pep Guardiola's team sat just a point above Liverpool in the table and the prospect of Gerrard, who had never won the Premier League as a player, potentially helping his former club win the title as a manager was the subject of countless column inches and dominated the pre-match discussion.

The head coach's phone was blowing up all week with messages and his staff – many with strong Liverpool connections – were inundated, too. Beale, close friends with Jurgen Klopp's assistant

Pep Lijnders, set out an aggressive and optimistic plan to pull City's defence apart.

For much of the afternoon it looked like it would work. Cash finished off a move identical to what had been worked on in training by heading Villa in front before Coutinho, who had not scored since the win at Leeds in March, showed a sublime touch to score with a little over 20 minutes to go. Gerrard looked set to provide a huge assist to Liverpool winning the title and record the best win of his Villa tenure to date.

Yet in what felt like in the blink of an eye, it all fell apart. Coutinho came off for the fit-again Nakamba but immediately Villa, bold from the first whistle, started playing 10 yards deeper. City pushed on and got one back through substitute İlkay Gündoğan – chosen to come off the bench ahead of ex-Villa captain, Jack Grealish, and five minutes later the German had put them ahead, Rodri having levelled the scores in between. City's class was indisputable but Villa's collapse was equally shocking. It was the second time in the season they had gone into the final 15 minutes of a match leading 2–0 and contrived to lose, the first being the 3–2 defeat to Wolves which had proved so damaging to Gerrard's predecessor Dean Smith. The pitch invasion which greeted the final whistle at the Etihad Stadium led to allegations Robin Olsen, making his first start in place of the injured Martinez, had been assaulted by supporters, something Manchester City would apologise for as they launched an official investigation into the trouble.[30] Rather than finish on a high, Villa completed the campaign 14th in the table with no-one left in any doubt there was plenty of work to do, not least the head coach who cut short a final press conference of the season, noticeably annoyed at the events of the day.

Much of the main summer transfer business was already complete. Despite diminishing returns the longer his loan progressed, Villa had already confirmed they would be signing

Coutinho on a permanent deal, Purslow having taken to the stage at the club's end of season awards to announce it. This was despite an acceptance in the club the Brazilian hadn't done enough to warrant Villa triggering the initial £33 million option to buy. Things changed when Purslow, on the insistence of Sawiris, was able to negotiate the price down to just over £17 million with a 50 per cent sell-on clause inserted. As Coutinho agreed a cut in wages from around £480,000 a week to £125,000 a week it was viewed as a deal worth doing, albeit the four-year contract handed to the 29-year-old raised some eyebrows.

A better-looking deal, financially, was for Boubacar Kamara, the Marseille midfielder Villa had been tracking for most of the season. Villa's recruitment team had done extensive work on the 22-year-old, with regular scouting trips, data analysis and several meetings with the player and his representatives. Head of recruitment Rob Mackenzie liked how Kamara could break up play and also move the ball around with precision. Lange was convinced and brought him to the attention of Gerrard, who helped get the free transfer over the line by visiting his house in southern France. Kamara had grown up watching Gerrard play in the Champions League and it was the personal touch which convinced him to join Villa and shun the advances of Atletico Madrid, then regulars in European competition. News of his imminent signing on a free transfer broke on the day of the Manchester City match and was confirmed within 24 hours.

Within a week Villa had added another key piece of Gerrard's proposed jigsaw in the shape of centre-back Diego Carlos. Unconvinced by both Ezri Konsa and Tyrone Mings and frustrated by the number of individual errors which led to goals, Gerrard had made signing another centre-back a top priority. Several options were considered, including Burnley's James Tarkowski who was available on a free transfer with his contract due to expire. Tarkowski had even visited Gerrard's house to discuss a move.

Borussia Dortmund's Manuel Akanji also featured highly as did Freiberg's Nico Schlotterbeck and Lille's Sven Botman, yet it was Sevilla's Carlos who Villa ended up moving for in a deal worth around £26 million.

Lange and his team of scouts spent significant time in Spain as they watched Sevilla, who had an impressive clean sheet record when the Brazilian played. His physicality, speed, aerial presence and durability were highlighted as his best qualities, alongside his flexibility to play either side of defence. It meant that Carlos could challenge Mings or Konsa for a starting place, while Gerrard was also taken by his winning mentality, having won the Europa League in 2020 with Sevilla as the skipper. Villa were sure that he would become a leading voice in the dressing room once his English improved. Signing a slightly younger alternative was considered but it was widely agreed that Carlos was the best option.

By the end of May, Villa had already made three significant signings in the shape of Coutinho, Kamara and Carlos. 'Bouba and Diego were brilliant signings for us in what felt like a really strong summer,' Purslow recalls. 'Everybody in the club was optimistic at this point.'

Yet it was an outgoing on the coaching staff which would have the biggest impact. Having turned down offers the previous year before moving with Gerrard from Rangers, Beale decided the time was right to strike out on his own by accepting the chance to become Queens Park Rangers head coach. This was hugely significant for Villa, as Beale was no ordinary assistant boss. His influence was such that some players had begun to question why Gerrard allowed him such authority.

Beale's departure left a huge, and according to insiders 'unexpected' hole in the coaching staff, which was quickly filled by Neil Critchley. On one hand, this looked almost like a coup. Critchley, a manager in his own right at Blackpool, had been convinced to quit the Championship club and join Villa as Gerrard's No. 2. The two knew each other from their time working together in Liverpool's academy and Critchley, the former Reds Under-23s boss, had even taken charge of a 'first-team' match against Villa when the Merseyside club were forced to field the kids in a Carabao Cup game due to a fixture clash with the Club World Cup. Yet a closer look at his CV confirmed he had never coached Premier League players and, while he was expected to take on just as big a responsibility as Beale, he was a very different character, nowhere near so forceful in his message, and now a part of the most populated coaching team in the Premier League where competition to be heard was growing.

Stamping his authority on the players became even trickier when an issue with his passport forced him to miss the pre-season tour to Australia. Valuable time to build relationships with players was lost and, with Beale no longer around, the coaching suffered.

The Australia trip, organised as a money-spinning commercial adventure, had its own issues. Long and arduous for all those on it, there was too much travelling, not enough quality training time, while some rather remote locations meant Villa stayed in substandard accommodation – at least for Premier League players. Almost every player was happy to get back and start preparing properly for the season but the difficulties Down Under undoubtedly hampered the mood.

After such a strong start to the transfer window, Sawiris, who often joined board meetings via a remote location on his yacht, outlined the importance of the season ahead. Villa were struggling to land other key targets, though, and the big headline in the days leading up to the season opener at Bournemouth was a departure as 18-year-old Carney Chukwuemeka joined Chelsea for a fee of around £20 million. The playmaker had long been tipped for greatness with Purslow once describing him as 'probably the best 16-year-old in England' before he inspired Villa to a Youth Cup win in 2021. Yet while Smith and then Gerrard had begun to offer the player increased opportunities in the first team, efforts to convince him to sign a long-term contract were proving fruitless despite Villa willing to make him the highest-paid teenager in club history.

With just one year remaining on Chukwuemeka's current deal, Villa risked losing him for virtually nothing in the near future and ultimately the deal with Chelsea suited both parties. The London club's new co-owner, Todd Boehly, first brought the player up when sitting next to Purslow at an informal get-together he had arranged, involving executives from the 19 other Premier League clubs. The sale – not that Villa wanted it – would help their PSR calculations later down the line as the growing number of graduates from the academy were used to balance the books.

While the circumstances surrounding Chukwuemeka were cause for some frustration, it was a player Villa failed to sign which would have the biggest knock-on effect on the existing squad. It can be revealed that, for much of the previous season, Gerrard had been eager to sign James Milner from Liverpool on a short-term deal. Milner, then aged 36, had made 100 Premier League appearances in two previous spells at Villa between 2005 and 2010 and had been an integral part of Martin O'Neill's team which came so close to qualifying for the Champions League during that period. Sold in 2010 to Manchester City, where he would win multiple Premier League titles, he remained a hugely popular figure among Villa supporters. Gerrard's plan was to install him as captain and ease the burden on Mings, whose performances the previous season he believed had suffered from the defender taking on too much responsibility.

When Milner rejected Villa's advances and instead signed a one-year extension at Anfield, Gerrard decided to make a change in any case and chose John McGinn as his new captain. Emi Martinez would take the role of vice-captain with Ashley Young club captain.

'It was a strange decision,' McGinn admits. 'I didn't see it coming. It was a proud moment for me but strange at the time.'

Though bold, the move was viewed as a good one by many inside Bodymoor Heath but, in an episode which would sum up his reign in a microcosm, Gerrard was unable to follow up an idea based on sound logic with effective execution.

Mings was told the news 24 hours before it was publicly announced on 27 July, a date much later than it was actually decided. Though the centre-back wasn't happy and didn't completely agree with the head coach's reasoning, he accepted the decision and vowed to knuckle down, knowing his performances in the latter half of the previous season had not been among his best.

McGinn, who says he has a 'brilliant relationship' with Mings, recalls the conversation between the two, which could easily have gone a number of different ways. 'We spoke about it at the time and he was very mature about it,' McGinn says. 'I'll never forget the message he sent me. He said he will support me with whatever I am doing and if I ever needed anything he'd be there. It was out of my hands but credit to the way he handled it.'

Gerrard assured Mings he remained a part of his plans but a groin strain sustained in the week before the Bournemouth game sowed the seeds of trouble. Mings declared himself fit to play, Gerrard deemed otherwise and left his now ex-captain on the bench, instead opting to pair Carlos and Konsa at centre-back. Villa contrived to concede from two set pieces in a dismal defeat.

'I was definitely fit because if someone had picked up an injury, I would have gone on and played,' Mings says. 'When I look back at the captaincy change, I don't think it was a bad thing. The reasons for Steven Gerrard taking it off me, which he said was for me to focus on my game and not worry about other people, were very fair. I was just surprised at what happened next because I think it would have been fair for him to give me that chance rather than drop me. I didn't really understand how not having the armband could benefit my game if I was on the bench.'

If being dropped had puzzled Mings, it was nothing compared to his bewilderment at comments Gerrard would then make in his post-match interview. Asked by a BBC Radio West Midlands reporter to explain Mings' omission, the head coach replied the defender would get back in the team when he 'looks me in the eye and shows that he's ready to play'. Publicly, it looked as though Gerrard was questioning Mings' attitude when, privately, there had been no such conversation. Those who regularly attended press conferences knew the 'look me in the eye' quote was one of the head coach's regular catchphrases yet in this context it appeared damning. What the Villa boss had intended to be a positive move for both the team and player was now shrouded in negativity and a major talking point in the week ahead. Writing in his national newspaper column, former Liverpool captain and manager Graeme Souness took aim at Mings and wrote of Gerrard's decision: 'This is you making a statement that there's something about this guy that is fundamentally wrong. You've embarrassed him.' Perhaps unsurprisingly because of their respective allegiances, Souness was supportive of Gerrard's decision.

Mings, meanwhile, began to fear the worst. He explains: 'I was thinking, how have I just gone from first or second centre-back to fourth in the space of a pre-season, because now if someone gets injured, maybe Calum (Chambers) goes on before me. I couldn't sit around and be fourth choice. I was trying to play for England. It was a really difficult time, there's no getting around that, but I always maintain that I do my best work in times of trouble.'

As luck would have it – at least for Mings anyway – within 24 hours of Souness' piece being published, on the eve of Villa's second game of the season at home to Everton, his argument was outdated as Mings was recalled in a 2–1 victory. The narrative now switched to whether the head coach had the courage of his convictions. More worryingly, after an entire summer to prepare, there were question marks over whether he knew his best team.

Mings' omission arguably wasn't the most controversial piece of team selection for the opening day defeat. That was leaving Ollie Watkins, Villa's top scorer in each of the previous two seasons, on the bench. Douglas Luiz was another left out of the starting XI and his future would come into focus later in the month on transfer deadline day when Villa rejected no fewer than four bids from Arsenal for the midfielder, on the insistence of Sawiris. Missing out on the chance to join a Champions League club was a huge blow to Luiz but the offer of a new, improved contract offered something in the way of compensation.

By deadline day Villa's season was already in trouble. The win over Everton, their only one in the first five Premier League matches, came at a huge cost as Carlos, a player who missed just five games in three years at Sevilla, suffered an Achilles injury which would keep him sidelined for most of the season. Gerrard had no option but to go back to the Konsa–Mings partnership of which he has been so unconvinced.

Three straight defeats followed, to Crystal Palace, West Ham and Arsenal and supporters were beginning to lose faith. Gerrard was keen to bring in another winger to compete with the inconsistent Leon Bailey but Villa saw a £25 million move for Watford's Ismaila Sarr collapse at the 11th hour due to an issue with personal terms.[31] Reinforcements eventually arrived on deadline day in the shape of centre-back Jan Bednarek, on loan from Southampton, with midfielder Leander Dendoncker arriving in a £13 million switch from neighbours Wolves.

On the pitch, the team lacked cohesion, Gerrard regularly switching between starting Emi Buendia or Philippe Coutinho or, in the case of a 1–1 draw with Manchester City, neither. Bailey's equaliser in that match raised spirits a little but the visit of Southampton, immediately before the September international break, was a colossal fixture with Villa's hierarchy prepared to make a change if necessary. Overtures had already been made to Graham

Potter before he was snapped up by Chelsea. A Jacob Ramsey goal, just before half-time, earned Villa three points and Gerrard survived. It would prove only a brief stay of execution.

The win came at a cost too, as Kamara suffered a knee injury which would rule him out until November. Gerrard might have made mistakes but neither was he bestowed much luck. Both of Villa's Premier League wins had been soured by losing one of his summer signings to injury. A few days later one of his main January signings, Lucas Digne, suffered an ankle injury in training. Gerrard might have been forgiven for thinking fate was conspiring against him.

Missed chances cost Villa dear in a 0–0 draw at Leeds when the season resumed after the break, before a 1–1 draw at newly promoted Nottingham Forest, then sat bottom of the table, prompted the first real public signs of agitation among the fanbase. McGinn, badly struggling for form, was sarcastically cheered off when substituted, an incredibly bruising moment for a player normally so popular. It wasn't the first negative reaction he had faced as he says, 'I've heard "McGinn's time is up here" many times since I joined.'

On the opening game of the season, members of his family clashed with supporters as they felt the level of criticism had become too personal, but at Nottingham Forest things got even worse and even his closest allies could see how much he was struggling.

'It was the lowest point in my Villa career. I'll never forget that night,' says McGinn. 'I knew it was a demanding club to play for but that was a massive low in my career. It affected me a lot.'

The result at the City Ground had extended Villa's unbeaten run to four matches, their longest under Gerrard. Yet the 16th-placed position in the table, with only seven goals scored in the first nine matches, rendered that statistic irrelevant.

Gerrard considered dropping McGinn for the following weekend's home match against Chelsea but backtracked. Mings, the team's most consistent performer since being recalled, then made the error which set Villa on their way to a 2–0 defeat. Now sat just one point above the bottom three, the pressure was on heading into a Thursday night trip to Fulham.

In the days before the game, Gerrard told support staff that he needed to win the next two games and hinted at a mini-celebration over the weekend if results went his way. In public he remained bullish, declaring a 'never say die spirit' was part of his DNA. Vastly experienced dealing with the press from his time with Liverpool and England, he always talked confidently, fronting up to every difficult question. As an orator he was hugely impressive, and in terms of competitiveness and wanting to win there are few like him.

But Gerrard's style off the pitch was not reflected by his team on it and the night at Fulham could not have gone worse. A change in defence saw Bednarek handed his first Villa start with Konsa pushed to right-back but the visitors were constantly on the back foot. The only surprise was it took Fulham 36 minutes to break the deadlock through Harrison Reed. Any hopes of a comeback then disintegrated when Luiz, who had signed a new contract a week earlier, was shown a straight red card following an altercation with Aleksandar Mitrovic. Sawiris charged out of the directors' box in frustration and Villa's evening only got worse. Mitrovic scored a penalty after Cash was rather harshly adjudged to have handled, before a shot deflected off Mings and past Martinez.

'*Steven Gerrard, get out of our club,*' sang a large portion of the away end, followed by coarse language and derogatory slurs.

'I have never been to a game where it has been so toxic among the away fans,' recalls Razzaq. 'That is the only word which can describe it. It was horrible. All of it was directed at Gerrard.

'As supporters, we always want it to work out. You don't desperately want to see another sacking because we have seen enough over the years. But it got to the point where it was only going one way.'

Mings, the third longest-serving member of the starting XI behind Jacob Ramsey and McGinn, agrees, saying: 'The team was suffering and when it comes to the end of a manager's tenure, it is pretty toxic around a club. The players have usually checked out of what he is saying, hence results aren't coming and the manager is also scratching his head thinking he is doing everything he can but nothing is working. By that point there is a real disconnect.' Just 90 minutes after the final whistle a club statement confirmed what was now inevitable. Gerrard and Villa had parted ways. The head coach had been told the news in person by Purslow shortly after completing his media duties. The fact the already deposed head coach then had to travel back with the team to Bodymoor Heath saw Villa accused of lacking respect by some observers, but in truth the circumstances were of Gerrard's doing.

'Is that me? Am I toast?' he is understood to have asked shortly after leaving the pitch. Rather than wait for the axe to fall, he wanted to know his fate up front. Long-serving members of Villa's media team would later speak of their admiration for how Gerrard, knowing his time was up, conducted himself during post-match press duties. That included during a bizarre scene when a reporter attempted to take a selfie with Gerrard, just after completing an interview, despite the obvious sensitivity of the moment. The manager remained dignified throughout.

Sensing the impending crisis, both Ashley Young and John McGinn offered to handle any media duties required after the game in a sign of strong leadership.

Gerrard would travel back on the team bus with the players in one of the strangest post-sacking scenes a Premier League manager will ever face.

'Things just didn't work out for him,' Purslow recalls. 'There were a few worrying signs after a brilliant start when his key objective of getting the club into safety was achieved extremely quickly. We faded at the back end of that season but we were all lifted by the signings.

'With hindsight, a number of things went wrong. He lost his trusted number two and then his chosen successor was unable to join the pre-season camp which was far from ideal. Then, after a positive run of matches in pre-season, the result at Bournemouth was a shock to the system.

'Losing Carlos and Kamara soon after was so unfortunate and he was unable to recover.'

Watkins now says that '99 per cent of the blame' for Gerrard's failure should be on the players, adding: 'Obviously you can be told what to do but at the end of the day it's us on the pitch who have to put in the performances. The manager can tell us what to do but it's us who are implementing it.'

When Villa arrived back at Bodymoor Heath in the early hours of Friday morning, Gerrard addressed the players for one final time, wished them luck for the future and then went to his office, packed up his belongings and went home. His 11-month reign was over. For Villa, the search for his replacement began in earnest.

15

A BLANK PIECE OF PAPER

Less than 96 hours after storming out of the Craven Cottage directors' box, Nassef Sawiris would be all smiles as he posed for a photograph in his London home with Villa's new head coach.

Just as 11 months previously when replacing Smith with Gerrard, Villa did not hang around when it came to bringing in the next man. This pursuit, however, would be very different to the one which had led to the appointment of Gerrard and indeed Smith before him. Rather than delegate to Purslow, this time it was Sawiris who led the search himself in a move which marked a significant shift in how the club conducted operations.

Having previously been happy to let others take the lead, this was the moment Sawiris decided to take more control, perhaps mindful that after four years his and Edens' reign as owners had reached a critical point. It was a view shared by supporters who, a decade earlier, had witnessed former owner Randy Lerner lose heart in the fight to break into the Premier League's elite. Now, for the first time since Dean Smith had been appointed four years earlier, momentum under the Sawiris and Edens regime had stalled.

Getting the next appointment right was crucial and Sawiris wanted to leave nothing to chance.

That is not to say the co-owner struck out completely on his own. He still sought advice from Villa's recruitment team, asking them to identify the best coach the club could realistically hire. While Gerrard had been a failure, there was still a belief in the playing squad and a confidence it simply required a good coach to get the best out of them. The key difference this time was having previously hired two head coaches who were on their way up in Smith and Gerrard, now Sawiris wanted someone with an established track record of success. He was prepared to pay for it too.

'For me, the key things about that change were the owners deciding on an elite, tier-one, manager,' says Christian Purslow. 'To do that as a club not competing in Europe was unusual but the owners made that decision. They wanted elite. It was a massive statement of intent because the easy thing for clubs to do when they are positioned between sixth and 16th in the league is to hire from a set of managers that cost a certain amount. When you hire managers who have won trophies, it becomes much more expensive.'

One of the two names given to Sawiris was Mauricio Pochettino. The 50-year-old Argentine had already been reported as a potential candidate in the press days before Villa's defeat at Fulham, when Gerrard was still in post. The former Tottenham boss had been out of work since being sacked by Paris St-Germain the previous July and while Villa were quick to dismiss the stories – and one well-known betting company was quick to make a joke of their reported interest – informal contact had been made with Pochettino's representatives during the final weeks of Gerrard's reign.

Pochettino had actually been on Sawiris' radar for some time. He had first been recommended to the Egyptian by Suso, just weeks before the latter was relieved of his duties in July 2020. Then still battling to stay in the Premier League, Villa's owners were planning for every eventuality and Sawiris wanted to know the best possible candidate should they survive in the Premier League but then struggle during the following season too and decide to move on from Smith. Pochettino listened carefully to Suso, who told him it was only a matter of time before Villa finished in the top four of the Premier League 'because of Sawiris' plan'.

In the end Smith kept Villa mostly on an upward curve through 2020–21 and by the time he was eventually axed Pochettino had taken over at PSG. Now he was a free agent, and with Graham Potter having joined Chelsea, the Argentine was under serious consideration.

Yet while Villa were genuine in their interest and indeed met with Pochettino, the move always felt a long shot. Pochettino's star remained high, despite his PSG sacking, and he had been courted by some of the biggest clubs in the world, including Manchester United and Real Madrid to name just two. Financially secure, the prospect of being thrown into what could well be a Premier League relegation battle was of little appeal, regardless of how much Villa were prepared to pay him. Villa, for their part, had concerns too. Just how much would Pochettino, who had spent much of the past decade playing in the Champions League and whose recent team had included Kylian Mbappe, Neymar and Lionel Messi, be prepared to get his hands dirty? The fit just didn't seem right.

Instead, the name thrown immediately into the frame the morning after Gerrard's sacking was Sporting Lisbon boss Ruben Amorim. The 37-year-old had established himself as one of the brightest young managerial talents in European football, having led Sporting to their first Portuguese title in nearly two decades the previous year. His team had already scored an impressive Champions League win over Tottenham a few weeks earlier. The fact Amorim also spoke perfect English meant he was a candidate given serious consideration.

Somewhat less appealing was the release clause Sporting had included in his contract after luring him from Braga in 2020. Reported in some places to be £30 million, it was in fact far lower than that, though still considerable at around £10 million. In any case, Amorim was not the other name Sawiris had been given by Villa's recruitment department. That was Unai Emery. Very quickly, it was Emery who became the club's No. 1 target.

Born in Hondarribia, a small coastal town in the Gipuzkoa province of the Basque Country, not far from the French border, Emery came from a family with football pedigree. Both of his father and grandfather were goalkeepers, the former playing for Real Union in the Spanish Second Division. One of four brothers, Unai was the only one of his generation to make it as a professional, making more than 300 appearances in a career which spanned more than a decade. A serious knee injury suffered early in his career, from which he never fully recovered, meant the vast majority of his matches came in the Second Division though he would later claim playing through the pain barrier helped develop the fighting mentality which has served him well in management.

His rise as a coach was rapid. After retiring as a player in 2004 while with Lorca Deportiva in the Third Division, he was offered the vacant managerial role by the club's chairman, promptly won promotion and almost took them up to the top flight the following season. A move to Almeria followed where, yet again, he won promotion in his first season, this time from the Second Division. When Emery then guided the Andalusian club to eighth in the top flight, he was now firmly on the radar of Spain's biggest clubs. Among them were Valencia. In four seasons at the Mestalla, Emery recorded three consecutive top three finishes, behind only Pep Guardiola's Barcelona and Jose Mourinho's Real Madrid, taking the club back into the Champions League. His methods, receiving growing acclaim in coaching circles across Europe, were studied by a young English coach named Dean Smith when the future Villa boss was working toward his UEFA licence.

After a brief stint with Spartak Moscow, Emery returned to Spain to take charge of Sevilla where he linked up with the sporting director, Monchi. Within months he had claimed his first major honour thanks to a penalty shoot-out win over Benfica in the Europa League final. Sevilla would win the competition in the next two seasons before Emery departed for Paris St-Germain. In two seasons with the Parisian club he won every domestic honour but could not deliver the Champions League title the Qatari owners craved, his team infamously blowing a 4–0 first leg advantage to lose 6–5 on aggregate to Barcelona in the Round of 16.

Emery would later describe it as his 'worst moment' in football. At this point questions were asked about whether he could cut it at the top, or if he was just a manager more suited to working for the underdog. On his PSG exit, he spoke to the author Martí Perarnau at length and was asked, as a 46-year-old coach, what he was lacking at this stage of his career.

'For my creations to be more complete creations. And for them to be my creations,' he replied.

In May 2018, Emery was unveiled as Arsene Wenger's successor at Arsenal, in what initially appeared to be his chance to make amends. Yet this 18-month stint with the Gunners represented comfortably the most disappointing spell of his coaching career. A poor finish to his first season in charge saw them finish fifth in the Premier League, miss out on Champions League qualification and then lose the Europa League final 4–1 to Chelsea. After an inconsistent start to the 2019–20 season, a run of seven matches without a win led to Emery being sacked in late November. Mercilessly mocked in the press for his efforts to speak English, he had almost come to be regarded as a figure of fun. A lack of control at the club would ultimately pave the way for his downfall. He wanted more of a say on the big decisions but was not afforded that freedom.

By the time Villa were looking for a new manager in October 2022, Emery's reputation in England had already undergone some revision. There was now an acknowledgement of the tough assignment he had taken in replacing the legendary Wenger, at a time when Arsenal were a club in need of rebuilding. An increasing number of observers felt Emery's own successor, Mikel Arteta, had benefited in part from the foundations his fellow Basque had put in place.

Most importantly, Emery had revived his own career. He had returned to Spain, taken charge of Villarreal and in 2021 masterminded the provincial club's first major honour, beating Manchester United to claim his fourth Europa League crown. Even more impressive achievements followed the next season with Bayern Munich and Juventus beaten en route to the semi-finals of the Champions League. Emery, it was now accepted, was a far better boss than that year-and-a-half at Arsenal might have suggested, although no closer to proving whether he could succeed at the highest level.

Villa were not the first club to try and tempt him back to the Premier League. Just a year previously, in October 2021, Emery had all but signed the contract to take charge at Newcastle, the club's Saudi Arabian owners having determined he was a better bet to lead their project than the other main candidate, Eddie Howe. A home Champions League tie against Swiss club Young Boys was going to be Emery's last. Yet at almost the final moment, the news he was bound for Tyneside leaked out in the English press. Emery became uneasy and Villarreal's owner Fernando Roig spent time before and after kick-off against Young Boys talking him round. Newcastle were told the deal was off. Howe got the job instead.

Mindful of the high price Emery places on his privacy and determined not to repeat the mistake of their Premier League rivals, Villa and Sawiris moved swiftly and with stealth. Only when the deal was virtually done bar the official announcement did rumours of Villa's interest in Emery first emerge in Spain.

It can be revealed, however, that during a secret meeting in Madrid almost a month earlier, Sawiris first held talks with Emery about his plans for the future.

Sawiris' relationship with super-agent Jorge Mendes was important. Though Mendes does not act as Emery's day-to-day agent, the pair have a longstanding relationship and it was Mendes, on Sawiris' behalf, who linked the two together. The co-owner was concerned with the form under Gerrard and wanted to know whether Emery would consider a more formal approach in the future. Villa were undoubtedly a club which piqued his interest and the initial meeting left Emery with a feeling of excitement. When Sawiris handed him a blank sheet of paper and said 'show me the way you would rebuild Aston Villa', he sensed the opportunity to create a special project.

While happy at Villarreal, there was a nagging sense his tenure had already witnessed its high point with the Europa League win and run to the Champions League semi-finals. The club simply did not have the financial backing to sustain a challenge in the long term against the likes of Barcelona, Real Madrid or Atletico Madrid. Surging gas prices on the back of the war between Russia and Ukraine made it even tougher for Villarreal's owner Roig, as his energy-intensive ceramics business suffered. Emery's contract at Villarreal had just seven months remaining and there was no progress on a new deal because of the financial uncertainty. Other clubs were also showing an interest but Sawiris was the first to request a meeting and the co-owner left with no doubt that Emery was the man he wanted in charge should a change be required.

When Villa officially pushed the button, Emery was in the middle of a hectic week which saw Villarreal play three matches in the space of just six days. He told Sawiris, via Mendes, he would be prepared to talk properly after the last of those games, a home fixture with Almeria, which took place on Sunday 23 October. In the meantime Sawiris began to establish an idea of how the deal would look financially. Emery's contract at Villarreal contained a £5.2 million buy-out clause and Sawiris indicated early on he would be prepared to pay it. Emery, meanwhile, began making discreet calls to the people he wanted on his backroom team.

One man already well-briefed on the situation was not a coach, but Damian Vidagany. A former journalist from Valencia, Vidagany had joined his hometown club as chief media officer in 2008, shortly before Emery was appointed head coach. The pair quickly established a bond which would persist beyond the latter's departure to Sevilla and when Vidagany later became chief executive of DV7, the media agency founded by former Spain striker David Villa, Emery became a client.

Ahead of the private meeting in Madrid, Emery asked Vidagany to join him and share his thoughts.

One of Emery's main frustrations, when reviewing his time at Arsenal, was the sense he had been left isolated. In his coaching team he had people he could trust, yet he needed someone at a higher level, a person to provide the link between the manager's office and the boardroom. Vidagany, in that regard, was a useful contact he could trust and add to his team in the event of a move.

'Unai wanted me to be an advisor because I have always been very close with him,' Vidagany says. 'When we met Nassef in Madrid, he was a little bit sick. His wife told him to stay at home but he insisted on holding the meeting because it was about the future of Aston Villa. Nassef was very clever in this meeting, because he explained what the club was, the aims and how he would be investing. Then he said to Unai about the blank piece of paper: "This is what I want, fill this paper and build me the club you have in mind."

'The approach from Nassef was perfect. It was for the future, but when results went down so fast at Aston Villa, the situation changed. Unai also had the wish to come back to the Premier League for a second opportunity so it appealed to him.'

Emery had carried out an extensive review of his time in charge at Arsenal, working out what he had done well and why things had gone wrong. Though it had been a bruising experience, in his own mind he had long determined he would one day return to the Premier League to prove the doubters wrong. Villa offered precisely that opportunity.

That said, it was still going to require some persuading on Villa's part. While Emery was interested enough to listen to what Sawiris was saying, the onus was still very much on the latter to put forward a convincing case for why he should take the job. Villa were, after all, a club languishing low down in the Premier League, with no European football to offer a coach who had spent 15 consecutive seasons competing in European competition. Never in Villa's 148-year history would they have appointed such a decorated manager. Pull this one off and it would rightly be declared a coup.

Aware there were no guarantees they would land their top choice, Villa were still speaking to other candidates. 'When you're running a good process, you have to prepare for not getting your first choice,' says Purslow. 'In the end Nassef met with Unai and was able to get it done. But over the weekend, we divided up and I was in London interviewing other candidates. Obviously, Unai was the first choice, but we didn't know if we were going to get him.'

On the same Sunday talks with Emery ramped up, Villa beat Brentford 4–0 under the guidance of interim boss Aaron Danks. The match was notable for being the first time Emi Buendia, Danny Ings and Leon Bailey, the three players bought to replace Jack Grealish 14 months previously, had started together. John McGinn, meanwhile, was omitted from the starting XI.

When the agreement with Emery was struck, the paperwork was completed within a day. The contract length was one of the longest Villa had ever given a head coach. Essentially, they had tied Emery down for four-and-a-half years with the final year an option in the club's favour. When the official announcement of his appointment was made shortly before 8 p.m. on the night of Monday 24 October, the reaction of supporters was a mixture of both shock and delight. Any fear Sawiris and Edens might be losing faith in the project was gone in an instant.

'It was like: "Wow". How have we gone from Steven Gerrard to appointing a tier one manager? A serial European trophy-winning manager?' says Mo Razzaq.

Shortly after the announcement, Villa's official Twitter account posted what has now become a famous photo, Emery and Sawiris stood side-by-side, holding up a Villa shirt. The chairman had got his man.

'I was thinking: "How have we pulled it out of the bag?"' continues Razzaq. 'It was a bit of a dream, to be honest. I had to start pinching myself to prove I hadn't just woken up! It was a reminder the owners of the club mean business. To have got Emery we knew they would have needed to sell him a really grand vision of the club.'

16

NO TIME WASTED

'I'm not here to waste my time.'

That one short sentence, which perhaps sums up better than any other how Unai Emery goes about his work, was first heard by supporters when he said it in a press conference nearly six months into his Villa reign.

His players, by contrast, heard it on the new head coach's very first day in charge, during an address in which he succinctly set out his stall, making clear both his ambitions and the demands which would be required of everyone at Bodymoor Heath under his leadership.

'I am not happy to be here,' he told them, explaining his appointment had only come about because another coach had been sacked, adding: 'When this happens it's because not only him, but everyone here didn't do their job properly.'

If that bit was the stick, Emery followed it up with the carrot. Telling the players his pride in having qualified for European competition in each of the past 14 seasons, he outlined his intention to continue the streak with Villa. Despite the team then sitting 17th in the Premier League, this was Emery's way of expressing belief in the group he had inherited.

'Maybe it will take time,' he told them. 'Maybe not all of you will be there, but many of you will because you have the potential to be there. Maybe you just don't know it yet.'

Just over a week had passed between Emery signing his contract and that first meeting with the players, the gap unavoidable as the new head coach and his entirely Spanish backroom team awaited the visas which would allow them to begin work. While Emery was keen to get cracking, the enforced interlude proved useful, in at least two ways.

For one, it meant his first match in charge of Villa would not be an away trip to Newcastle, a fixture which would be seriously testing with the hosts then sitting fourth in the Premier League. On a personal level, it also had the chance to be awkward for Emery, with the build-up guaranteed to be dominated by questions of why Villa's new boss had turned down the Magpies at the last minute a year previously. Aaron Danks instead took caretaker charge for the second weekend running, though this one went rather less well than the first, Villa crumbling to a 4–0 defeat.

It was that afternoon which again highlighted the team's frail mentality yet Emery, watching on from Spain, was already well on the way to understanding the difficulties he was inheriting, having begun a study of every match played to that point of the season. Another added benefit of having to wait to start work was it provided time to prepare.

'Unai had some doubts about some players. He had some information about others,' says Damian Vidagany. 'But while it was clear that maybe half of the squad were not at the level required to be in Europe, it was also clear that there were some amazing players who had potential but it needed to be unlocked.

'That's why Unai always says the first thing to do is develop the players. If you do that, the results start to come and then you have success.

'Sometimes a manager will say the players are shit. Unai analysed it deeper and realised at Villa there were 10–12 players who had high potential. They needed to be developed to get better.'

One of those was John McGinn, the captain who had lost his way and his place in the team under Danks. Emery was advised upon his arrival to hand the armband to one of McGinn's team-mates, and so tough was his situation at Villa that his agent had started responding to requests from rival Premier League clubs interested in signing him in the next transfer window. 'I was actively for sale at that moment in time, maybe not by the manager but by the powers that be, who were in charge,' McGinn says.

'I am not saying it had anything to do with Steven Gerrard, either, but the club were looking to see if anyone was interested. I did have a lot of interest at that time, several clubs but probably West Ham mostly at that point. There was a chance I could be away. It was a bit strange. I had prepared myself for leaving and as a footballer you get used to these things because sometimes you have to get used to moving on.'

Emery, though, had other ideas, as McGinn adds: 'When the manager joined he called me into a meeting and asked "Why does everyone keep saying we need to sell John McGinn when I've watched the games in detail, and although the last ten haven't been great, the ten before were great, and I believe you can be one of the best players here. Am I missing something?"'

McGinn admits he immediately felt a sense of relief. Never one to hide behind excuses, he says the difficult period was partly down to his form and playing in a position not entirely conducive to his own game. The midfielder maintains he was not feeling any added pressure because of the captaincy but says: 'I was starting to become a bit paranoid, thinking "Who is trying to do me in?" You don't expect it from a club where you have given so much, and played through injuries and tough moments personally, all to try and get the best result for the club.'

During extensive research Emery had seen enough in McGinn's performances to suggest he was talented enough to be a part of the future and Vidagany says: 'When we arrived we were told that McGinn was not a good captain but when I saw him as a person, the first thing I thought was "What a great guy."

'What had happened with Tyrone as the captain, when he was replaced, is not normal. This should not happen at a football club. You cannot push out a captain unless he did something very, very bad. We did not want this so we put all our trust into McGinn.'

Before making key decisions on other players, among Emery's most important tasks was assembling his backroom team, though in truth it was a relatively straightforward job as he had already sounded out most of those he planned to bring with him. During his 17 years in management, Emery had built a trusted core of coaching assistants, all of whom mirrored his own relentless work ethic. After agreeing to join Villa, it was already assumed most of his backroom team would be moving to the UK as well. That included first-team coach Pablo Villanueva and data analyst Victor Manuel Manas, both of whom had worked with Emery since his time in charge with Sevilla, along with strength and conditioning coach Moises de Hoyo. Individual performance coach Antonio Rodriguez Saravia, better known by his nickname Rodri, who had impressed Emery since joining Villarreal the previous year, was another brought across. So too was goalkeeper coach Javi Garcia, a long-time Emery assistant.

That move spelled the end for Neil Cutler, after nearly four years at the club. His departure prompted Emi Martinez to pen an emotional farewell message on social media.

There was room for another face on Emery's team, and again he had worked with Emery before. Joining him at Villa as assistant head coach was Pako Ayestarán, a former fitness coach at Valencia during Emery's time in charge. The 59-year-old had been out of work since being sacked by Portuguese club Tondela but remained a hugely respected coach with vast experience. Of most interest to Emery was Ayestarán's time as assistant to Rafa Benitez. The pair had worked together for more than a decade, winning four trophies together at Liverpool between 2004 and 2007, including the Champions League, before Ayestarán left to pursue his own ambitions in management. Emery believed his knowledge, not least of the Premier League, would be hugely beneficial.

Aaron Danks subsequently became another casualty in the ruthless cull, leaving with his reputation still relatively high, although perhaps not in the eyes of McGinn who had been demoted to the bench for the two games under his watch. The other remaining senior member of the coaching staff, Austin MacPhee, was given time to impress, largely because of Emery's own interest in set-pieces. Players who worked with Emery in Spain said the interest bordered on an 'obsession' as he looked at alternative ways to gain an advantage against opponents with a stronger starting line-up, and believed set-pieces were a clear area of opportunity.

When the well-worked free-kick and corner-kick routines started to become a heavy source of goals, the players quickly bought into it. At PSG, however, that all fell apart as Emery had to allow the 'genius' of Neymar to dictate the direction at set-plays. Finding the right balance between being demanding and keeping his star players happy at PSG was perhaps his toughest task.

With Villa in need of a kick up the backside, he would not encounter the same problems.

A new way of working followed and MacPhee had a short window to impress. If he wasn't good enough, he'd be out the door because his sessions would now take on greater significance. Unlike before when Gerrard and Beale, and to a lesser extent Smith, completed their own training drills and sent the players off for some extra work with MacPhee, Emery was fully engaged and got involved in every session, adding input of his own along the way. It wasn't long before the players started recognising the expert advice of MacPhee – and the modern technology he used – could be hugely beneficial if incorporated in the right way.

When he was headhunted from FC Midtjylland a year earlier, MacPhee told Villa he would only join if they purchased a data-measuring device called TrackMan which had been used to great effect in Denmark. TrackMan is a launch monitor used mainly by professional golfers but also a growing number of football clubs.

Within time, specific training with MacPhee and his analyst, Jose Rodriguez Calvo, who also joined from Midtjylland, would become more of a science as the players learned signals for movement based on foot patterns of the set-piece taker. The level of preparation became so detailed that players had to learn which arm to use to block certain opponents.

Phone applications were also used to share routines and improve the kicking technique of each player. Ahead of games MacPhee even briefed the team on the referee's previous history in a clear sign of his commitment to leaving no stone unturned, something Emery looks for in all his support staff.

Vidagany, meanwhile, having played such an essential part in Emery joining Villa in the first place, was appointed the club's chief of staff, an all-encompassing role in which he would not only be the head coach's personal PR man but an advisor and most importantly a friend. It is Vidagany, for example, who most impresses on Emery the importance of setting the right tone in his messaging with both the media and supporters. Conscious this was perhaps an area Emery had neglected while at Arsenal, it was immediately notable how the new boss sought to praise fans at every opportunity after taking charge at Villa. Vidagany takes huge pressure off Emery by shielding him from commercial duties and essentially overseeing his daily agenda so the manager has the freedom to complete the tasks of most importance. It is also Vidagany who helps draft the head coach's programme notes which have become legendary among journalists for their inspiring and passionate language.

Another of his duties is that of translator at press conferences, should Emery have any trouble understanding questions from the floor. One of the few media briefings Vidagany was not at Emery's side was the new head coach's official unveiling, which took place in the directors' lounge inside the Trinity Road Stand at Villa Park on Friday 4 November. On that occasion, Emery was flanked by Christian Purslow and Johan Lange, while Tommy Jordan also sat at the top table. Vidagany, who would later be introduced in person to the attending media, stood watching from the side along with members of Emery's family, including his brother Igor and son Lander.

Mindful of the difficulties Emery had often experienced in making himself understood at Arsenal, Villa had a translator on hand ready to relay any answers in Spanish should the new head coach wish to use his mother tongue to better expand on any answers. Yet this was an option Emery declined during the filmed section of the briefing. Those in attendance noted how, while not perfect, his use of English already seemed far more confident than during his time with the Gunners.

Just as he had been open in outlining his ambitions with his players, there was no attempt to hide them from the media either. 'My dream is to win a trophy with Aston Villa,' said Emery, having been asked just three questions into the session whether qualifying for Europe that season was a realistic ambition. Yet there was no attempt to ignore the club's current predicament, with the new boss quick to stress the first challenge would be getting the team out of its lowly league position.

Purslow, sat in the same spot as when introducing Gerrard less than a year earlier, described Emery's appointment as: 'Perhaps the most important moment and most important step our club has taken since our promotion from the Championship.' Villa's chief executive also gave public thanks to Jorge Mendes' agency, Gestifute, for their part in making the deal 'so smooth and fast'.

A light-hearted moment saw Emery quizzed about his love for *Peaky Blinders*, the popular TV series based on the lives of Birmingham gangsters. Asked if it might help him better understand the local accent, Purslow quipped he 'couldn't understand it' himself.

Further colour came from the fact Emery had turned 51 the previous day. The Spaniard claimed to have been so busy preparing for the home match against Manchester United the following Sunday, he'd had no time to celebrate. 'My birthday will be on Sunday, if we win,' he smiled. At the time, those members of the press present would have been forgiven for wondering whether the new head coach was kidding and simply delivering a nice line for their benefit. On the contrary, it would quickly come to be remembered as an early insight into Emery's workaholic character.

'We didn't have too many days working with him prior to the game but he brought a clear understanding and a structure to the team that was different to Gerrard's style,' explains Ollie Watkins. 'He told us to believe in ourselves, believe in the style he wanted us to play.'

Right from the get-go players understood how methodical Emery would be in his approach. The sessions leading up to the United match were often played at walking pace, players told precisely where to stand as the ball was worked slowly up the pitch from the feet of Emi Martinez, through the defence and midfield to the forwards. Key to the plan was creating space for Emi Buendia to attack the opposition back line. When Sunday rolled around it was, as one observer of those training sessions remarked, as though the 'fast forward' button had been pressed, with the same patterns of play seen at snail's pace on the training pitch sped up to devastating effect when the real action began.

On paper, Emery could not have been handed a tougher assignment than Manchester United at home. It is not that the Red Devils were the class of the division. Erik ten Hag's team sat fifth in the table after what could only be described as a steady start at best under the Dutchman, who had been appointed the previous summer. Of bigger issue for Villa was their rotten home record against United, which stretched back into the previous century. Not since August 1995 had Villa beaten them on their own patch in a league fixture. That 3–1 victory, under the management of Brian Little, had become famous for prompting former Liverpool captain turned television pundit Alan Hansen to look at a United side which featured largely unknown youngsters including David Beckham, Paul Scholes, Nicky Butt and Gary Neville and proclaim they 'would never win anything with kids'. Villa's home record against United since that day read: played 23, drawn eight, lost 15. Supporters were hard-wired to expect the worst in this fixture and usually that is precisely what they got.

This day, however, would be different. Results 24 hours earlier meant Villa kicked off one place outside the bottom three, only above Southampton courtesy of their win over the Saints earlier in the season. Yet right from the first whistle, they did not look like a team playing with any sense of pressure.

'I told my dad that when he watched the game, he was going to see a very different version of me playing because I will slow the ball down, wait for the pressure to come and find solutions,' Mings recalls.

Emery had kept his new players on their toes, only telling them his team selection at the final team meeting less than three hours before the game. There were only two changes from the XI beaten so heavily at Newcastle the previous weekend but both of those players brought into the line-up, Jacob Ramsey and Lucas Digne, would have a huge impact.

Less than seven minutes had elapsed when Ramsey picked up a pass from Ollie Watkins, turned and sent Leon Bailey racing into the box, the winger firing a finish beyond David de Gea to send noise levels inside Villa Park soaring. Things quickly got even better. Ramsey pounced on a loose ball, was brought down by a lunging Luke Shaw and with Emi Martinez stood near the halfway line, seemingly directing Villa's players where to stand in the wall, Digne curled a free-kick over the wall and inside the post for his first goal for the club, in what was an early win for MacPhee as Emery was immediately impressed.

Villa were rampant but just a minute before half-time United got back into the game courtesy of a fluke when Shaw's speculative shot, heading well wide, struck Ramsey and looped over Martinez into the corner of the net. It was the kind of huge luck which always seemed to fall United's way at Villa Park and, as well as their team had played, many home supporters headed for a half-time pie suspecting the rest of the afternoon would play out the way it usually did, with the visitors mounting a comeback.

Instead, it was Villa who grasped back the initiative. Three minutes after the break, Watkins picked up the ball on the left, drove at the visiting defence and crossed for Ramsey to thump a finish into the top corner. In doing so, the youngster created a small part of Premier League history, becoming the first player to register a goal, assist and own goal in the same match. From there, a Villa team which had so often folded at the first sign of adversity saw out the win with relative ease. For United's captain, Cristiano Ronaldo, it would be his final game in the Premier League, departing after an insipid display where he lacked effort, energy and any genuine goal threat. For Emery, it was the perfect start.

The new head coach made a quick exit at the final whistle. After shaking hands with Ten Hag, Emery had time to make a couple of small fist bumps in the direction of supporters, while there was also just the flash of a brief smile as he marched down the touchline before disappearing down the tunnel.

In the post-match press conference he was just slightly more ebullient. 'I was dreaming of it and I am so happy,' he said, before quickly switching back to reality, adding: 'Today was perfect but I am going to have to remain calm myself and remind the players we have only made the first step.'

A lengthy debrief inside the auditorium at Bodymoor Heath followed the next day and it gave both the players and some high-ranking club officials further insight into the head coach's character.

Emery had almost completed his talk, having slowly worked through the duration of the game. There were just a few minutes left to debrief when the door swung open from the back of the room and in entered Purslow who had Prince William alongside him as a special guest.

Many of the players expected the pair to be welcomed in as the meeting was almost complete, yet Emery shocked the room by asking for them to leave as his talk was not finished. He would later exchange pleasantries with the future King but that set a clear tone within the club that he was the boss, and warned everyone in the room of the importance he places on concentration when he is talking.

Not everything was rushed with Emery, as Mings recalls: 'He didn't give us all the information straight away, but there was extreme clarity in his message. Against United it was simple. He told us when we didn't have the ball to sit in a 4–4–2 and if someone comes into the area go and close them down.' The luck of the Carabao Cup draw meant Emery's second match in charge would also be against United, this time at Old Trafford in a third round tie. Though Villa had won at the venue under Dean Smith the previous season, their record in away fixtures against United was almost as bad as at home, while they had also lost their last six cup meetings with the Red Devils since a 3–0 victory in 1999 against what was an opposing side largely made up of youth team players. It was a streak which would be extended to seven, though only after Villa had again played well, twice taking the lead through Watkins and a Diogo Dalot own goal but being pegged back on both occasions before conceding twice late on to lose 4–2.

While the defeat was disappointing, not least for the 7,500 travelling supporters who had journeyed north, more than anything this felt a night when Emery was testing out the squad he had inherited to better inform his opinion of the way forward. There were seven changes from the team which had beaten United the previous weekend, including a first start of the season for Calum Chambers in the heart of defence and a rare outing for back-up goalkeeper Robin Olsen. Boubacar Kamara also returned after two months out injured and in the final stages in particular, with his substitutions, you got the sense Emery was using the cup tie as a training exercise.

A Sunday afternoon Premier League trip to Brighton just 64 hours after the final whistle at Old Trafford was of far greater importance but Villa were dealt a blow when Watkins, impressive in both matches under the new boss, fell ill. In the hours before kick-off it became clear the striker could not play while Bailey, another standout performer in both matches against United, was also under the weather and could only be named on the bench.

The match itself then got off to the worst possible start when Alexis Mac Allister pounced on a mistake by Douglas Luiz to fire the home side in front after just 49 seconds. Another long afternoon looked to be in store for a Villa team which had taken only two points from its first seven away league matches.

Yet Villa hit back with Danny Ings, who had replaced Watkins in the line-up, levelling from the penalty spot after Lewis Dunk had brought down John McGinn, the latter also starting for the first time in the league under Emery. Nine minutes into the second half, Ings then put Villa ahead after Luiz had taken revenge on Mac Allister by robbing his opposite number deep in home territory. Though Brighton pushed hard for a leveller, Villa held out to record their first away league win of the season. It was also the first time they had come from behind to win away from home in the Premier League in nearly 18 months and moved them five points clear of the relegation zone. The fact they were now closer to sixth-placed Liverpool than 18th-placed Nottingham Forest allowed Emery to claim with confidence his team were now 'looking up' the table, rather than worrying about what was beneath them. A team which had scored just 11 goals in its first 13 league matches had now netted five in their opening two under new management.

'I think these six points give us a calmness for the work ahead,' declared Emery. For the next six weeks that work would take place exclusively on the training pitch, with the World Cup in Qatar meaning Villa would not play another competitive match until after Christmas. It meant Emery would effectively have a pre-season to work with his new squad and the fact Argentina's Emi Martinez, the Polish duo of Matty Cash and Jan Bednarek and Belgium's Leander Dendoncker were the only players selected by their respective nations for the tournament was another advantage.

Lifting the players who had missed out on a dream trip to the World Cup was Emery's first task. Mings and Watkins were overlooked by England, Digne and Kamara failed to make the cut for France, Buendia did not squeeze into the Argentina squad while Coutinho, now injured, and Luiz were cast aside by Brazil.

An 11-day break allowed many of those to get away with their families before a warm-weather training camp in Dubai was set up for Emery to get to work. The resort where Villa stayed was quiet and in a low-key area, but popular with football clubs because of the privacy. Brighton and Bournemouth were also at the same facility but they ate in separate rooms and trained on a different pitch. Emery had his own conference room on site for team meetings and it was on this trip where the players began to realise just how meticulous the Spaniard was in his planning.

During the early days in the camp, the fitness training was tough, but the trip was more about changing the culture, the outlook, and bringing the players back together.

Bailey spoke about the need to improve the team spirit and was a standout individual who felt refreshed by the change in management. Raised in the underprivileged ghetto of Cassava Piece, north of Jamaica's capital city of Kingston, he was no stranger to struggle, having trekked through Europe with his adopted father in search of a trial during his younger years. After spells at lower-tier clubs in Austria and false dawns at Ajax and Trencin, Bailey signed for Genk in Belgium and kicked on but his time at Villa needed a serious boost and Emery was about to provide it.

A friendly game against Brighton saw Villa work on new patterns of play but it was far from free-flowing. In another game against Chelsea, 70 miles away in Abu Dhabi a few days later, the same teething problems continued. Having these weeks to practise, without the pressure of getting results, was so important.

Purslow had made the trip over and sat on the sidelines among only a handful of other spectators flicking between English, Spanish and French to encourage players through the games. Emery, meanwhile, was as commanding as he is on a proper matchday. He pulled players into position, also switching between English and Spanish to tell them exactly where to stand and how to receive the ball. It was a stark contrast to the final days of the Gerrard era when the man leading the way had struggled to offer any direction.

One player who stood out on that trip was Danny Ings. He looked fired up and scored another goal against Brighton, fresh after scoring two in the Premier League before the break.

Ollie Watkins, however, was at a particularly low point. He was struggling to shake off the frustration of missing out on the

England squad and felt even more aggrieved that he was now in Dubai when the World Cup was nearby in Qatar. That his brother was a resident in the UAE only added to the pain. The pair had planned for a Middle East reunion but the goals dried up and England manager Gareth Southgate looked elsewhere.

After breakfast one morning, and for over an hour, he sat outside the hotel discussing his disappointment. Watkins knew in advance that, because his goalscoring record was not as good as Harry Kane, Marcus Rashford or Callum Wilson – the three strikers chosen to represent England – he would be overlooked.

'I want my name to be mentioned when these big tournaments are coming up so I'm pushing to get those extra goals,' he said with conviction over a coffee.

Emery's plan for the striker would help him achieve that. It was simple. No longer would Watkins be running deep into the channels, and instead the focus would switch to playing centrally and within the lines of the penalty box.

Rodri, the new individual coach, pulled up clips of Carlos Bacca, the former Sevilla striker who starred for Emery up front, and showed Watkins the moves he had to make to succeed in the manager's system.

On the flight back home there was renewed confidence and a spring in his step again. Others were pumped up too and couldn't wait to get started back in the Premier League. Many felt refreshed after the break but more importantly that they were already becoming better players by working under Emery and his staff. The work of Rodri, in particular, was proving eye-opening for several players who had rarely experienced such attention to detail over their specific roles.

'One of the first things he did with me was show me on a whiteboard how I was all over the defence,' Mings says. 'He said I just need you to stay in your position, play as a left-sided centre-back and trust other people to do their jobs. That was music to my ears.

The clarity and the simplifying of your job in a small area of the pitch allowed everyone to understand what was required.

'The Dubai camp really helped, so while I was disappointed to not go to the World Cup, I also knew that for my long-term Villa career, these three or four weeks were going to be so crucial to understand how the manager wanted us to play.'

The next time Villa supporters saw their team play in the UK was on 15 December, a bitterly cold night when Villarreal visited for a friendly. A late goal from Étienne Capoue earned the Spanish team victory, though Villa largely performed well with both Mings and Buendia hitting the post and Watkins missing several good chances. By then, much of the talk around Villa Park was of the one player still away at the World Cup, Emi Martinez, who two nights earlier had reached the tournament final with Argentina courtesy of a 3–0 semi-final win over Croatia.

Martinez had already established himself as a hero by saving two penalties in a quarter-final shoot-out win over the Netherlands and he would go on to replicate that feat on the grandest stage of all, saving Kingsley Coman's spot-kick in the final after a thrilling match against France had finished 3–3 as Argentina won their third World Cup title. It capped the incredible rise of a player who had only made his senior international debut less than 18 months previously. For Villa, it was also a proud moment, with Martinez becoming the club's first-ever World Cup winner. That five-and-a-half year contract they had convinced him to sign at the start of the year now looked a seriously savvy move.

Yet Martinez, who had provided some insight into Emery's coaching style before departing for Qatar, explaining how the Villa boss had told his players not to fear making mistakes, would cause the first awkward questions of his new club manager's reign. A lewd gesture performed by the goalkeeper with the Golden Glove Trophy – which he had been presented as the best shot-stopper of the tournament – combined with his taunting of Kylian

Mbappé, which drew a formal complaint from the French FA, were the subjects which dominated Emery's first post-World Cup press conference.

'I am going to speak with him because I want to control him about that as well, his emotions,' said Emery, while also stressing the importance of the bigger picture. 'I prefer to focus on how he performed and how he is going to win with us after,' he added.

The real downside to Martinez's World Cup success from Emery's perspective was his No. 1 goalkeeper would not be available for the Boxing Day visit of Liverpool, which came just eight days after the final. Robin Olsen instead made just his second Premier League start but could do little to prevent a 3–1 defeat in an entertaining match where Villa competed well yet paid the price for not taking their chances.

'I am disappointed, angry but I think the attitude of our team was amazing,' said Emery. Just how demanding the new head coach would be was again demonstrated when he dismissed the positive start prior to the World Cup as 'not good enough for us'.

Players too had changed their tone. While there had been no shortage of encouragement to take from Villa's performance against the Reds, in a fixture the majority of people expected them to lose, Mings, a player also refreshed by the managerial change, instead chose to focus on the 'frustration' of having let the visitors off the hook.

In their next match Villa would not be so generous. A 2–0 New Year's Day win at Tottenham was the biggest sign yet Emery had his team on the rise. In some respects, the afternoon was a tale of three goalkeepers, the first of them being Martinez who, despite being back at Bodymoor Heath and available following his exploits in Qatar, was kept on the bench by Villa's boss. Olsen, who had participated in the majority of training sessions that week, was instead handed his second start in succession and rewarded Emery's faith with an assured performance. The same could not be said for

Tottenham keeper Hugo Lloris. Back in action just a fortnight after losing out to Martinez and Argentina at the World Cup, the France international was responsible for Villa's opening goal early in the second half when he spilled a Douglas Luiz shot. This owed a little to Emery's meticulous planning. Aware Lloris sometimes had trouble holding the ball at the first attempt, he told Watkins to stay near the keeper any time shots were hit from distance. It was the striker who pounced on the loose ball, diverting it for Buendia to stroke home. Luiz would go on to get Villa's second with 17 minutes remaining following a neat exchange with McGinn. 'There is a clear way of playing. The manager is finding strengths in people's games we probably didn't realise ourselves,' remarked the latter when asked to assess Villa's rapid upturn.

Matty Cash, who returned immediately after the World Cup with Lionel Messi's shirt after Poland lost to Argentina, explains some of the finer details he began to notice under Emery, saying: 'I had to change in terms of my positioning and how I approached certain situations. The manager is such a good coach and tactically he's so clever. All the players quickly noticed that.'

This was only the beginning.

17

MARCH TO EUROPE

Unai Emery wore a look of thunder.

'We can't continue like that,' the Villa boss almost shouted into a room of journalists, the majority of whom were taken aback by his anger.

Granted, Villa had just been beaten 4–2 at home by Arsenal, their third Premier League defeat in succession. Yet their performance, against a Gunners team who went back top of the table courtesy of two stoppage time goals, had been impressive. Villa had led twice through Ollie Watkins and Philippe Coutinho and, though they had been pegged back, had chances themselves to win in what had truly been a game decided by inches, the visitors going ahead for the first time when Jorginho's shot hit the bar and bounced down onto the head of Emi Martinez before going over the line. Villa, in the eyes of almost everyone in the stadium's press conference room, had been unlucky.

Emery was having none of it. 'I am very disappointed, very frustrated. It is embarrassing,' he said. A large focus of Emery's ire was Martinez, who having conceded the third goal in such unfortunate fashion, had let in the fourth after being stranded upfield, having ignored his head coach's pleas to stay back by going up into the opposition box when Villa won a corner in the final minute of stoppage time.

'He decided and sometimes it is good. But I don't like it. I told him after the match,' said Emery. 'Statistically, you can go up 100 times and maybe score one or two times. But the transition helped them. To lose 4–2 to me is worse.'

Some context might help explain Emery's annoyance. Much as he had refuted the suggestion during the build-up to the visit of Arsenal that the club who had sacked him after just 18 months in charge might mean a little more to him than the standard league fixture, there was a sense the Spaniard would rather have enjoyed putting one over on his former employers.

Even more pertinent were Villa's recent results. While the second of their three defeats, a 3–1 reverse at Manchester City, was the kind suffered by most teams in the league when they faced the reigning champions, the first had been a frenetic home loss to relegation-threatened Leicester, when Villa twice blew leads and were beaten 4–2. It was the chaos Emery couldn't stand and when the scoreline was repeated a fortnight later against Arsenal, he vowed to do something about it. The work done in the following days would not only turn Villa's results around, but it would ultimately set them on their way to qualifying for Europe for the first time in more than a decade.

Results and performances up to the Leicester defeat at the start of February had been mixed and included one of the worst afternoons in Villa's history. The 2–1 FA Cup third round home defeat to Stevenage, then playing in English football's fourth tier, was probably the second-most embarrassing result the club had ever been on the end of, beaten in the nadir stakes only by a 5–4 aggregate loss to Bradford City in a League Cup semi-final a decade previously. It was the kind of setback which would in many eras have prompted supporters to call for a head coach to be sacked and the fortune for Emery was it occurred in just the sixth match of a reign which had otherwise begun promisingly. The Spaniard could also point to the fact he had named a much-changed team and by the end of the month the Stevenage result was significant for the fact four of the starting XI had departed the club, either permanently or on loan.

It also helped Emery that Villa were able to win their next game. The victory over Leeds five days later was notable for being the debut of the new boss's first signing, Alex Moreno. The 29-year-old left-back had joined in a £13.2 million deal from Real Betis, with Emery keen to add more competition for Lucas Digne in a position which, when taking into account his tactical set-up, was among the most important in the team. Emery likes his left-backs to play high up the pitch, almost to the point where they become wingers, and to counter-balance that, his right-back would often sit deep or become a third centre-back. Moreno, generally regarded as the best Spanish player in the position never to receive an international cap, was seen as the ideal fit and the fee good value.

With the deal completed on 11 January, his Premier League baptism came quicker than expected 48 hours later when Digne was forced off with injury just 10 minutes into the match against Leeds. Moreno, who had trained just twice with his new teammates, entered the fray and performed impressively, his goal-line clearance in the first half proving a critical moment and an early demonstration of the pace he would add to the team. The match was also memorable for Villa repeatedly catching Leeds offside as they played a high defensive line, something which would quickly become a feature of Emery's team. Speaking afterwards, Tyrone Mings explained how defenders were now 'celebrating' offsides, such had been the attention placed on the tactic in training. The defender also claimed Emery's methods, on a personal level, were giving him a 'new lease of life'.

If Moreno was an example of Emery identifying a player and Villa following through on his request to sign them, the same could not be said for the second January arrival, Jhon Durán. Emery had never heard of the 19-year-old Colombia international until he was put forward by the club's recruitment department.

Durán had been tracked by Villa's data analyst Joe Bucknall since making his breakthrough at Envigado aged just 15, where he had become the youngest ever player to score in the Colombian League. By January 2023 he was on the radar of dozens of European clubs thanks to his exploits for Chicago Fire, who had signed him for £1.8 million two years earlier. Durán, the youngest international signing in MLS history, had actually only been in Chicago for a year as the transfer could not be completed until he turned 18. Among those who watched him in person in the USA during the early part of 2023 was Rob Mackenzie, who stayed behind following a business trip with Johan Lange to visit the Milwaukee Bucks.

Villa's recruitment team were quick to note how Durán possessed both physical and technical abilities rare in a player so young. The player was invited to visit Villa Park, together with his agent and father, where the club put forward a big sales pitch which included a video of former Villa and Colombia international striker Juan Pablo Angel, who like Durán hailed from the city of Medellín. Ben Hackney, the head of scouting operations, created the video which was used and Lange held further FaceTime conversations with Durán, using a translator, to further push the club's cause.

Emery would also need convincing. Villa's recruitment staff prepared videos of Durán in action and after viewing them the head coach agreed with their assessment and gave the green light to complete the deal. Emery also held a FaceTime conversation with the player to help it over the line. Like Moreno, he would need time to get used to Emery's demands and specific requirements in his position. The manager gave both of the new signings clips to study at home in order to speed up the process.

Durán's signing was then followed just a few days later by the sale of Danny Ings to West Ham in a deal worth £15 million. Of all the calls Emery made during his first transfer window, this was the biggest. Ings was still Villa's top scorer with seven goals, including five in his last eight Premier League appearances, the most recent an equaliser in a 1–1 draw against Wolves earlier that month.

But while Emery was hugely respectful of the 30-year-old's ability, there were doubts about whether he was quite the right fit for Villa's new style of play. Watkins looked a better option and in the 18 months since Ings had joined from Southampton there had been little evidence the pair could play together effectively. If anything, there was a long-held suspicion the presence of Ings was an unwanted distraction for Watkins, something the latter would effectively confirm in an interview with *The Times* later in 2023, telling Charlotte Duncker that Ings' depature 'definitely did help me' because 'Before, I used to think if I had a bad game was Ingsy going to start the next game, and there was always that doubt that if I hadn't scored after 60 minutes he was going to come on.'[32]

Emery was happy to keep both on board but the offer from West Ham, of £12 million up front and a further £3 million if the Hammers avoided relegation, for a player whose re-sale value was only going to decrease as he approached the final year of his contract, ultimately proved too good to turn down. Purslow played a leading role in the sale, first holding tight as four clubs all battling for Premier League survival registered an interest.

In a frank and candid conversation with Emery, the CEO then explained why it made financial sense to sell Ings in this particular window. Emery listened carefully and sanctioned the move, even though it left him with only Watkins and the raw and unproven Durán as his back-up.

If it felt like a gamble, the failure to bring in a replacement, even on loan, before the end of the window looked even more so. Emery and Villa were essentially placing their full trust in Watkins and his durability, an act of faith for which they would be repaid handsomely. Watkins began what would turn out to be a superb second half of the season by scoring the only goal in a win at Southampton, the day after Ings had been sold.

Emery was reluctant to bring in another striker who would at best only take up space in the dressing room and at worst disrupt Watkins, but that was only after it became clear he could not land any of his top targets.

Discussions around signing Joao Felix on loan from Atletico Madrid had taken place but it quickly became clear he was only interested in joining a club in the Champions League. 'It wasn't impossible,' Emery would later say, but Chelsea, the club the forward did eventually join, had far more to offer than Villa at that stage and the plan was to close the gap in the times ahead.

Emery was only thinking big. It's understood he asked his team about whether a move for Victor Osimhen at Napoli was realistic, but also quickly discovered it was a non-starter, especially so late into the window.

Content at sitting tight in the hope of landing the right players in the summer, rather than rushing through moves in January when Villa's books were already pushed to the limit, Emery identified two top targets: the Spanish attacker Nico Williams at Athletic Bilbao, a player who would almost certainly command a record-breaking transfer fee, and Marco Asensio, the No. 10 coming towards the end of his contract at Real Madrid.

There was a push for Weston McKennie, the USA midfielder, but his loan move to Leeds United had already been agreed and even a hijacked attempt would prove to be too late. One player Emery did get frustrated about not signing sooner was the defender from his former club, Villarreal, Pau Torres, but there was hope a deal could be done in the summer.

The focus, therefore, was on moving players out. Jan Bednarek and Ludwig Augustinsson's forgettable stays were cut short after only six months, while Marvelous Nakamba joined Luton on loan and Cameron Archer was moved out to Middlesbrough.

Frederic Guilbert went to Strasbourg on loan, while Morgan Sanson became the final member of the starting XI from the Stevenage nightmare to depart when he joined Nice, in a deal which would eventually become permanent that summer. Emery had concluded that while the Frenchman had talent, too much water had passed under the bridge for him ever to be effective at Villa. The last time he started a Premier League game at Villa Park, against Manchester United over a year before his exit, it ended with the midfielder kicking a water bottle in rage after being substituted following a mistake that gifted Bruno Fernandes the opening goal in a 2–2 draw.

The win at Southampton in late January had been followed by Ashley Young becoming the first Villa player to claim they should be targeting European football over the second half of the season. It did not seem too crazy a suggestion. With five wins from their first seven league games under Emery, including a perfect record of three wins from three on the road, Villa were one of the country's most in-form teams and sat 11th in the table, just three points behind seventh-placed Fulham. Yet after losing to Arsenal a month later the outlook had changed. Now the gap to seventh was seven points and though the chance of being sucked back into trouble at the wrong end of the table seemed remote, there was a real danger the season might now fizzle out.

Emery's anger in defeat to the Gunners was because he believed his team had paid the price for abandoning the game plan. Rather than carry out the head coach's instruction of keeping possession and staying patient, Villa had kicked the ball long and given it back to Arsenal on countless occasions inside the final 15 minutes. That had invited pressure which eventually told with their opponents twice scoring late to snatch the points. In the training sessions which followed that week, there was a renewed focus on playing out from the back, with players urged not to panic and give in to the desire to clear the ball to the other end of the pitch when under pressure.

'Everything had been so positive until then,' says McGinn. 'It is normal and natural, you are in one of the best leagues in the world and at some point you are going to come up against better teams. But he stayed calm. He might not have looked so calm on the sidelines at the time, but he managed to stay calm in the dressing room and tried to find the solutions.'

By now, more than three months into his reign, Villa's players had become used to Emery's coaching methods and the early success they had experienced meant they were buying into them. To describe Emery as a workaholic might be underselling the point. Damian Vidagany probably puts it best when he describes his friend as being like a 'nuclear plant of energy' – almost always on the go. It is typical for the head coach to spend 12 hours a day at Bodymoor Heath and the important aspect is he is never working for the sake of it. There is always a purpose and no moment is wasted. Emery regularly uses the training ground gym after players have departed for the day but has never been seen without his laptop, watching a game and studying the next opponent, when on the exercise bike or treadmill. Team meetings, meanwhile, have become legendary in length. Carefully put together by Emery, his coaching staff and analysts, they have been known to last for hours and there are typically at least two on the day of a game, sometimes three. To stay focused those in attendance drink plenty of coffee but that sparks a growing need to empty the bladder and only one man, Jhon Durán, has been brave enough to request permission to leave midway through a meeting in all of Emery's time and he never asked again.

'Look at the people who do Ted Talks, they are motivating,' says Vidagany. 'Unai has to do a different one for every match because he's talking and in front of the players for three hours each game.

'Meetings cover gameplan, the opponent, set-pieces. It's a big mental task. It's very hard to do this.

'Imagine having to deliver a speech to a university every three days and it has to be different and unique? It's difficult. You need a mental strength and passion. Then there's the challenge of identifying the patterns, the tactical things. You have to be a master.'

If the meetings feel long for the players then consider the work Emery has put in to prepare them. He watches each opponent at least five times before adding his own solutions to the opposition report which is put together by Victor Manas. Emery also clips up various parts of the presentations himself and uses the meetings to prompt and provoke his players. His personality is completely different to when he's public facing and many have said that he's more like an actor than a manager when he's presenting.

On one occasion he repeatedly hid behind his trusted whiteboard to replicate an on-field action, showing how the passing lane to a player was blocked off by his incorrect starting position.

As the team would find out in later times, the lower the level of opposition, the greater his focus would become.

For the first three months of his time at Villa, Emery lived in The Belfry Hotel near the training ground, in part because, as Vidagany jokes: 'He had no time to find a house!'

Success might have brought financial rewards but for Emery that has never been the motivation. 'He's 20 years doing this now. He doesn't know what he's worth financially,' says Vidagany. 'He doesn't care about the car or the house. He lives in a nice three-bedroom apartment but he doesn't need a big house. He's just focused on football!

'He likes to enjoy life when there is a break, but when there isn't a break, he lives like a monk in a tracksuit. He'll go home wearing it and then come back. He's working for the success, not for the money or recognition. You don't see him (around) a lot. He doesn't like the exposure. He works for the glory, he wants to win.'

Among Emery's first moves was to change the pre-match routine with players staying in a hotel the night before home matches. Those with larger windows are preferred as they provide more natural light and therefore – the head coach believes – helps create a brighter atmosphere for his squad.

For a man so meticulous in his planning, it may sound unusual Emery rarely sets a training schedule any longer than a fortnight in advance, but that's just the way he likes it. With Emery, everything is open to change, and players have learned to adapt to that.

One player who was doing precisely what the manager wanted in the early months at Villa was Watkins. His opener against Arsenal meant he had scored in all four matches since Ings' departure and when he netted again the following weekend, firing home from the penalty spot in a 2–0 win at Everton, he became the first Villa player since Paul Rideout in 1985 to score in five consecutive league matches. The post-match claim he was targeting a goal-a-game for the rest of the campaign might have sounded bullish but also demonstrated a player whose confidence had been fully restored. No longer down in the dumps like in Dubai, he was now the player leading the charge.

Emi Buendia, who scored Villa's second goal in the win at Everton, was another visibly benefiting from the Spaniard's methods. The goal at Goodison was the Argentine's third in nine matches and he was finally beginning to show the form befitting the club's record signing. Through Buendia's first 18 months at Villa Park there was a sense he was almost trying too hard to live up to the tag. Emery's advice was to slow down and to not be afraid of taking more touches, or feeling he had to play the match-defining pass every time he was on the ball. For the first time since joining Villa, meanwhile, Buendia was getting an extended run of matches, starting every one since Emery had walked through the door.

'Now I understand maybe it is better to touch the ball less but make better opportunities for my team-mates. That is one of the things I am learning,' he said, during an interview with the *Express & Star*.

The win at Everton made it four from five away matches for Villa under Emery. It was a different story at home, however, where they had lost three out of six. The 1–0 win over Crystal Palace the following weekend, therefore, felt like the moment they truly hit the reset button. Though the match, decided by Joachim Andersen's first half own goal, was a largely turgid affair for the neutral with few chances at either end of the pitch, for Emery it was the perfect response to the chaos witnessed against Arsenal a fortnight previously. This time Villa stuck to the plan in the closing stages when defending their one-goal lead, continuing to play out from the back regardless of how nervy it might have made the home crowd.

'The fans have to be patient and we have to be patient because it is possession football in risky areas,' acknowledged Matty Cash after the final whistle. 'It can go a bit edgy. That is where we have to stay brave and they have to be brave with us, knowing we are going to do that.'

It might not have been thrilling but Villa's attacking play was improving, the last two goals at Villa Park both 19-pass sequences from back to front showing just that. They were also nudging their way back into the race for Europe. A 1–1 draw at West Ham was followed by a 3–0 win over Bournemouth in front of both Sawiris and Edens, prior to the international break in which Buendia, Douglas Luiz and Jacob Ramsey all scored.

The owners were now in town on a more regular basis, jumping firmly on the bandwagon as, under Emery, it was cool to be at games again. Until this point they tended to hand-pick the matches they attended, usually based on the level of opposition or importance of the game. Given that a game against Bournemouth, with all due respect, was hardly an encounter to set pulses racing in advance, the fact Sawiris and Edens had jetted in was a measure of just how well Villa were now performing.

That Ramsey got on the scoresheet, in a week where he had stood in wellington boots and a hard hat on the building site across the road that would soon become the club's new inner-city academy, was also fitting. He showed the owners why their £8 million pledge to the project was a sound investment and could help discover more first-team stars from the local area, just like himself, in the future.

Though Villa had not moved from 11th in the table since a 1–1 draw with Wolves on 4 January, they were back to within four points of seventh and having seemingly overcome the first blip of Emery's reign. Just one goal had been conceded – and that a contentious penalty – in the four matches since Arsenal. Only the Gunners, Manchester City and Manchester United had taken more points than Villa since Emery's arrival.

The wins kept coming as the season moved into April. A 2–0 victory at Chelsea, in which Watkins scored his 10th league goal of the season – making it three consecutive campaigns in which he had hit double figures – moved Villa into the top half of the table. Just three days later they were up to seventh, occupying what was likely to be a European place come the end of the season, after a 2–1 triumph at Leicester City thanks to the most unlikely of match-winners.

It would be fair to say most Villa supporters presumed they had seen the last of Bertrand Traoré when he had joined Istanbul Basaksehir on loan the previous summer. After scoring eight goals in his first season at the club following his £17 million move from Lyon in 2021, the Chelsea academy product had been limited to only 10 appearances in his second due to injury and inconsistent form. Traoré's tendency to always be fit for international duty for Burkina Faso but return to Villa with a knock had been of increasing frustration for Steven Gerrard, who eventually lost faith and decided the player was not going to be part of his future plans. The 27-year-old had been sent to train with the youth team before going out on loan. Fast forward six months and Villa's failure to find a suitable loan back-up to Watkins in the January window prompted Emery to recall him. The match at Leicester was just Traoré's third substitute appearance since returning but the night he would make his mark on Villa's push for Europe. Two minutes after coming on and with just three minutes of the 90 remaining, the winger pounced on a misplaced pass 25 yards out and – ignoring the pleas of team-mates not to shoot – lifted a first-time effort over Foxes goalkeeper Daniel Iversen and into the top corner.

It was a sublime goal which a few weeks later would be voted Villa's best of the season by supporters. Traoré, who later paid an emotional tribute to his friend Christian Atsu, among the 56,000 killed two months earlier in an earthquake which struck Turkey and Syria, was not finished there. The following Saturday he scored the opener in a 2–0 win over Nottingham Forest, Villa's fourth victory in a row. Emery, largely dismissive of his team's European chances to that point, now had to concede they were in the race.

'You have to be ready when you have that opportunity in front. We have that now,' he said. In seven matches since the defeat to Arsenal, his team had dropped just two points and conceded only two goals. It was hugely impressive, though any sceptics could point to the fact that, bar the trip to Chelsea, the fixture list had exclusively pitted Villa against teams in the bottom half of the table. The next match, at home to a Newcastle team who were themselves on a five-match winning streak and firmly in the race for Champions League football, would provide the real test.

'Villa are on fire? Let them know the fire brigade are in town,' joked Magpies striker Callum Wilson in the build-up, during an appearance on the *Footballer's Football Podcast*.

They were words which would come back to haunt him, after an afternoon where any doubt about Villa's European credentials was firmly extinguished. Watkins set up Ramsey for an 11th minute opener and then scored twice himself in the second half. The striker, who also hit the post and saw another effort controversially chalked off by VAR, was simply unplayable as he took his tally to five goals in the previous four matches. John McGinn, later alerted to Wilson's pre-match comments while being interviewed in the mixed zone, smiled before replying: 'Like a lot of emergency services at the minute, the fire brigade must have been on strike.'

Villa were now sixth in the table, just six points behind the fourth-placed Magpies and with seven matches to play there were even some supporters wondering whether they could gatecrash the Champions League race. The victory over Newcastle was not only great for momentum but also the most complete Premier League performance many inside Villa Park had seen for almost a decade.

'You look back and think, hang on, this is pretty much the same team Steven Gerrard had,' says Mo Razzaq. 'But we were now getting a different set of results because there was suddenly a belief within the team. Every player knew what they had to do. Emery's man-management was completely different.

'Every game you went to, particularly home games, was like a cup game. Everything counts, everything matters. To think where we were, teetering above relegation, and where we ended up. It was a miraculous turnaround. I have never experienced one so quick. We went from being relegation fodder to one of the toughest teams to beat in the league.'

A 1–1 draw at Brentford the following weekend, in which Douglas Luiz netted an 87th minute equaliser, halted momentum and offered a reality check, and though a rare Mings goal was enough to see Villa past Fulham, their surge up the table was about to hit a stumbling block.

Mings' goal saw Villa set a new Premier League record as the first team to score in their first 20 matches under a new manager. But at what felt the worst possible time, Villa were about to lose their shooting boots.

While a narrow 1–0 defeat at Manchester United, who boasted one of the best home records in the division, could be stomached, a reverse by the same scoreline at lowly Wolves the next weekend felt far more damaging. Villa found themselves back down in eighth with Tottenham, their main rivals for the seventh spot which would earn a place in the Europa Conference League, three points better off. In the kind of script journalists love, the two teams faced each other in their next game. Villa were suddenly in must-win territory.

'We've made it extremely difficult for ourselves but the challenge is still there,' said McGinn.

Emery described the visit of Tottenham as a 'cup final' and his message, in public, was for his players to enjoy the occasion. Despite seeing his team beaten on consecutive weekends, the head coach felt there had not been a huge amount wrong with either performance. There was also an insistence most of the pressure was on Tottenham, European regulars who were now under the guidance of interim boss Ryan Mason following Antonio Conte's exit by mutual agreement six weeks earlier. While talented, Spurs were also woefully inconsistent and had conceded 10 goals in their previous two away matches.

Villa, by contrast, had won five straight at home without conceding since losing to Arsenal. Emery went through a unique approach before the game by showing his team clips of how Real Madrid's defenders had stopped Manchester City's Erling Haaland in the Champions League semi-final he had watched during the week. Though their defence would finally be breached on this occasion, courtesy of a stoppage-time Harry Kane penalty, earlier goals from Jacob Ramsey and Douglas Luiz ensured Emery's team claimed a win which kept them firmly in the European hunt.

The odds still favoured Tottenham. Goal difference meant they were still above Villa in the table and they certainly had the easier run-in, hosting Brentford before visiting relegation-threatened Leeds on the final day. Villa had to play two teams who were themselves in the thick of the European race, first away to Liverpool and then at home to Brighton on the final day.

Tottenham's match with Brentford was the first to kick off on the penultimate weekend and members of Villa staff watched from the press room at Anfield knowing a big win for their rivals would leave them with something of a mountain to climb. Those fears looked like being realised when Kane fired his team into an early lead yet in the second half Spurs' flakiness returned. Bryan Mbuemo scored twice in quick succession to turn the game around before Yoane Wissa scored late on to seal a 3–1 win for the Bees. For Villa, there was suddenly an opportunity and it was one they grasped, Ramsey firing them in front against the Reds after Watkins had missed an early penalty. Emery had worked all week on a plan to expose Trent Alexander-Arnold – playing in a hybrid right-back/midfield role – and Ibrahima Konate on the right side of the Liverpool defence by building out to the corner flag and then flipping balls into space for Watkins. A late Roberto Firmino equaliser denied Emery's team a fine victory but the point was enough to move them above Tottenham and into seventh. Destiny was back in their own hands. McGinn later confirmed players had been informed of Spurs' defeat prior to kick-off at Anfield.

After weeks of working out all the permutations, the equation for Villa was now wonderfully simple. Beat Brighton at home on the final day and they would be back in European competition for the first time since 2010. Anything less would leave the door open for either Tottenham or Brentford to pip them on the line.

'It was actually really strange, knowing we had put ourselves in the position to achieve something really special,' says McGinn. 'I was just so excited because I never thought [it would happen], with the journey we had as players. Me and Tyrone spoke before the game about how mental it was, we were one win away from Europe. Brighton are a team who, on paper, people think aye, you will beat them. People think Aston Villa are a bigger club and they are at home so if they need to win, they will win. It doesn't work like that.'

'This is our time, this is our moment and we have to enjoy it,' proclaimed Emery in the build-up. With the Spaniard having built his reputation on excelling in cup competitions, there was a sense Villa could not ask for a better man to be at the helm for a match where everything was on the line.

Inside Villa Park it felt like one of those big semi-final nights, the pre-match entertainment cranked up and a mixture of excitement and tension in the stands. Emi Martinez had long been asking for an enhanced build-up and was a big supporter of the stadium announcer adding a catchy tagline onto each player's name when the starting line-up was revealed.

Villa flew out of the blocks, Luiz firing them ahead inside eight minutes following impressive work by Ramsey. The latter then teed up Watkins for his first goal since the win over Newcastle. Brighton, who had earlier seen a goal chalked off for the most marginal of offside calls, pulled one back through Denis Undav but a Villa team which had not conceded more than once in a match since the Arsenal defeat was not about to forget the lessons of that afternoon now. This was going to be their 10th win in 15 matches after Emery's post-match rant, a run which had seen them concede only eight goals. The final whistle sounded to a huge roar and Emery, reserved throughout, now allowed himself time to take in the achievement. At one point the head coach was lifted in the air by a beaming Damian Vidagany and after a lap of honour alongside Nassef Sawiris and Wes Edens he was passed a microphone to address the crowd.

'This is a champagne moment,' he said, before adding: 'But this is only our first step.'

18

CONTROL

As players and staff celebrated the long-awaited return to European football on the Villa Park pitch, there was one notable absentee.

Christian Purslow, for so long front and centre since becoming chief executive in 2018, was nowhere to be seen. Just over a fortnight later he was out of the club completely, following a shift in power which had begun the moment Emery had walked through the door seven months previously. The promises made to Emery on his appointment, coupled with the willingness of co-owner Nassef Sawiris to take a more hands-on role, meant the model in which Purslow had long held a vital position started to change. By the time Villa were beating Brighton on the final day of the 2022–23 season, the triangle of power consisting of chief executive, head coach and sporting director had been broken up. Instead the club's day-to-day operations had effectively been split in two, Emery and his growing number of Spanish allies calling the shots on the one half in the football department at Bodymoor Heath, while the commercial half at Villa Park was headed up by a new arrival in president of business operations Chris Heck.

Even under this new structure, few were under any doubts as to who was really in charge. Authority now lay in the hands of one man: Unai Emery.

It was in early February that those who deal with Villa on a regular basis first detected a change. Impressed by the performances of Tyrone Mings, Emery decided he wanted the defender to be given a new contract yet during negotiations over the deal Purslow was conspicuous by his absence. Signings and contract extensions were typically the kind of thing the chief executive would be all over. That had certainly been the case when Mings had agreed his previous deal a little over two years earlier. This time Purslow's involvement consisted of a phone call of congratulations once the centre-back had signed on the dotted line.

It was Johan Lange who had instead taken the lead during discussions with Mings' representatives but any idea the sporting director's own power base might be expanding proved wide of the mark. While Emery and his staff had huge respect for Lange, there was a sense the sporting director was tied too closely to the existing regime. It is also natural for any recruitment chief to be loyal to those players they had brought in. While aware of Lange's capabilities, Emery wanted his own man as part of a rebuild which would shift power away from the boardroom and toward the training ground, with the head coach at the centre of it all.

'We always liked the way Man City created a structure in the club, of full-confidence, brilliant people like Txiki Begiristain and Omar Berrada,' explains Damian Vidagany. 'That helps Guardiola to be protected. Even though Guardiola was doing well in the Premier League the big challenge was to win the Champions League. For six or seven years he couldn't do it.

'Why Man City finally won the Champions League was because of their consistency. They had time to fail, fail, fail and then succeed.

'Look at PSG, who have been chasing the Champions League for some time. They have had many managers, whereas sometimes you need five or ten years with one coach, but that isn't always in the DNA of some clubs.

'We were always talking about the club working well when there's a strong structure helping the manager to make the club be aligned with the football. We explained that to Nassef and he was very excited.'

The first notable changes to Villa's recruitment structure took place in April, with the appointments of Alberto Benito and Pablo Rodriguez. The latter had been part of Emery's coaching staff at Villarreal, where he had also worked as a senior scout. Benito, who was given a job described as a 'global technical role' in Villa's official statement, ranks as arguably Emery's closest ally in football. Former team-mates at Toledo, they had enjoyed success together at Almeria with Emery as head coach and Benito as sporting director. The latter then recommended his friend to Valencia in 2008. He joined Villa from Real Betis, where he had been chief scout.

Officially, Benito was brought in to work alongside head of recruitment Rob Mackenzie, though it rapidly became apparent to the latter his department was in the process of being overhauled. For one thing, it had now been publicly confirmed Villa would be bringing in a new sporting director to effectively replace Lange.

The prospective appointment appeared quite the coup. Mateu Alemany, who was known to both Emery and Vidagany and had worked briefly with the latter at Valencia, had spent the previous two years as Barcelona's director of football. The 60-year-old was one of two names on a shortlist drawn up by Emery and Vidagany, with the assistance of Sawiris. Though the deal had not been formally agreed, when news of Villa's approach broke in the Spanish press Emery was confident enough to talk about Alemany on the record.

'If he [Alemany] is coming here because it is a possibility, it will be a very good opportunity to create a strong structure with him,' he said.

Yet just a few days later, after visiting Bodymoor Heath, Alemany performed a U-turn and decided to stay at Barcelona. 'Aston Villa has an impressive project and one of the best coaches in Europe,' he later told DAZN Espana. 'But after a personal reflection, I saw that my place was here [at Barcelona].'

'It was very difficult. He's my good friend, amazing guy, super professional,' says Vidagany now. 'But it was a long process to convince him to come and at the end of the day he was at Barcelona. Even if he had agreed to come, sometimes it's still hard to leave Barcelona!'

Undeterred by Alemany's change of heart, Villa set off in pursuit of the other candidate on their list. Ramon Rodriguez Verdejo, better known throughout the football world as Monchi, had been sporting director at Sevilla when Emery won three Europa League titles. In fact, barring a two-year stint at Roma, the 54-year-old's association with the Spanish club stretched back more than two decades, during which he had established a reputation as one of the best talent spotters in Europe. Under his watch, Sevilla also became renowned for buying young players at a low price and selling them on for huge profit, the Croatian international Ivan Rakitic being just one example. Monchi was also responsible for developing an academy which produced the likes of Spain legend Sergio Ramos.

The approach to Monchi was another ambitious move by Villa, and Emery for one had major doubts about their ability to recruit his former colleague. Just four years earlier, Monchi had been close to joining Emery at Arsenal, following the end of his stay with Roma, only to change his mind at the last minute and go back to Sevilla.

'That upset Unai and he said: "He will not come, he will do it again!"' explains Vidagany. The approach was made in any case and

Monchi indicated he would be interested. A meeting was arranged for the start of June, just days after Sevilla defeated Roma to claim their seventh Europa League title of his time as sporting director. Quite understandably, considering his track record, the Spanish club were very reluctant to let him depart. In a farewell press conference, Monchi would later claim Villa had ended up paying more than the £1.7 million release clause thought to be in his deal.

'Sevilla have reached an agreement with Aston Villa, paying more than the clause because they wanted me and considered that I could be important for the project,' he said. 'My pocket thinks the opposite. Everything that Aston Villa have paid I have stopped earning, as I said it is a personal issue, not an economic one.'

'It was like a war!' explains Vidagany, who led the negotiations from Villa's side. 'I was trying to steal the jewel from their crown. At the end, we got him.'

While Alemany's U-turn had initially been a blow, there was now a sense it may have worked in Villa's favour with the appointment of a recruitment chief who already knew all about Emery and his working methods.

'Unai and Alemany don't know each other deeply, but with Monchi everything was fast because of the relationship,' says Vidagany. 'It [Alemany's U-turn] was not a big setback. Always look at the bright side of life, as they say!'

Monchi's appointment would be officially announced on 16 June. His title was president of football operations and in Villa's statement Sawiris described him as a 'serial winner' while Monchi called Emery 'one of the best managers in football'.

Vidagany's importance at Bodymoor Heath, meanwhile, was highlighted by his promotion from chief of staff to director of football operations. There would be a further appointment, on the eve of the new season, with Arnaldo Abrantes recruited from Nottingham Forest to become head of medical services, replacing longstanding club doctor Ricky Shamji.

For Lange, meanwhile, there was reassignment as he became global director of football development and international academies, as both Sawiris and Edens believed he was still an important figure in the business. The statement described the position as a 'key role' and he was still in control of Villa's scouting network. Yet the fact he would be reporting in to Monchi made it almost impossible to paint the move as anything other than a demotion. Lange was told he would not be required to attend Bodymoor Heath on a day-to-day basis, should he choose. In October, he would leave to become technical director at Tottenham, having spent the majority of his final months at Villa back in Denmark. Just as when he joined Villa in 2021, Mackenzie would be one of his first appointments, the latter moving south to become Spurs' chief scout just a month later.

'In Aston Villa the authority now is Unai,' says Vidagany. 'It's compatible to have people like myself and Monchi around Unai. We can discuss or argue sometimes with Unai, but he knows that the project is not at risk. There is no doubt about the key of the project.

'This is why we are bringing players and helping them realign and building a consistent message with the communication of Unai. When there are so many heads, it's difficult to align everyone.

'That's why we thought this was the right structure for Villa. We really felt that the right model is to build a strong structure on the football side who can really have the decisions of the football side. With the owners and the club having a business side. But football must be the heart of the club. Sometimes when there is a CEO who is not a football person, football is contradictory, but at Aston Villa, football is the priority.'

* * *

By the time these structural changes were announced, Purslow had already chosen to depart. The announcement early on the morning of Monday 12 June, while initially coming as a jolt as such things typically do, was in truth no huge surprise. In under a year he had gone from being arguably the most powerful person at the club, behind the two owners, to the odd-man-out.

Having already seen his influence at Bodymoor Heath reduced as Emery took greater charge, the chief executive also saw some of his responsibilities on the business side reduced by the appointment in May of Chris Heck as the new president of business operations of V Sports, Villa's holding company. The obvious question at that announcement was where it left Purslow and it would take only a few weeks to find out.

Those present in the directors' box for the triumphant final match of the season spoke of the atmosphere being 'strange and awkward'. By that stage, Purslow had already told his family he was leaving. No more living out of an apartment close to New Street Station for the bulk of the week and away from his family home just outside of London. While being interviewed for this book, he admitted that although he loved his job, on reflection it was tiring and lonely at times as well as all-encompassing.

Sawiris and Edens, the pair who had for so long leaned on his expertise, offered the 59-year-old a role with reduced responsibilities but that never appealed. Purslow was all-in at Villa and fought hard for everything he believed in, so leaving on a high felt right. With Sawiris ready to dedicate more time towards the day-to-day running of the club, the baton had been passed.

Anyone who spends nearly five years as chief executive of a professional club is going to experience failures. The ill-fated appointment of Steven Gerrard will, fairly or unfairly, be something with which Purslow is always associated in the eyes of supporters. Yet across the whole piece, his tenure was one of huge success. Arriving at a club rooted in the Championship, he left it back in Europe. Among Purslow's first actions on his appointment was to create a strategic five-year plan addressing all areas of under-performance at the club. So detailed and precise was the blueprint, Purslow even had a glossy brochure created to outline exactly what he wanted to achieve.

On his exit he could be satisfied at having hit almost every target with the team in Europe, Villa Park sold out every week, the training facilities vastly improved, a new academy built, and the women's team professionalised and at the time fifth in the Women's Super League.

In a statement, owners Sawiris and Edens said: 'We are grateful for all he has done. He has overseen a transformation of the club both on and off the pitch and delivered the ambitious turnaround plan he presented to us when he arrived in 2018.'

Heck's remit would not be nearly so wide, as unlike Purslow he would have absolutely no influence on footballing decisions. His role was strictly business. The 49-year-old American, whose appointment was very much driven by Edens, had most recently been president of the Philadelphia 76ers NBA franchise. At Villa, he was given the simple instruction of increasing revenues which, while much larger than when the club was first promoted back to the Premier League, still lagged a long way behind the so-called Big Six. This was an essential part of the club's business model as the greater the income, the greater the opportunity to spend under PSR. Heck presented Sawiris and Edens with a four-year plan to effectively double Villa's revenue from £200 million to £400 million by 2027 and while the target seemed ambitious the new man did not lack confidence, telling a meeting of the fans advisory board (FAB) he was 'fucking good at selling sponsorship'. A raft of new appointments followed to what was described as the Senior Leadership Team at Villa Park. They included former Blackpool managing director Ben Hatton as chief operating officer and Ron Erskine as chief commercial officer. Yet the new regime did not get off to the best of starts, particularly when it came to keeping supporters onside.

Among the more notable business-related announcements in Purslow's final weeks had been an increase in season ticket prices of around 15 per cent for the 2023–24 campaign. This marked the second significant rise in consecutive years and was met with frustration and in some cases anger by supporters. Though the move is understood to have been driven entirely by Sawiris and Edens – with Purslow having voiced his opposition – it was the new man Heck who would quickly become the main target for criticism over increased costs at Villa Park. Early in the season it was announced the Holte Suite, a venue inside the Holte End which for years had been available to season ticket holders for free both before and after matches, was being rebranded as a hospitality area, with entry priced at £60-per-match. Heck's biggest move, meanwhile, came in December when he announced the postponement of a planned rebuild of the North Stand which would have increased the capacity of Villa Park from just under 43,000 to more than 50,000.

That project, which had first been unveiled in 2022 and given the green light by Birmingham city council later that year, would have represented the biggest development at the stadium for more than 20 years. The speed with which planning permission was granted was among Purslow's proudest achievements and consolidated Villa Park's position as a venue for the 2028 European Championships, which will be hosted by the UK and Ireland. Yet the renovation would also have taken time to complete and left the ground with a reduced capacity for at least a season. With Emery's team at that point in contention for the Champions League spot they would eventually claim, there were concerns Villa risked playing some of their most high-profile matches in years in what would effectively be a three-sided stadium.

Heck's proposal, in short, was to do more with the space already available though, as supporters correctly suspected, this would also equate to rising costs. Early in the 2024–25 season, with Villa having achieved the dream of qualifying for the Champions League, it was announced tickets for group stage matches would be priced between £85 and £97 for non-season-ticket holders. Though the first fixture against Bayern Munich sold out, in record time, for many long-term fans there has become a sense their loyalty is being exploited.

'There's been a core of supporters who have followed the club through the bad times, such as when part of the stadium was closed during the Championship years,' says Mo Razzaq. 'Since getting back into the Premier League there have been some significant price increases and some of those people are being priced out. There's definitely a feeling the club has forgotten about these loyal fans. Even those who can afford it are buying through gritted teeth.'

It is not only in the relationship between club and supporters that Villa's rapid ascent under Emery has caused growing pains. While the club qualifying for Europe for the first time in more than a decade was something for Sawiris and Edens to celebrate, it did cause complications for a major deal struck earlier in 2023. In February, it had been announced V Sports, Villa's Luxembourg-based holding company controlled by the billionaire duo, had purchased a 46 per cent stake in Portuguese First Division club Vitoria Guimaraes. The agreement followed more than two years of negotiations and marked an important breakthrough in Sawiris and Edens' efforts to expand the V Sports brand across the globe.

Yet Villa qualifying for Europe created a snag. UEFA rules prohibit an ownership group from holding a significant interest in more than one club playing in the same competition and with Vitoria also due to participate in the Conference League, it meant V Sports had no choice but to reduce its shareholding to 29 per cent just four months on from the original deal being rubber-stamped.

Multi-club ownership has become increasingly common in modern football with the Abu Dhabi-controlled City Football

Group, which owns Manchester City and a further 12 clubs across five continents, the most obvious example. Villa were merely the latest to try and follow in their footsteps. Indeed, a plan to build a network of clubs with which to share resources and aid player development had first been touted by Tony Xia following his take-over in 2016 though, like most of the grand plans during his two-year tenure, it never got off the ground.

Vitoria was in essence the first step on the ladder for V Sports, which had previously experienced frustration in its efforts to bring a Major League Soccer franchise to Las Vegas. Sawiris and Edens had even trademarked the name Las Vegas Villains, with the latter speaking openly about his plans to build a stadium in the gambling capital of the world. In early 2022, it was reported V Sports had entered into a period of exclusivity with the MLS in the hope of getting a deal, which was expected to cost Villa's owners up to $1 billion, over the line. In the end, it never happened and MLS instead awarded a franchise to San Diego.

The Vitoria deal, thought to be worth around £4.9 million, was far lower in cost. By the end of 2023, Villa had agreed a further three partnerships with Egyptian club Zed FC, Japanese outfit Vissel Kobe and Spanish Third Division side Real Union.

It is the latter deal which particularly stands out as a prime example of how Emery is now the most powerful man at Villa. Both the head coach's father and grandfather played for Union and in 2021, more than a year before he joined Villa, the head coach had purchased a controlling stake in a club dear to his heart. Emery's brother, Igor, is president of the Basque club. Several prospects from Villa's academy, including midfielder Tommi O'Reilly, defender Josh Feeney and goalkeeper James Wright, have joined Union on loan since the partnership was founded.

While his predecessors, Smith and Gerrard, had to push for changes at the training ground, it is now a case, as one club insider remarks: 'What Unai wants, Unai gets.' The same applies to his staff if Emery believes it is of benefit to the team. Strength and conditioning coach Moises De Hoyo was able to procure a state-of-the-art DEXA machine for more accurately measuring players' body mass index (BMI). Emery had also requested the need for floodlights to be installed on training pitches, so his team can work outside of daylight hours if required.

For a head coach or manager to hold such sway is almost unheard of in the modern game. Yet in the 2023–24 season the club's willingness to cede such responsibility and effectively bet the house on Emery's ability was going to pay dividends in a manner few ever really dreamed imaginable.

19

THE GIANT IS AWAKE

Never in the 150-year history of Aston Villa had a 5–0 defeat hurt so little. Every other team to wear the famous claret and blue jersey to have lost by that scoreline had left the pitch to boos from their supporters and faced a major inquest. Yet when the final whistle went at Selhurst Park on the afternoon of 19 May 2024, there were only cheers from the 2,500 or so visiting supporters in one corner of the stadium. Players beaten emphatically in their final Premier League match of the season wore only smiles.

The last-day trip to Crystal Palace had been rendered the most meaningless match of Unai Emery's reign by the fact that five days earlier his team had secured a fourth-placed finish and qualification for the Champions League. Plausible for months and probable for weeks, it was a seismic achievement, comfortably Villa's greatest since their last major trophy win in 1996 and arguably even before that, when placed in the context of the modern game. With two additional days off after the end-of-season awards night, some members of the squad had partied a little too hard, yet it was deserved because for everyone present on that afternoon in south London, from fans to players and even journalists, it still felt a little surreal.

This was, unquestionably, Emery's triumph. A man handed so much control that he was even able to name his son, Lander, on the bench for the final game of the season, he had justified the faith shown in him by the powers above. But this was also the point at which all of the good work since Nassef Sawiris and Wes Edens had swooped in to rescue Villa from the jaws of financial disaster six years earlier came together. All the bold calls, all the good recruitment decisions, all those times things went Villa's way at the crucial moment. This was a journey on which many could claim a portion of the credit for helping the club on its way.

It was certainly no fluke. If fortune might have favoured Villa earlier on their climb from the Championship to the top half of the Premier League, the 2023–24 season was the moment it tried to conspire against them and it required Emery's brilliant coaching methods and man-management skills to keep his team on track.

And yet this most celebrated of seasons could hardly have got off to a worse start.

Just like everyone else associated with Villa, Emi Buendia could rarely remember looking forward to a campaign more. After a difficult first 18 months following his then club record £38 million move from Norwich in the summer of 2021, the playmaker had finally begun to feel at home during the second half of the 2022–23 season under Emery. Heading into the new campaign, he looked primed to play a major role, scoring in the final pre-season friendly at Valencia. Just a couple of days before, Buendia had learned he was due to become a father for the third time. Even at a club already full of excitement for the months ahead, you would have been hard pressed to find anyone in better spirits.

A planned expansion to the Champions League for the following season, meanwhile, appeared to present clubs like Villa with an opportunity. The larger tournament would mean more places available for the leagues who performed strongest in Europe that year and there was an expectation a fifth-placed Premier League finish would likely be sufficient to qualify for the continent's elite competition. Emery certainly had it on his mind, when he sat down for an interview with broadcaster Sky Sports a week or so before the season was due to begin.

'The present and the future for me at Aston Villa is to try and play in the Champions League. That is my dream,' he declared.

Yet just three days before the season was due to begin with a long away trip to Newcastle United, the mood of optimism was punctured. Villa's players were just moments from leaving the field at the end of a training session when Buendia went down. Immediately, the 26-year-old knew he was in trouble. Scans later confirmed his worst fears. Buendia had suffered damage to the anterior cruciate and medial collateral ligaments in his left knee. One of the most important players in Emery's plan for the season would play no part in it. If only, for Villa, that had been the end of it.

Players wore T-shirts expressing support for Buendia in the warm-up at Newcastle but just midway through the first half it was another team-mate central to their concerns. Tyrone Mings raced back to challenge Magpies forward Alexander Isak but as he did so his right leg appeared to buckle. The defender left the pitch on a stretcher in tears. In the space of 72 hours, two of the most important cogs in Emery's Villa machine had suffered injuries which would keep them out for the entire season.

Mings' injury was particularly nasty. Complications and additional cartilage damage in his knee in addition to torn ligaments meant he underwent three surgeries and it would be more than 14 months before he would be seen in a Villa shirt again. Even as recently as May 2024 there were doubts over whether he would be able to make a return.

'Even the surgeon that did my surgery couldn't guarantee that I was going to be fine,' says Mings. 'The guy I later went to see in America couldn't guarantee that when he did the rehab with me, I'd be fine. Such was the size of the cartilage injury I had, he was like until you get back playing and training, you won't know.

'I was at my lowest in April/May of last year. That's nearly 10 months after the injury. People think you should be coming out the other end but I was in the worst part, probably because I had three surgeries and I didn't start rehabbing until November. I was doing rehab, having surgery, doing rehab, having surgery. It was a tough time. I was in such a painful place for 11 months thinking I don't know if I will get back. But I wouldn't change any of the experience.

'I think everything happens for a reason. Even when I got injured I thought, you know what, if that saved me from a really serious head injury the following game then you can't get away from what is meant to be for you.'

Villa had been trailing 2–1 at the time of Mings' injury and it was hard not to think his departure contributed in part to an eventual 5–1 defeat which further added to the mood of disbelief. It had certainly resulted in an earlier Premier League baptism than expected for Pau Torres. The Spain international centre-back had been one of three big summer signings for Villa in a £31 million move from Villarreal and Emery's plan to ease him in gently to English football was now out of the window.

While Villa's boss had made clear early in his reign he had no desire to go raiding his old club for players, with Torres he was prepared to make an exception, such was his belief in the 25-year-old's ability. A key member of the Villarreal team which won the Europa League and reached the semi-finals of the Champions League under Emery, Torres had caught the eye of many of the top clubs in Europe and was considered one of the finest ball-playing defenders on the continent. But concerns over his physicality and a large release clause of more than £43 million in his contract had prevented many suitors from making a serious approach. That was not the case with Villa, Emery having pencilled Torres in as a target right from his first days back in the Premier League. He was frustrated at being unable to make him the first signing in the previous window and so keen was Emery to land his man he even called Torres when the player was on his honeymoon early in the close season.

'I had to tell him to let us enjoy our holiday, that a honeymoon is something you only experience once in your life, and that we leave it until I was back,' Torres would later explain in an interview with Sky Sports. 'He respected that for the days before I came here.'

Emery's relentless nature, whether it be on the training pitch or when trying to persuade a player to join, was nothing new to Torres and a big factor in him eventually agreeing to join. Monchi was able to agree a fee with Villarreal significantly lower than the release clause as Villa landed one of their main summer targets.

The other big money buy of the window was Moussa Diaby, who joined in a club record £43 million deal from Bayer Leverkusen, having turned down a lucrative offer to join Al Nassr in the Saudi Pro League in order to play on the bigger stage in England. Leon Bailey, whose place appeared most under threat by the arrival of the new man, also played a part in convincing his former team-mate to make the move.

Villa's other signing ahead of the season's start was Belgium international midfielder Youri Tielemans on a free transfer. The first deal over the line, it was announced out of the blue just a few hours before Manchester City defeated Inter Milan to win the Champions League final on 10 June. Tielemans was available after the expiry of his contract at relegated Leicester City. In four years with the Foxes, who he had joined from Monaco for £40 million, he had written his name into club folklore by scoring the only goal in their 2021 FA Cup final win over Chelsea. At that time he had been tracked by some of the Premier League's biggest clubs before a loss of form, particularly in his final season in the East Midlands, saw his star fall just slightly. Emery was convinced he could be an asset for Villa and persuaded him to join by outlining his Champions League ambitions and making him one of the highest-paid players at the club.

Whatever plans Villa originally had for the final weeks of the window changed with the injuries to Buendia and Mings. Replacements were required and found with Italy attacker Nicolo Zaniolo, a player Monchi knew from his time at Roma, arriving on a season-long loan from Galatasaray. Defender Clement Lenglet, who had played under Emery at PSG, joined in a deadline day loan move from Barcelona to fill the gap left by Mings.

While the incomings were the type to spark excitement, the outgoings were arguably more fascinating with three academy players – who had barely kicked a ball in anger for the first team – leaving for combined fees of £37 million. In fact, midfielder Aaron Ramsey, younger brother of Jacob, had never made a senior appearance for the club before moving to Burnley in a £14 million deal which included a buy-back clause. So complicated was the agreement, it took the Premier League and EFL more than a week to ratify but once signed-off it provided the blueprint for striker Cameron Archer's £18 million switch to Sheffield United and winger Jaden Philogene's £5 million move to Hull. Archer's transfer also included a buy-back clause, along with an obligation on Villa's part to take him back should the Blades, newly-promoted to the Premier League, be relegated at the end of the season. Philogene's move featured a matching clause which allowed Villa the chance to match any bids the Tigers received for the player in the future. All three deals, while complex, were constructed to help Villa's efforts to remain within PSR in the 2023–24 season as the fees could be banked as pure profit. At the same time, they were able to retain some control over the futures of players developed at Bodymoor Heath.[33]

Qualifying for Europe meant Villa also had to take notice of UEFA's own cost control measures. These rules, which run separately to the Premier League's PSR, allowed clubs to spend just 90 per cent of their revenues on transfer fees, player wages and agents' fees. Reducing this figure was among the reasons they were open to selling Lucas Digne, who on £125,000 a week was among the biggest earners in the squad. Yet the fact the France international, who had serious interest from the Saudi Pro League, remained at Villa was a reminder sometimes the best deals you do are the ones you don't.

Emery had arrived at the club with doubts about Digne, having received a less than flattering report on the Frenchman's performances while at Everton from connections in football. His first move as Villa boss was to bring in competition at left-back in the shape of Alex Moreno. But though Digne found himself out of the team, he never sulked and endeavoured to prove to Emery his initial assessment had been wrong. With Moreno still recovering from a hamstring injury at the start of 2023–24 season and a move for Sevilla's Marcos Acuna having fallen through, Digne had to play and through his performances established himself as a key member of the team. Even when Moreno returned, he found Digne hard to displace. The latter even became an unlikely fan favourite through a ritual of shouting 'Another one!' into the club's social media cameras after every win. Speaking to his players in a team meeting some months later, Emery would hold Digne up as an example of precisely the kind of character he wants at Villa.

In another sign of how relentless he is around developing players, Emery helped his goalkeeping coach Javi Garcia put together a presentation for the club's most consistent and reliable performer, Martinez, before the season started. Believing that every player can still improve, Emery and Garcia pinpointed areas the goalkeeper could work on in the season ahead to make him even more rounded and important to the team.

It was clear the opening day thrashing at Newcastle would be a test of Villa's mettle but they were about to get words of encouragement from the most surprising of places. During an interview with US broadcaster NBC on the following Monday, Sir Alex Ferguson claimed Emery's team were the most impressive he had seen over the opening weekend of the season.

'I watched Aston Villa and Newcastle and I can't believe the scoreline,' he said. 'Aston Villa played fantastic football and just lost bad goals. It's a surprising game, football. You can play teams off the pitch and not score. That is what happened to Aston Villa.'

While it was true Villa's performance had been nowhere near so bad as the scoreline suggested, it would also be fair to say Ferguson's comments were the cause of a few raised eyebrows. Just a few months later they would appear more like an example of clairvoyance and a reminder of why the Scot is among the greatest managers of all time.

Villa were quickly back on track with a 4–0 home win over Everton which wiped out the damage to their goal difference done at St James' Park and was the catalyst for a run of five victories in six matches, which included an 8–0 aggregate triumph over Hibernian in the play-off round of the Europa Conference League. A 3–0 defeat at Liverpool was the only setback, though it did mean Villa had won two and lost two of their opening league matches and the season's first turning point occurred in a home game against Crystal Palace, immediately after the international break. Trailing 1–0 as the match entered the closing stages and indebted to two fine Emi Martinez saves for keeping them in it, Villa roared back to win 3–1 with Jhon Durán thumping in an 87th minute equaliser and Douglas Luiz and Bailey then scoring in stoppage time. The latter had undergone a heart-to-heart with Emery after being subbed on and then subbed off in the defeat at Liverpool, a talk the head coach would later credit as a factor in the Jamaica international, then still to win over the vast majority of supporters two years after joining, going on to enjoy the best season of his career. Luiz, whose Villa career had also experienced its share of ups and downs, was another hitting previously unseen levels of consistency. The goal against Palace was his third of a season in which he would go on to hit double figures in all competitions and prove a reliable penalty taker. Emery spoke at length with Austin MacPhee about penalties and the set-piece specialist then worked tirelessly with Luiz on developing a new technique that would go on to help Villa secure many valuable points.

Villa's defence, meanwhile, was coping well with the loss of Mings, in part because Torres was adapting quickly to the demands of the Premier League but mainly because of Ezri Konsa, who had stepped up to become more of a leader at the back. Though a naturally humble person who prefers to lead by example rather than shout, Konsa made the conscious effort to be more vocal, realising he was now the most experienced central defender remaining after Mings. In mid-September, his performances were rewarded with a new five-year contract. Konsa, who had seen his progress stall under Steven Gerrard, had been among those players Emery had identified as having vast untapped potential when he joined the club and the head coach had told the defender as much.

'The boss has said it before in an interview that he believes in me more than I believe in myself,' says Konsa. 'Having a manager that believes in you so much gives me a big confidence boost. I think it's important and it's helped my game a lot.

'Not only that, but my leadership skills, I think I've really grown into that role ever since Tyrone got injured. I feel like I had to really step up into that role.'

Another player continuing to go from strength to strength was Ollie Watkins and the striker was the next player to be handed a new extended deal just a few weeks after Konsa. Watkins, who had opened his account for the season with a hat-trick in a 5–0 thrashing of Hibernian, grabbed his second treble of the campaign in a 6–1 hammering of Brighton in late September.

'It won't be my last [hat-trick] of the season, that is for sure,' declared Watkins, a comment which both epitomised his own levels of confidence and those of the team. You could hardly blame Villa, particularly when it came to playing at home. The thumping win over the Seagulls, who had arrived in the Midlands sitting third in the table having won five of their first six matches, was both a statement to the rest of the Premier League and their 10th consecutive home league win. It was the manner in which Villa were winning which most impressed. West Ham, another team with aspirations of challenging in the top half, were swatted aside 4–1, while both Luton and Fulham were beaten 3–1 with ease.

That took Villa to within one win of equalling a 91-year-old club record of 14 consecutive home league wins. The only snag was their next opponents were champions Manchester City, to be followed just three days later by the visit of Arsenal, runners-up the previous season. Presumed by many to be the point reality set in for Villa, instead it was the week which sent expectations to new, almost unprecedented levels. Martinez, in a display of his self-confidence and desire to win, posed a frank question to the management team ahead of the two games, asking for each player to be gifted a new watch if they beat both City and Arsenal.

Villa had just 72 hours to prepare for City's visit after a late Watkins header earned them a 2–2 draw at Bournemouth. Emery, conscious of the workload his players were facing, decided to shake up their normal routine. Though a naturally intense character, there are times when, as one club insider puts it, the Villa boss 'goes into a different orbit'. This was one such week. While some managers will set a training schedule weeks in advance, Emery prefers to work on instinct and feel and is not afraid to make late changes if he believes they will help his team. With City visiting on the Wednesday night, Emery took the unusual decision to give his players the Tuesday off, rather than the Monday immediately following the Bournemouth draw. On the morning of the City match he told his squad to report to Villa Park, rather than Bodymoor Heath, and held a walkthrough session on the pitch. Just a few hours later, on that same surface his men would produce a performance which ranked as perhaps the finest delivered by a Villa team in decades.

City, admittedly, arrived amid something of a wobble having failed to win any of their previous three league matches and were without key midfielder Rodri, who would go on to win the Ballon d'Or a year later. Yet never before had a Pep Guardiola team been so comprehensively dominated as they were at Villa Park. The champions managed only two attempts on target and the only surprise was it took until the 74th minute for the hosts to break the deadlock, Bailey's shot deflecting up and over Ederson to earn Villa the most deserved of victories.

'I still feel that is our best performance to date,' says Konsa. 'We controlled that game throughout the 90 minutes.

'The stats said something about we had 22 shots to their two and I just felt like going into that game we knew we could win.'

Guardiola's response was to declare Villa title contenders, something Emery was quick to dismiss. The boss had begun repeating in press conferences how there were 'seven contenders' with more of a chance to finish in the top seven than his own team, essentially consisting of the traditional Big Six plus Newcastle. But Villa were now up to third and when they followed up the win over City by beating Arsenal 1–0, to move within two points off top spot, putting a lid on the excitement was proving harder and harder.

There had been just two full days between the matches and, conscious of the emotional and physical exertion which had gone into beating the champions on the Wednesday night, Emery surprised both his players and staff again by giving them Friday off, a move most players had never experienced in their career. The unusual schedule worked as Villa, though visibly weary from their midweek heroics, held on to John McGinn's early goal to beat the Gunners. Martinez and his team-mates had their new watches and Villa countless new admirers.

'Those two games at Villa Park were probably the pinnacle of what has been created over the past few years, the atmosphere and belief and everything really,' says McGinn. 'The performance against City was incredible, the best I have ever been involved in. The Arsenal one was just a complete test of strength and character and thankfully we managed to come through that one. It was a special week, one we will never forget.'

Returning to Europe had also created a buzz among travelling supporters although Villa's form was far from convincing. First, a 3–2 defeat at Legia Warsaw, then Villa needed a stoppage time strike from McGinn to break the deadlock in one of the most one-sided games Villa Park has ever seen when Bosnian minnows Zrinjski Mostar arrived in town.

Home and away victories over AZ Alkmaar helped steady the ship but Villa could only squeeze past Legia in the home fixture, amid violent scenes from the travelling supporters.

A 1–1 draw away at Zrinjski just days after the stunning double over City and Arsenal served as another reminder that they needed to sharpen up on the road and Emery knew it. Within seconds of the final whistle, he created a temporary 'mini office' outside of the away dressing room by pulling together two boxes from the kitman to create a table. Sitting on another equipment box he pulled out his laptop, plugged in his mouse and USB and began picking clips from the game to show his players in a meeting the following day.

His team may have achieved their target of finishing top of the Europa Conference League qualifying group but Emery knew the hard work was only getting started.

The long-term losses of Buendia and Mings were far from the only injury setbacks Emery and Villa would suffer during a marathon season in which they would play 56 matches, 15 more than the previous year. They had also entered the campaign without Moreno and Jacob Ramsey and for the latter, who had suffered a broken foot while playing for England at the European Under-21 Championships, this would turn out to be a year of huge frustration. On returning to action in September, the 22-year-old outlined his ambition to break into the senior England squad in time for Euro 2024. But just a few weeks later he would suffer a reoccurrence of his foot injury shortly after scoring what would be his only goal of the season in the 6–1 win over Brighton. Though he returned again in late November, further niggles and the form of others limited his chances and he struggled to find any rhythm. After he sustained yet another foot injury in early March, during a 3–2 win at Luton, his season was over.

Elsewhere, it would be easier to list the players who didn't spend time on the treatment table. Torres missed two months between December and February with a foot injury, while Digne was absent for more than a month in the New Year with a hamstring problem. Konsa missed several weeks with a knee injury sustained in a 5–0 win at Sheffield United while Bailey, who would finish the season as Villa's second top scorer behind Watkins with 14 goals in all competitions, played through the pain barrier over the closing weeks.

The injuries undoubtedly disrupted Villa's rhythm, none more so than the serious knee injury suffered by Boubacar Kamara in a 2–1 defeat to Manchester United in early February, which ruled the France international out for the rest of the season. Kamara, who became the third Villa player to sustain such an injury after Buendia and Mings, had played an integral role in the team, his ability to cover the defence providing the likes of Luiz and Tielemans the freedom to advance further up the pitch. Without him, Villa became a lot less solid at the back. Even before his injury, their form had begun to dip. The defeat to United made it three matches without a win at home, bottom club Sheffield United having ended the winning streak in stunning fashion when they claimed a 1–1 draw just prior to Christmas. Now eight points off the top and no longer dark horses for the title, Villa found themselves down in fifth place which, the longer the season progressed, no longer looked the certainty to deliver Champions League football many had presumed. Indeed, by the time Villa became the last English club to exit European competition, losing 6–2 on aggregate to Olympiacos in the semi-finals of the Europa Conference League in probably the season's biggest disappointment, it was already confirmed an extra Champions League place would not be going to the Premier League. Villa had seen off Ajax and Lille in the previous knockout rounds and it felt like momentum was building for a trophy win, but now it was top-four or bust.

The good news for Emery was the two most irreplaceable players in his team, Watkins and Martinez, remained fit. The former got the winner and the latter made a vital last-minute save in a 2–1 victory at Fulham the week after the loss to United which lifted both the mood and the team back above Tottenham and into fourth place.

The final three months of the season essentially became a battle between the two teams for that place and a question of who best could hold their nerve. There were at least a couple of occasions when Villa appeared to have lost theirs, not least with a 4–0 home defeat to their rivals in which McGinn was sent off and banned for three matches for a rash challenge on Destiny Udogie. Tottenham, with a match in hand, moved to within two points of Villa yet afterward Emery sounded a note of defiance.

'We are sad, we are disappointed, but we are fourth,' he said in his post-match press conference. For Villa supporters of a certain generation, the remark had echoes of when the club's most revered manager, Ron Saunders, asked reporters whether they were prepared to bet against his team after they lost to closest challengers Ipswich en route to winning the title in 1981. The manner in which Tottenham's players celebrated at the final whistle had also not gone unnoticed.

'They celebrated like it was already done,' says McGinn. 'That helped us, giving us that little bit of extra motivation. Our pride was dented. We knew we had a point to prove. The manager said after that game, there are 38 matches in the season, don't forget that.'

Tottenham duly missed the chance to climb above Villa and further increase the pressure when they lost at Fulham the following weekend. Zaniolo, who had endured a disappointing loan spell, promptly netted just his second goal of the season to earn Emery's men a precious point at West Ham the next day. That match was notable for being the full Premier League debut of Morgan Rogers. Signed from Middlesbrough in January, the 21-year-old midfielder was considered a player for the future but the loss of Ramsey meant he ended up playing a far larger role much earlier than expected. There could be no denying he rose to the challenge, scoring three goals in his final eight league appearances of the season.

Villa had moved for Rogers after he caught Emery's eye while the head coach was analysing Middlesbrough, ahead of his team playing them in an FA Cup third round tie at the start of January. Stopping the former West Bromwich Albion academy product, who had joined Manchester City at the age of 16, became a key part of Villa's game plan. Emery was determined to make Rogers the first English player he had ever signed and though the fee, of an initial £8 million rising to a potential £15 million, for a player who had moved to Boro from City for just a fraction of that amount the previous summer was met with scorn in some quarters, it quickly began to look a bargain.

Rogers scored his first Villa goal in a 3–3 draw against Brentford on 6 April, an afternoon which looked a big setback for Emery's men after they surrendered a two-goal lead to draw at home. Yet it was the following weekend which would ultimately prove pivotal in the Champions League race. Tottenham were thumped 4–0 at Newcastle on the Saturday lunchtime before, just a little more than 24 hours later, Villa pulled off a huge shock by winning at title-chasing Arsenal.

This was another of those occasions in which Emery 'went into orbit' in the build-up. Few gave Villa a chance at the Emirates against an Arsenal team which had dropped just two points since the turn of the year and was, at that point, in control of the title race. Villa, meanwhile, had played the opening leg of a Europa Conference League quarter-final tie against Lille less than 72 hours before.

Emery held three team meetings in the build-up to the late Sunday afternoon kick-off and then watched his team produce perhaps the finest performance of his reign to that point. Having frustrated Arsenal in the early stages, with Martinez producing a world class save to deny Kai Havertz, Villa gradually took control and won it late through goals from Bailey and Watkins, the latter producing a lovely, lifted finish over David Raya to spark memorable scenes in the away end.

Emery, who in every press conference up to that point had played down his team's top-four chances, finally conceded they were now contenders. 'Inside the club we always had the ambition,' says McGinn. 'But we knew how difficult it would be because as a lot of people know, a lot of teams have the ability to spend more than us because of PSR. The manager helped take the heat off us and the pressure. I think he had been in the game long enough to know in that moment it would help and it really did help. We were the underdogs for the majority of the time. He was supporting us in that moment and giving us the space we needed.'

Closing out the deal would not prove easy. Villa beat Bournemouth but then drew 2–2 with Chelsea, another home match in which they blew a two-goal lead. Another missed opportunity came with a 1–0 defeat at Brighton yet the consolation was Tottenham were floundering, on a run of four straight defeats. Villa hosted Liverpool in the penultimate match of the season knowing a win would secure fourth place. They didn't get it, though two late goals from substitute Jhon Durán earned a dramatic 3–3 draw and meant Spurs had to beat Manchester City, then back in pole position for the title, the following night to keep the race alive. By sheer twist of fortune, the match would be taking place at the same time as Villa's end of season awards, with players, staff and several hundred fans together at the stadium.

'If the result didn't go our way, we would have had to get the job done ourselves that weekend,' says McGinn. 'The beer was on ice, no-one was celebrating.'

All that changed when Erling Haaland put City ahead shortly after half-time and then, in stoppage time, scored the penalty which put the result beyond doubt. At that point the noise inside The Lower Grounds suite at Villa Park was perhaps almost as deafening as in the blue half of Manchester. Emery exchanged embraces with his coaching staff and players, his suit jacket very quickly glistening with the champagne sprayed by Martinez and others. After all the work, all the tension which had built up in the previous weeks and months, this was sheer release. The head coach was soon on the stage to deliver an emotional speech in which he thanked his staff, players, supporters, and claimed having now qualified for the Champions League, Villa's next challenge was to win it.[34]

'It is easier if we are in it than if we are not!' he shouted.

McGinn also spoke, as did Mings. For both, having been on the journey from the Championship, it was a particularly surreal moment.

'People asked me whether it was harder that the team were doing well and I was not playing,' says Mings. 'The answer was a definite no because it was one less thing to worry about. There is nothing worse than wanting to contribute. I had been at Bournemouth in a relegation battle while being injured.

'You don't want to be sitting there injured thinking will I be coming back to the Premier League or the Championship. I was sitting there thinking I don't know if we're going to qualify for the Conference League, Europa League or Champions League. It's a very different mindset!'

Asked if he thought qualifying for the Champions League was possible, when he first stepped through the doors of Villa Park in 2018, McGinn replies: 'There's a small part of you that hopes and believes, but there was also a small part of me thinking that I would play for Barcelona and lift the Champions League when I was younger!

'When you look back and be honest, the answer is no. It has been surreal. It has been a whirlwind few years. It is probably what the owners envisaged when they joined, having not had the history of being involved in football. But it's not always so plain sailing and getting to the top is not easy.

'There's been a few times where we have been on the brink. We've had our fair share of luck. But I look back to that first season in the Premier League, we were seven points away from safety with four games to go, we were absolutely written off and finished. That would have been tough to recover from. Credit to everyone there. We had a hero in Trezeguet to get us over the line.'

If there is a single lesson to take from the story of Aston Villa since 2018 it is perhaps that football moves quickly and there have been numerous further examples since the 2023–24 season finished. Barely a week after the campaign had been completed came the first big news of the summer, with Emery signing a new five-year contract through to 2029. Villa had already triggered the extra year option in his previous deal a few weeks earlier, aimed as a warning to any clubs who might be considering an approach for their most prized asset. Tying Emery down for the longer-term was always the primary aim for the club, and just as he had been throughout his reign, from the whirlwind 2018 takeover onward, Nassef Sawiris was decisive in his action. For Emery, there was also a change of title. No longer head coach, he was now Villa's manager, a moniker far more fitting for the power he holds.

'We are really excited to continue this journey with no limits to our dreams,' he said in the official statement announcing the deal.

Since taking charge in 2022, Emery has completely altered the outlook in terms of what many believed possible at Villa Park. Yet the weeks which followed his new contract served as a reminder of the challenges which still lie ahead. Villa's battle to comply with PSR, detailed regularly in this book, has never been so fierce as in June 2024. Losses of nearly £120 million for the 2022–23 season had left the club with what Damian Vidagany would later describe as a 'ticking bomb' which necessitated the swift sale of Luiz to Juventus for £42.5 million in order to remain within the limits. Villa would also later sell Diaby, who had perhaps not lived up to the promise of his early weeks at the club, to Saudi Pro League outfit Al-Ittihad for £51 million to further help the equation down the line. There were also big additions, with Belgium international midfielder Amadou Onana surpassing Diaby as record signing when he joined from Everton for £50 million.

Villa made their strongest start to a Premier League season for a quarter of a century but the challenge of juggling domestic and European ambitions, coupled with a growing injury list, has at times proved tough. Perhaps the clearest demonstration of the speed with which fortunes can change arrived on the night of 29 January 2025 when, at around the same time Morgan Rogers was becoming the first player to ever score twice in the opening five minutes of a

Champions League match to set Villa on their way to a 4–2 win over Celtic which secured a last-16 berth, news broke that the club had agreed a deal in principle to sell Durán to Al-Nassr for a fee which could eventually be worth more than £70 million.

Within 48 hours of the final whistle the hero of Bayern was gone. In his place came the loan arrivals of Manchester United forward Marcus Rashford and three-time Champions League winner Marco Asensio from Paris St-Germain. The combined wages Villa will pay the pair for the remainder of the season comes in somewhere around £500,000 a week and while the sale of Durán demonstrated the need for the club to be opportunistic and compromise in the world of PSR, the Rashford and Asensio deals underscored Emery's desire to never remain idle and his need to win now, rather than later.

Getting things right off the field will undoubtedly be vital to maintaining long-term success on it. Villa are a vastly changed club to the one Sawiris and Edens saved in 2018, with revenues having increased by more than £200 million. But just as in the Lerner years, the club lags behind its bigger domestic rivals. With Chris Heck leaving at the end of the 2024–25 season, the onus will be on his replacement to increase commercial income almost as quickly as Emery transformed the fortunes of the team. It is no easy task. Villa are expected to be in breach of UEFA's cost control measures for the 2024–25 season, which limits clubs to spending 80 per cent of their revenues on transfer fees, salaries and agents' fees.[35] Though there will be no sporting sanction, Villa are likely to be fined.

Just as it was difficult to pinpoint the place to start this book, so the ending must remain unwritten. Yet with Emery at the helm and the ambition of Sawiris and Edens still strong, everyone connected to Aston Villa, from supporters to players and even journalists, has a genuine reason to believe the best days remain ahead.

'You don't get much chance to look back, though there are certain times you do reflect and think wow, that's actually happened,' says McGinn. 'It's been an amazing journey but I don't like to reflect too much because I think there is much more to come.'

ACKNOWLEDGEMENTS

The authors would like to extend huge thanks to Unai Emery, Damian Vidagany, Monchi, Christian Purslow, Jesus Garcia Pitarch, Dean Smith, Jack Grealish, John McGinn, Tyrone Mings, Ollie Watkins, Ezri Konsa, James Chester, Conor Hourihane, Albert Adomah, Neil Taylor, Ahmed Elmohamady, Anwar El Ghazi, Andre Green, Jed Steer, Mbwana Samatta, Neil Cutler, Keith Wyness, Tommy Jordan, Tom Otrebski, Warwick Horton, Mo Razzaq, Howard Hodgson, the many others who spoke to us for this book on condition of anonymity and all of those people, whether executives, managers, players, supporters or staff, at every level of the club, who picked up the phone or had time for a conversation over the past decade and made the experience of chronicling Aston Villa's remarkable journey everything it has been.

REFERENCES

1. 'Everton delay Russian deal', BBC Sport, 23 August 2004. http://news.bbc.co.uk/sport1/hi/football/teams/e/everton/3588046.stm
2. Nabil Hassan, 'Reading: Sir John Madejski confirms Anton Zingarevich exit', BBC Sport, 2 June 2014. https://www.bbc.co.uk/sport/football/27663506 and Jack de Menezes, 'Want to own a football club? Buy Reading for just £1 after owner Anton Zingarevich puts Royals up for sale', *The Independent*, 26 May 2014. https://www.independent.co.uk/sport/football/football-league/want-to-own-a-football-club-buy-reading-for-just-ps1-after-owner-anton-zingarevich-puts-royals-up-for-sale-9435428.html
3. 'China aims to become football superpower "by 2050"', BBC Sport, 11 April 2016. https://www.bbc.co.uk/news/world-asia-china-36015657
4. 'Full statement on Albion takeover', West Bromwich Albion website, 5 August 2016. https://www.wba.co.uk/news/2016/august/full-statement-on-albion-takeover
5. Steve Wollaston, 'Who is Dr Tony Xia? The lowdown on the new owner of Aston Villa', *Birmingham Mail*, 14 June 2016.

https://www.birminghammail.co.uk/sport/football/football-news/who-dr-tony-xia-lowdown-11469502

6. Aston Villa, 'Club statement: Sale confirmed', 18 May 2016. https://www.avfc.co.uk/News/2016/05/18/club-statement-sale-confirmed
7. Nick Harris, 'Saviour or dreamer? Sportsmail talks to Aston Villa's owner-in-waiting, Dr Tony Xia'. *Mail on Sunday*, 22 May 2016. https://www.dailymail.co.uk/sport/football/article-3602825/Saviour-dreamer-Sportsmail-talks-Aston-Villa-s-owner-waiting-Dr-Tony-Xia.html
8. Nick Harris, ibid.
9. Laurie Whitwell, 'Aston Villa takeover facing Premier League and Football League probe before ratifying purchase of club by Dr Tony Xia', *Daily Mail*, 20 May 2016. https://www.dailymail.co.uk/sport/football/article-3601731/Aston-Villa-takeover-facing-Premier-League-Football-League-probe-ratifying-purchase-club-Dr-Tony-Xia.html and John Percy, 'Aston Villa's £65m takeover to be scrutinised by Premier League amid doubts over new Chinese owner', *Telegraph*, 20 May 2016. https://www.telegraph.co.uk/football/2016/05/20/aston-villas-65m-takeover-to-be-scrutinised-by-premier-league-an/?utm_source=chatgpt.com
10. Charles Clover, 'Questions over Aston Villa's Chinese buyer', *Financial Times*, 20 May 2016. https://www.ft.com/content/9969d8b0-1e63-11e6-b286-cddde55ca122
11. Nick Harris, 'Saviour or dreamer? Sportsmail talks to Aston Villa's owner-in-waiting, Dr Tony Xia'. *Mail on Sunday*, 22 May 2016. https://www.dailymail.co.uk/sport/football/article-3602825/Saviour-dreamer-Sportsmail-talks-Aston-Villa-s-owner-waiting-Dr-Tony-Xia.html
12. Gregg Evans, 'Elphick on players drunk at Villa training, "bad attitudes" and the "mess" of 2016', *The Athletic*, 13 May 2020. https://www.nytimes.com/

athletic/1810172/2020/05/13/elphick-villa-captain-drunk-training-bruce/

13. Samuel Agini, 'European football clubs' route to easy borrowing under threat', *Financial Times*, 12 June 2020. https://www.ft.com/content/40b1be0b-1503-4cfb-97e6-0fdd1abcfc29 and Ed Aarons, 'Why Premier League clubs are turning to an Australian bank in big numbers', *Guardian*, 11 February 2020. https://www.theguardian.com/football/2020/feb/11/premier-league-clubs-australian-bank-macquarie-loans
14. Dan Colquhoun, 'Former Aston Villa hero discusses "chaotic" times under Dr Tony', Claret Villans, 14 October 2024. https://claretvillans.com/former-aston-villa-hero-discusses-chaotic-times-under-dr-tony-01ja534aecqn
15. Mark Kleinman, 'Aston Villa suspends CEO as club races to meet HMRC tax bill', Sky News, 6 June 2018. https://news.sky.com/story/aston-villa-suspends-ceo-as-club-races-to-meet-hmrc-taxbill-11395857
16. Mark Kleinman, 'Aston Villa suspends CEO as club races to meet HMRC tax bill', Sky News, 6 June 2018. https://news.sky.com/story/aston-villa-suspends-ceo-as-club-races-to-meet-hmrc-tax-bill-11395857
17. Gregg Evans, 'Meet Aston Villa's ambitious owners: Nassef Sawiris and Wes Edens', *The Athletic*, 30 November 2020. https://www.nytimes.com/athletic/2223968/2020/11/29/aston-villa-owners-edens-sawiris/
18. Gregg Evans, 'Cash-strapped Aston Villa use their staff car park to get another loan', *Birmingham Mail*, 12 July 2018. https://www.birminghammail.co.uk/sport/football/football-news/aston-villa-tony-xia-loan-14894967
19. Aston Villa, 'Club statement: Dr Tony Xia on future plans', 30 May 2018. https://www.avfc.co.uk/News/2018/05/30/club-statement-dr-tony-xia-on-future-plans

20. Gregg Evans, 'Meet Aston Villa's ambitious owners: Nassef Sawiris and Wes Edens', *The Athletic*, 30 November 2020. https://www.nytimes.com/athletic/2223968/2020/11/29/aston-villa-owners-edens-sawiris/
21. BBC Sport, 'Aston Villa report £36.1m pre-tax loss for 2017–18 season', 6 March 2019. https://www.bbc.co.uk/sport/football/47468115#:~:text=More%20from%20Sport%20*%20Aston%20Villa.%20*%20Table
22. 'Aston Villa's final appeal for Lovre Kalinic work permit rejected by FA', ESPN, 30 January 2016. https://www.espn.co.uk/football/story/_/id/37453158/aston-villa-appeal-lovre-kalinic-work-permit-rejected
23. https://x.com/Dr_TonyXia/status/1133084938104901633
24. Simon Stone, 'Aston Villa: Dr Tony Xia's Villa involvement over after new owners' cash injection', BBC Sport, 9 August 2019. https://www.bbc.co.uk/sport/football/49289990
25. James Nursey, 'Arrest warrant issued for former Aston Villa owner Dr Tony Xia in China', *Mirror*, 18 October 2019. https://www.mirror.co.uk/sport/football/news/arrest-warrant-issued-former-aston-20648242
26. https://x.com/Dr_TonyXia/status/1185241428428853249
27. Jonathan White, 'Ex-Aston Villa owner Tony Xia "detained for six months before arrest": report', *South China Morning Post*, 7 February 2021.
28. Gregg Evans, 'Villa masseur texted his family in case he didn't make it. Now he's fighting fit', *The Athletic*, 19 April 2020. https://www.nytimes.com/athletic/1754680/2020/04/19/villa-masseur-texted-his-family-in-case-he-didnt-make-it-now-hes-fighting-fit/
29. Toby Miles, 'Aston Villa boss Dean Smith reveals he slept in his training ground OFFICE after drinking shots with Jack Grealish in a "heavy night" that lasted until the early hours after confirming Premier League survival', *Daily Mail*, 27

July 2020. https://www.dailymail.co.uk/sport/football/article-8563863/Aston-Villa-boss-Dean-Smith-reveals-slept-OFFICE-heavy-night-celebrating-survival.html

30. 'Club Statement: Aston Villa', Manchester City website, 22 May 2022. https://www.mancity.com/news/mens/club-statement-aston-villa-63788839
31. Phil McNulty, 'Aston Villa move for Watford forward Ismaila Sarr falls through', BBC Sport, 22 August 2022. https://www.bbc.co.uk/sport/football/62629580
32. Charlotte Duncker, 'Ollie Watkins: I want to get people talking about me', *The Times*, 24 Augsut 2023. https://www.thetimes.com/article/ollie-watkins-i-want-to-get-people-talking-about-me-fzblwm8wf
33. Jacob Tanswell and Gregg Evans, 'Aston Villa and FFP: The Jack Grealish money, creativity and selling academy talent', *The Athletic*, 12 January 2024. https://www.nytimes.com/athletic/4815655/2024/01/12/aston-villa-financial-fair-play/ and https://www.nytimes.com/athletic/5555475/2024/06/13/aston-villas-complex-transfers-douglas-luiz/
34. https://x.com/AVFCOfficial/status/1790515433831043444?lang=en
35. Matt Hughes, 'Aston Villa in talks with Uefa over deal after breach of squad cost rules', *Guardian*, 11 April 2025, https://www.theguardian.com/football/2025/apr/11/aston-villa-in-talks-with-uefa-over-deal-after-breach-of-squad-cost-rules and Matt Maher, 'Walking the PSR tightrope is nothing new for Aston Villa', *Express & Star*, 12 April 2025, https://www.expressandstar.com/sport/football/aston-villa/2025/04/12/matt-maher-walking-the-psr-tightrope-is-nothing-new-for-aston-villa/

BOOK CREDITS

HarperNorth would like to thank the following staff and contributors for their involvement in making this book a reality:

Sarah Allen-Sutter
Fionnuala Barrett
Sarah Burke
Alan Cracknell
Jonathan de Peyer
Tom Dunstan
Kate Elton
Sarah Emsley
Simon Gerratt
Lydia Grainge
Monica Green
Natassa Hadjinicolaou
Emma Hatlen
Jess Haycox
Grace Howarth
Megan Jones
Jean-Marie Kelly
Taslima Khatun
Dan Mogford
Alice Murphy-Pyle
Adam Murray
Genevieve Pegg
Amanda Percival
Dean Russell
Eleanor Slater
Hilary Stein
Emma Sullivan
Katrina Troy
Inigo Vivyan
Tom Whiting

Harper
North